ENERGY, TRADE AND FINANCE IN ASIA:
A POLITICAL AND ECONOMIC ANALYSIS

Perspectives in Economic and Social History

Series Editors: Robert E. Wright
                  Andrew August

Titles in this Series

FORTHCOMING TITLES

ENERGY, TRADE AND FINANCE IN ASIA: A POLITICAL AND ECONOMIC ANALYSIS

BY

Justin Dargin and Tai Wei Lim

Routledge
Taylor & Francis Group

LONDON AND NEW YORK

First published 2012 by Pickering & Chatto (Publishers) Limited

Published 2016 by Routledge
2 Park Square, Milton Park, Abingdon, Oxfordshire OX14 4RN
711 Third Avenue, New York, NY 10017, USA

First issued in paperback 2015

Routledge is an imprint of the Taylor & Francis Group, an informa business

BRITISH LIBRARY CATALOGUING IN PUBLICATION DATA

Dargin, Justin.
Energy, trade and finance in Asia : a political economic analysis. – (Perspectives
in economic and social history)
1. East Asia – Foreign economic relations – Persian Gulf States. 2. Persian Gulf
states – Foreign economic relations – East Asia. 3. East Asia – Economic policy.
4. Persian Gulf States – Economic policy. 5. East Asia – Commercial policy.
6. Persian Gulf States—Commercial policy. 7. Energy policy – East Asia. 8.
Energy policy – Persian Gulf States.
I. Title II. Series III. Lim, Tai-Wei.
337.5'0536-dc22

ISBN-13: 978-1-138-66153-0 (pbk)
ISBN-13: 978-1-8489-3155-8 (hbk)

Typeset by Pickering & Chatto (Publishers) Limited

CONTENTS

LIST OF FIGURES AND TABLES

Figures

Tables

PREFACE

The impetus for this research was to instigate a thorough examination of the historiographical survey and history of inter-regional ties between the Middle East and North-East Asia. It remains a work in progress, given the complexity of the topic and evolving interrelationships between the two regions. The text may also be used to study how energy inter-regionalism is studied, imagined and discussed in addition to implementation and exchange. In surveying the inter-regional literature between North-East Asia and the Middle East, several entities appear to be commonly mentioned, studied or researched. They included Japan and China, but India and particularly the US were indispensible in such discussions given their important and significant influence. In the history between the two regions, contemporary literature, particularly the recent ones, also highlight the non-energy aspect of the trade between the two regions.

The discussions may allude to the presence of inter-regional ties between the two regions. Surveying the literature, it appears the dominant feature discussed may be a definitional feature of a region's ties with one important or large economy/entity/state (e.g. India, Japan, US and China in this case). Given the lack of a macro-regional framework or a North-East Asian regional organization in dealing with the Middle East as a region, the dominant format of inter-regional ties appears to be the Middle East's region's relations with each individual large economy or state.

In conjunction with the focus on inter-regional trade ties, the arguments appear to allude that inter-regional ties appears to increasingly embed bilateral energy trade within non-energy trade. The arguments presented do not put forward the replacement of energy ties with non-energy trade ties, instead both reinforce each other and given the still-growing industrial capabilities and output, the discourse argues that this aspect of the overall relationship may become increasingly important if not as important as the energy ties in the near future.

This also implies that a conventional strain of thought on inter-regional ties between the two regions and the US may be evolving. The Middle East's main export of energy to Asia (including North-East Asia) provides the region with the commodity for industrial production and the output to the developed markets (including the US) may provide Asia (including North-East Asia) with surplus for oil purchase. Both the oil revenue surplus from the Gulf and trade surplus from North-East Asia may fund the sophisticated financial markets of the developed economies (including, and perhaps predominantly, the US).

The modifications to this system may include the fact that the Middle East has diversified its economic output away from sole reliance or dominant reliance on energy and moved into other varieties of economic output such as trade, manufacturing and financial investments. Moreover, Middle Eastern economies themselves are now increasingly reliant on energy for their growing population and manufacturing capabilities.

As part of diversification of economic portfolio, Middle Eastern investments are also moving into growth areas of Asia (including North-East Asia and India) in this diversification exercise. Diversification into non-energy investments may be made possible by the accumulation of oil revenue surplus and such funds' ability to provide the Middle East with overseas acquisitions that can augment, build up its technological capabilities overseas and even produce industrial goods overseas. Among other interests, Middle Eastern funds are also interested in the growth prospects of Asia (including North-East Asia and India).

Another modification to the conventional discourse is the interest of Asia (including North-East Asia and India) in trading with the Middle East in non-energy, non-oil sectors and move into non-energy sectors because of their interests in new markets in the Middle East (particularly consumer classes in economies enriched by oil revenues) and its potential to generate trade surplus to balance the deficit from energy trade, particularly for energy-scarce economies such as Japan's.

In both cases, these investments are made by the private sector and sovereign funds that are augmented by oil revenues due to favourable oil prices in the case of the Middle East and the trade surpluses made possible by the industrial output and export-orientation of Asian economies (including India and North-East Asia). In the case of sovereign funds and government-linked companies involved in such trade exchanges, they may be guided by long-term interests that may be associated with national priorities.

As these national priorities become increasingly competitive among Asian (particularly large emerging Asian economies like India and China in addition to mature large economies like Japan), they may become competitive and brush up against each other. Therefore, the argument made is that it may be possible for Asian economies and government-linked companies to collaborate and approach oil purchases and acquisition based on a coordinated and/or consultative mechanisms rather than outright competition.

If this occurs, then it may be a landscape of inter-regionalism through regionalism (within North-East Asia for example). Similar arguments are made for the

Gulf states, that their regionalism may create the economy of scale needed for their economic engagements with other regions or integrate better into globalization. One example may be the gas cooperation and collaboration among the Gulf states. If this argument is followed, in the ideal situation then, instead of inter-regionalism between a region and a large economy, it may be macro-regional ties between two regional bodies (a North-East Asian one and a Middle Eastern one). But is this possible?

Currently, this may be difficult, given the differing interests within North-East Asia or within Asia (between India and North-East Asia) or East Asia for energy needs and other priorities in their interactions with the Middle East. Internally, there are also many internal contradictions of development that prevent alignment of first level common interests. These internal contradictions include different capabilities and abilities in efficient energy consumption, domestic oil availability, financial strength, environmental considerations and a whole host of developmental considerations, particularly for large emerging economies like India and China. The needs of large emerging economies and those of mature developed economies like Japan may not always be complementary.

But this may not preclude the possibility of an open form of regionalism if external parties, particularly the US are involved. An open form of loose regionalism may help information exchange and confidence-building but reflect the realities of the region at the same time. Open North-East Asian regionalism may also involve India whose influence over the Indian Ocean and its domains through which overland pipelines and cross-regional energy infrastructure may need to traverse.

The US is particularly important for any regionalism, inter-regionalism or macro-regionalism because it is a hyperpower whose influence is crucial to the success of any schemes in regional and inter-regional relations. The US ability to encourage or obstruct any aspects of regional and/or inter-regional initiatives can mean the successes and failures of those initiatives. The US is also the only entity with deep and long-entrenched interests in North-East Asia, India and the Middle East and the nature of its relationship is comprehensive involving all facets, not solely or predominantly on economic aspects. The US may also be inter-regionally transcendental above the regionally specific mistrust that each component within the North-East Asian or Middle Eastern region may have vis-a-vis others in the region.

The US may be imagined as a hub where the inter-regional spokes of the Middle East and North-East Asia may pass through and connect with. Within this hub and spokes model, each dominant entity in the two regions may transact their needs accordingly. This does not diminish their roles in any way because without the important and significant role of India, China, Japan, along with the Middle East energy producers, the regional or inter-regional system cannot reach an equilibrium that is satisfactory to meet the trade and energy needs of each party.

The previous assumption of Middle East energy for Asian industrial output and financial investments and consumer products for the developed markets may not be as strong but facets of this system will continue to exist with some modifications. Instead of more specialized roles within the system, the element of greater interdependence may be enhanced further, given the more diversified needs and capabilities of each player.

Yet, some semblance to the old system may continue, given that large internal contradictions of the large emerging economies. For the near future at least, despite the important and significant achievements by India and China in development, they will continue to meet with internal challenges that may consume their resources and may affect the outward emanation of their immediate needs and priorities. Important domestic priorities may prevent India and China from concentrating on inter-regional issues beyond meeting their immediate economic needs, unlike the US comfortable reach into the global and inter-regional space. But at the same time, the US is likely to find greater dependence on its Asian partners and other members within the inter-regional system.

Some aspects may be somewhat de-emphasized and/or deprivileged in some contemporary literature on the energy sector of North-East Asia and the Middle East. First in discussions about oil, which may probably be the most important energy commodity in bilateral trade between the two regions, coal which remains the main energy source in India and China and remains important to Japan may be neglected. Coal is also available to a large extent in China, India and nearby Russia, making it the most accessible and convenient energy source. Therefore this publication introduces coal literature into discussions about energy and trade issues between the two regions.

Secondly, despite the well-publicized and maybe even exceptionalized focus on the industrialization of large emerging economies of India and China, it may be easy to bypass the fact that this industrialization depended on Western and Japanese firms that are located in China producing for the rest of the world, without which industrialization in large emerging Asian and even Gulf economies would not be possible. Therefore the interdependence factor remains strong and influential in bilateral exchanges between the Middle East, North-East Asia and India.

Just as large emerging economies and regions depend on the West for investments and manufacturing foreign direct investments (FDIs), the global landscape for investments is also likely to see more outward-oriented cross-border investments from the Gulf economies, North-East Asian investors and their sovereign funds. The global landscape including the West may likely see more collaboration with the large emerging economies and Gulf economies through areas like equity investments, joint ventures and loan dispensing. Overseas energy investments may likely be a priority for the large emerging economies in Asia and their sovereign funds. Energy-rich recipients are also likely to benefit from this.

In making such investments, the large emerging Asian economies are likely to set sustainability and environmentalism, as well as renewable and green energy investments, as important priorities for their acquisitions. It may be possible that carbon neutral, renewable energy sources may also be a simultaneous priority with fossil fuel. The procedure is part of the overall efforts to reduce dependence on fossil fuels.

In the near-medium term, attempts are made by North-East Asia and India to mitigate the use of oil and increase reliance on natural gas. Nuclear technologies are also another possible priority, although in the short and medium term, this aspect may be slowed down or mitigated by nuclear accident at the Fukushima nuclear plant in Japan as countries reassess their dependence on nuclear energy. The main challenge may be on to minimize the risk factor.

Interdependence is be likely to rise and not decline with Asian industrialization as pollution gets into the cities and as population shift into urban areas increases, factors which induce Asian cities to be dependent on and partner with Western and Japanese firms for environmentally friendly and green technologies. At least in the area of urban planning, the scenario appears to have the potential for cooperation instead of a zero-sum game. Greater areas of interdependence may have the net effect of promoting conflict avoidance if it can overcome the potential for conflict.

Interdependence is needed as the large middle classes of large emerging economies aspire to have the same lifestyles as their advanced economies' counterparts. If the outcome of this aspiration is zero-sum competition between developed economies, large emerging and mature economies and/or between mature economies, then a conflictual landscape may be highly possible, and this may pertain not just to the fossil fuel market but also nuclear fuel market as well in the clamor for carbon-friendlier fuels in the near and medium term future.

Another issue that may be often neglected or downplayed in inter-regional energy exchange literature between North-East Asia and the Middle East is the fact that green energy may not just be renewable energy but also the capability to use, develop and implement energy-saving technologies, energy conservation techniques and managing and producing the next generations of energy-saving products.

On a more discourse and narrative level, literature on inter-regional energy ties between the Middle East and North-East Asia may also fail to ask questions concerning the relationship between energy and security. In exchanges over this subject area, some scholars posed the question why there is a tendency among realist scholars to emphasize the association of energy commodities with security perspectives. The answer appears to be apparent given the scarcity of these commodities, their strategic nature and their importance to national security. To scholars who do not agree with the link between security and energy, they argue that overly associating the two may create a vicious cycle of insecurity on the part of its consumers.

Imagining them as the commons or a public good, such as air or water, the cross-boundary natural species that nature takes charge of, may help to remove some of those insecurities. But this remains at the discourse level and narrative idealism as long as aspirations continue to exist for material-based consumption. The next best thing therefore may be to cooperate, compromise and reduce consumption, something that will be a long-term venture.

Equilibrium may also need to be reached between market forces and state-guided energy management and acquisition. Suggestions of possibility to liberalize the energy market may be mitigated by the fact that uncontrolled economic competition without consultation and cooperation may not be ideal in securing reasonable pricing nor would zero-sum competition between state-owned companies. Given that competition between energy firms is a global one, interdependence and cooperation may also prevent disruptions to existing global regimes and organizations that regulate energy development. The international rules and regimes can help to accommodate the rise of large emerging economies and their burgeoning middle classes.

This volume acknowledges the contributions of Stephen Nagy (Assistant Professor, Chinese University of Hong Kong, CUHK) and Ms Chan Yim Ting, Helen (Research Assistant, CUHK).

1 INTRODUCTION

Energy may be one of the most contentious issues in the world and there are many discourses, narratives, explanations and arguments about the use of energy, including its role in inter-regional exchanges between the Middle East and North-East Asia. Increasingly, trade and energy exchanges are spoken together and this appears to be the case in recent works by Kemp, Simpfendorfer and Davidson.[1] Narratives and discourses that highlight the inter-connectedness of non-energy trade and energy exchanges as an interrelated item in the inter-regional exchange between the Middle East and North-East Asia appear to be favorable to maintaining this inter-regional exchange. The bundling of energy and goods in trade and exchanges between the two regions acts as a form of interdependence through a spaghetti effect whereby greater intermingling promotes greater interdependence, analogous to spaghetti criss-crossing each other.

There are a number of centrifugal forces to mitigate the sustainability of energy trade inter-regionally between North-East Asia and the Middle East. Centrifugal forces may include increasing energy needs of the Middle East diminishing the potentialities of future energy export trade, for example the fast-growing Gulf states, their natural gas needs and their growing interdependence in forming regional energy systems. Regionalism is complicated and mitigated by growing inter-regionalism.

But because the two regions themselves are not institutionally regionalized and integrated politically as blocs, the inter-regionalism between the two regions remain organic, ad hoc and loose. Because of the nature of Middle East/North-East Asia inter-regionalism as a platform for open, export-driven, FDI-based interaction and exchange, it includes, requires and involves the active and extensive participation of two other influential entities, India and US which are indispensable to inter-regional trade. The US acts as a hub for many transactions that occur in the region, given its global orientation and deep economic and political engagements with both regions, India as well is an increasingly important conduit and node in this exchange. Between the two large democracies, both India and the US are co-sponsors of the United Nations Democracy Fund in 2005 and enjoy mutual solidarity.[2]

The US node remains important because other major energy consumers in North-East Asia (largest consumers due to their sizes) like Japan, US, India, China Energy (abbreviated as JUICE in this publication) consumers, though important, dominant and influential, may find it difficult to achieve regionalism without its support (direct or indirect). Gilbert Rozman probably represent the least positive interpretation of regionalism, arguing that differential emphasis and progress in development has resulted in domestic sectors (not including the US) within the JUICE grouping at times focusing on niche and more parochial interests rather than regional and globalized ones.[3]

The US on the other hand has clear, important, capacity-building and entrenched interests in both regions, the Middle East and North-East Asia. Intra-regionally, the US also has solid and essential alliances with important and major regional stakeholders such as South Korea and Japan. For example, Christopher Dent argues that, in North-East Asia, a meeting point of four dominant entities (US, Japan, China and Russia) exists, the US has maintained a clearly mapped out interest in the region and remains an important balancer between North-East Asian entities in times of geopolitical rivalry and is strategically positioned to tilt opinions on issues related to North-East Asian regionalism in one direction or the other.[4]

The US is also a highly adaptable entity which can accommodate different interests and priorities that shape the region. This adaptability may also follow different administration as their own different distinctive styles, whether Republicans or Democrats, shape the outcome of events in both the Middle East and North-East Asia. Very often, regional entities are influenced by the external environment for inter-regionalism crafted by the US in the interest of open, free and vibrant trade and exchanges for the interests of the stakeholders. Its balancing and tilting factor in final decision-making processes and its agreement or support lent to processes taking place in both regions can make an initiative a success or reality from the proposal stage.

This is not to argue that dominant regional entities like China and India or the Gulf states are unimportant, neither does it downplay smaller and medium-sized entities. The regional entities have their own space and leeway for exerting their influence and power, while limited regionally, are globally important. They exert their influence economically, demographically, diplomatically reflective of their capabilities and resources among various other means. Such influence may not even be defined by state boundaries. As Vali Nasr succinctly noted, the global Islamic populace (a transnational entity) is equal to India and China's demographics with more than 1 billion and in 2008, the GDP of Iran, Pakistan, Saudi Arabia and Turkey with 420 million people was US$3.3 trillion, equivalent to India, but India has triple the number of people.[5]

There are other ways through which the middle power economics/states/ entities are exerting their influence. For example, Saudi Aramco, according to David Rothkopf, is undergoing localization of manpower personnel.[6] Such shifts may not be globally tectonic in nature but can have global implications which regional entities in the inter-regional energy trade as well as hyperpowers[7] may have to accommodate. The interdependence factor between these groups of economic entities, states and economies within the complex inter-regional flora and fauna lubricate the system as it has done so in the past when empires collaborated with middle and small economies and powers to make trade and exchanges a reality.

The role of the US is equally valuable as working partners for middle or medium-sized powers/states/economies. In the inter-regional sphere of the Middle East and North-East Asia, the US also plays the role, but this volume argues that it is not an empire. It argues that the US is a benign entity that acts as a hub (de facto or in reality) for transmitting and intersecting priorities and needs for entities within the Middle East as well as within North-East Asia. It is the hub that many if not almost all spokes plug into within the two regions.

The US value system and worldview have also influenced the normative behavior of the international systems, including its partners in both regions of the Middle East and North-East Asia. These values are democratic, market-driven and carefully crafted to maximize free flow of goods and energy that respond differentially to most major and minor entities within the inter-regional trade between the Middle East and North-East Asia. The values are not absorbed and taken wholesale by the stakeholder entities in both regions. Instead, they are localized, adapted, adjusted and assimilated selectively to fit local and regional conditions according to their national interests and domestic priorities.

US developmentalism values were also disseminated to the developing economies in the post-war era. Though they were not absorbed lock, stock and barrel, these important ideas of development and economic growth were adapted first by various successful economies that embarked on market-driven systems and later also adapted, hybridized, localized by former command/socialist economies. The basic foundations were based on American ideas of market-driven capitalism and free trade. Some examples of local, regional, ideological and religious adaptations to these ideas and also resistance towards complete borrowing can be found in Howard J. Wiarda's *Non-Western Theories of Development* that is potentially thought-provoking.[8]

The current global system from a broad perspective is a combination of historical ideas and tradition of far-reaching and permeable global trade based on: stakeholders in the form of dominant economic entities along with their regional systemic components of small and medium sized economies/states (systemic); European contributions in the industrial age and their influence on contemporary features (historical); and localized/indigenously adapted American values and ideas of trade, energy exchanges and technological development (knowledge-based adaptation).

The conceptualization of history comes into play as trade had once been a past element in inter-regional trade between the Middle East and North-East Asia but the historical Silk Road declined and the rise of maritime trade overtook it. Nevertheless, the increasing trade links, sometimes along the same traditional Silk Road routes, appear to conjure imageries of a historical trading relationship. Even if this is so, the inter-regional trading relationship takes place against a new backdrop with important and significant participants such as the US and its vast transnational global reach, transnational companies, state-owned companies, sovereign funds, alternative energy advocates, and many other new players.

Conceptually, both North-East Asia and the Middle East are individually and in and by themselves not coherent institutional blocs that resemble or represent advanced or even institutional stages of regionalism although some early preliminary initiatives/mechanisms are in place to form the foundation of a loose form of regionalism and issue-specific cooperation (particularly in the economic aspect).

Consequently, North-East Asia-Middle East inter-regional trade and exchanges have been based on the trade between individual regional economies, typically represented by regional suppliers dealing with single large economies or energy consumers in North-East Asia. Such arrangements give rise to some scholarly and practitioner arguments of 'Asian premium' or price differentials based on competing interests between large energy consumers in North-East Asia vying for the same oil or fossil fuel products which they are dependent on from the Middle East.

Discourses of the interrelatedness of trade and energy in Middle-East and North-East Asia trading relationship appear to be foregrounded more in the present compared to past literature on contemporary inter-regional exchange between the two regions. This may be due to perceptions (and also reality, backed up by economic quantitative figures) of the increased wealth of both regions in the Middle East and North-East Asia stimulating trade and consumption. Both regions, through export-orientation (North-East Asia) and accumulation of oil revenues (Middle East), have more resources to spend and consume.

Among the entities involved in the inter-regional trade between the Middle East and North-East Asia, the economies and entities of JUICE consumers are highlighted in the study between North-East Asia and the Middle East. The US and India are included due to their important impact and influence on the inter-regional trade between North-East Asia and the Middle East. Other than the US, almost all other economies and energy consumers in North-East

Asia are busy with economic growth (including the large emerging economy of India) and/or other pressing priorities. The US alone has the global reach, capacity, multifaceted engagement and interest in managing the system of energy exchange that straddles the two regions of North-East Asia and the Middle East. The discussion of its role is indispensable in inter-regional trade and exchanges between the Middle East and North-East Asia.

In this equation between energy importers and producers in the inter-regional trade, demography appears to be an important factor in determining usage and also influence on the energy trade. Demography may make a direct impact on consumption, when it is paired off with rising development and economic progress and prosperity. Demography may also provide large emerging economies with sizeable workforces to produce products that supply mature economies, generating trade surplus for these large emerging economies known as BRICS (Brazil, Russia, India, China and the recently joined South Africa into this league).

India's rising demand is often paired off with China to highlight the growing energy needs of emerging and developing economies. Competition and cooperation between them often have global impact. And their consumption adds on to existing consumption found in mature JUICE entities like the US and Japan, often without the same technological efficiency and sophistication like them to use the energy more efficiently. Increased consumption of course may be predicated upon the unproblematic portrayal of the sustained and continued rise of emerging large economies. It is also predicated upon the imageries of the desires of tens of millions to get out of energy-scarcity situations with no access to electricity and more individuals within the middle class to attain similar lifestyles akin to their counterparts in developed economies.

This assumption of linear development associated with energy scarcity and the aspirations of the middle-class emergence in large emerging economies like India and China however, may not be unproblematic, given the number of internal contradictions that both India and China face and it may affect both economies in terms of energy consumption. It may also be dependent on the fact that both large emerging economies are unable, in the short and medium term, to reinvent themselves and formulate new energy-saving technologies or alternative energy development that may either reduce the amount of energy used or pare down reliance on fossil fuels.

Even fossil fuels formerly (and contemporarily) perceived as polluting continue to appear in the discourse on energy alternatives in North-East Asia with coal, for example, as seen in energy narratives and discourses as plentiful and affordable. But it is also seen as an output of back-breaking work that is risky and dangerous.[9] Focusing on the positives only, if the characterization for coal is affordability and abundance, then the discourse on gas energy is one of long-term commitment and supply with the imagery of a cleaner form of fossil fuel for future utilization and development.

The discourse of scarcity is strong, entrenched and dominant in North-East Asia. First applied to Japan in the modern era when it embarked on modernization after the 1868 Meiji Restoration and emerged as an energy consumer whose dependence on fossil fuels became intertwined with its industrialization process. The discourse is then applied to post-market reform China where fast growth based on the pattern of accelerated state-led growth which eventually saw demand outstrip supply even though it has a significant and sizeable domestic output in oil and a globally significant share of coal. The discourse drives the urgency of North-East Asian energy consumers to search globally for more energy resources and also led to anxiety of consumers and stakeholders to compete for more energy resources. Energy scarcity both real and imagined drives oil prices and its speculation.

Lisa Margonelli argued that 2003 was the defining year when the rise of Indian and Chinese demand for energy made the jump in global demand for oil prominent after years of retrenchment (twenty years' worth) in refining jobs.[10] 2003 was also memorable for other reasons. According to Margonelli, China overtook Japan to become globally the number two biggest importer of oil.[11] The discourses and narratives on the reasons behind the increased energy usage in North-East Asia vary, often greatly. For example, Margonelli pointed out the impact of rumors and speculation on energy prices, including Chinese production of ceramic toilets and kilns that are energy-intensive ventures directly related to energy price hikes.[12] Other explanations including that of John Hofmeister (former president of Shell) included attributing increased fuel usage for example in first half of 2008 to increased use of oil for the airline industry and the hosting of the Olympic games in China.[13]

Consumption pattern was also another possible reason for increased oil use in China. Margonelli argued that diesel generators by Chinese consumers to manage blackouts resulted in nearly an additional million barrels of oil consumed on a daily basis in 2004 compared with 2003.[14] Consumption is in fact something desired and banked on by oil producers eager for more economic revenues and so some oil producers have strategically offered oil supplies under market rates and better quality supplies (e.g. with lower sulphur), for example in the case of Saudi supplies to China.[15]

The Saudis enjoy the status of having the largest oil reserves, as the second largest producer of oil after Russia and the largest exporter. In the popular discourse and narrative in energy literature, Saudi Arabia is both statistically and comparatively the largest supplier in the market with the Ghawar oil facility the biggest ever discovered oilfield in energy history.[16] According to Geoffrey

Heal, Saudi Arabia has proven oil reserves of 262.7 billion barrels and outputs approximately 8 million barrels per day for yearly revenue of US$175 billion.[17]

While the narratives on oil suppliers are those of harnessing the future perceived potential needs and imports of rising emerging economies, others are producing discourses on mitigating increased oil and energy consumption. In the discourse on mitigating consumption, there appears to be a potential debate between incrementalism and radical energy innovation and/or supply. Incrementalism suggests the long-drawn effects of a paced but step-by-step conservation of energy leading to an accumulative effect. It is a gradual process that requires patience to negotiate a challenging road to eventual energy saving.

Incrementalism may also suggest the possibility of looking at alternative sources of energy such that their slow development and technological introduction into daily lives through market needs may make an eventual difference as consumers transition from fossil-fuel lifestyles to comparatively carbon-cleaner lifestyles. Strong advocates of incremental conservation even argue that it can displace fossil fuels and signal the so-called obsolescence of oil energy, for example Paul Roberts has suggested that the manner in which governments of developed economies like the US and Japan have invested substantially in energy-saving technologies and automobiles may in turn signal lower demand for OPEC (Organization of Petroleum Exporting Countries) oil.[18]

Radical innovation advocates may not be able to have the same patience as incrementalists. They posit that radical changes may be possible through the myriad of existing technological developments that can be further developed to move away from polluting (or what they perceived as) polluting sources of energy including, primarily, fossil fuel-based options to cleaner and more carbon-free energy utilization. Regardless of incremental or radical innovation adherents, precedents in the late modern era appear to have a track record of less than positive success in completely replacing the need for oil energy and there continues to be reliance on fossil fuels.

Paradigm shift and radical change as opposed to slow transition away from fossil fuels may be underlined by the urgency of fast-emerging energy consumers who may join an already overcrowded group of developed economies that are major energy users. They may also be motivated by oil-peak theories or less positive projections of the impact of energy on limiting growth and economic development. It may also be motivated by narratives and discourses that link energy shortages and its negative effects on contemporary civilizations and lifestyles. The discourse and narrative in this aspect is underlined by the real-life example of one and a half billion individuals or 25 per cent of the global populace without reach to electricity or fossil fuels.[19]

Within the rubric of the narrative of the alternatives, scholarly arguments have turned to alternative fuel and also alternative energy sources as a means for lessening reliance on the Middle East in terms of North-East Asian energy consumers.

The narrative of alternative sources of energy (either in terms of geographical locations or energy-conserving technologies) in North-East Asia may historically be traced back to Japan in the 1970s with the outbreak of the oil crisis that necessitated Japan's global outreach for energy, something emulated and/ or evolved independently by later developers in North-East Asia, including China and South Korea, both of whom have embarked on accelerated processes of global energy searches. Before the oil crisis, the only time Japan experienced energy and oil scarcity was during the immediate post-war period when Sony founder Akio Morita observed that due to petroleum shortage, vehicles and public transport had to rely on waste oil, charcoal and usable solid fuels.[20]

Energy diversification policies and diplomacy in North-East Asia was also pioneered by Japan after the oil crisis as it sought to reduce overreliance on a single source, namely the Middle Eastern suppliers. This is a pattern that other North-East Asian economies and India have followed after their own phases of economic development. Japan for example, does not have any reliance on single sources, no matter how large (e.g. Russian prolific gas reserves) but relies on a variety of Middle Eastern and Asian suppliers.[21]

The nearest alternative energy-rich region to North-East Asia is Russia and this awareness is well understood by the Russians who visualized its role as a 'fuel tank' for North-East Asia as early as the late 1990s by scholars such as Vladimir I. Ivanov.[22] According to Stephen King, Russia has globally the largest output of oil and natural gas combined, accounting for 12.4 per cent of world oil output (ranking after Saudi Arabia) and 19.6 per cent for gas.[23] The earliest example of North-East Asian interest in importing Russian oil may have been in the autumn of 1973 when Prime Minister Tanaka visited the Soviet Union and talked about the Tyumen oil facilities in Siberia with their Russian counterparts.[24] After Japan, later developers in Asia also followed suit with their own interest in Russian resources. The discourse and narrative on Russia conceptualizes the resource-rich energy producer as the greatest hope for fossil fuel energy-scarce North-East Asia based on the argument of complementarity derived from Russia's increasing economic yield from energy revenues. According to Paul Roberts, Russia relies on petroleum trade for 33 per cent of its total revenues and sees the incoming revenue as an economic resource for developing north Russia.[25]

Offer of developmental aid and capacity-building help in exchange for energy appears to be a pattern found among Asia's large economies during their fast-growth phases. Japan energy diplomacy that was initiated in the 1970s based energy diplomacy on friendship, goodwill, infrastructure development and financial aid and help. This template appears to be replicated in other North-East Asian energy consumers, with adaptation to local conditions and capabilities.

For example, China promised infrastructure construction in exchange for fuel, one example according to Margonelli, China provided US$3 billion and a refinery facility for Nigeria.[26]

The main thesis or theme of this volume is based on the idea of inter-regional exchange between North-East Asia and the Middle East (including the Gulf region). Two items, trade and energy, are specially highlighted as case studies. Energy (particularly oil and natural gas) is chosen given that it is an established commodity in the exchanges between the two regions while trade is more historical but nevertheless important due to increasing economic contacts between the two regions. Trade and energy may be bundled into one single package as the economies found within the two regions may be interacting through comprehensive economic deals as part of a conscious effort to deemphasize energy due to efforts (in both North-East Asia and the Middle East) to diversify away from it and to utilize trade as a leverage to move into a post-energy interactive platform. For the foreseeable future, however, energy remains an important component and may not be eliminated from the exchange totally.

Rising energy use and increased trade between the Middle East and North-East Asia may be considered as part of the perceived concept of 'rising' Asia. Given that the discourse and narrative of 'rising Asia' has built up to a certain extent both in popular perceptions and perceptions among specialists and is now an industry by itself, the narrative appears to assume that there is an unproblematic continuity in the growth of Asian economies, particularly among the large emerging economies, such as India and China. Based on this unproblematic projection of growth, there are projections of increased energy use.

The chapter on 'Progress and Development' discusses the popularly cited ingredients for Asian economic growth, including that of science and technological development, education, demographic growth and rapid industrialization. But the same ingredients that have brought about fast growth have also stimulated the contradictions of development. Industrialization, and its consequents, increased urbanization and the spread of personal vehicles, are several popularly cited causes of challenges to the emerging economies' environments. This is the counterbalance to the perceptions of the so-called shift of gravity of the world economy to the Asia-Pacific economies.

Demographic growth which has also created a large market for some emerging economies may also be responsible for competitive use of resources, diseases in overcrowded cities, etc. These contradictions of development centres upon the ability to feed populations of developing areas, keeping them employed, locating enough resources for them to utilize. These priorities appear to lead to several major challenges, including depleting resources, diseases from overcrowding and socio-economic gap from fast development.

In the worst case scenario, such contradictions in development have been argued by some scholars to have possibly caused the collapse of previously flourishing societies. Resource-use shortage may have contributed to the collapse of some civilizations, economies and states and therefore it may be a common challenge faced by fast growth experienced in both large developing economies and developed economies. In defining resource use as a common problem, it may then be possible to imagine resource as something that is shared between different peoples, societies and end-users including local communities.

For energy resources, shared use may pose a formidable challenge given its strategic nature, its universal application by all types of economies and perceptions of its depletion. In such a case, consensus may be necessary for its sustainable use into the future, especially since depletion may proceed at a slow and unnoticeable pace before it hits crisis levels. Then the question becomes whether there can be incremental solutions (e.g. energy conservation) for this issue or alternative sources of energy that can help to alleviate the problem. Arguments are made for functionalist cooperation in this field, utilizing the massive resources of both developed and emerging economies.

Having cited the contradictions of development, China and India must be celebrated for their achievements which have benefited a large portion of humanity. The emergence of the Gulf economies also opened up a developmental model option in the Middle East. India's democratic system serves as an important model of inspiration as it is believed that the free system may yield benefits in the long run. India's influence stretches beyond its border through effective soft power, migrant workers and its English-proficiency in terms of working language. Indian successes in the hi-tech industry serve as possible evidence of emerging economies' leapfrogging possibilities.

China may be symbolic of the manufacturing model of development, attaining the image and perception of the world's factory. Its skilled labor force stands testimony to the enormous progress made in the fields of education and skills dissemination. In the field of education, China is turning out graduates not just in basic skills but also researchers and postgraduate students in advanced technological sectors. It may be based on this educational achievement that successes in developing the hi-tech sectors are built upon. The achievement of China in lifting millions out of poverty is also cited as a contribution to the world economy. Human resource development may also be a considered as an inspiring feature in Chinese economic development.

China is also contributing to the region as a consumer market for goods made by the rest of the world. In this sense, it appears to be becoming both a manufacturing platform as well as a major consumption centre, with its role as an engine of growth in the world economy. East Asia which had benefitted from inexpensive items produced in China may also be benefitting from selling their own products and services to China. Given its importance in this sense, China may be playing an increasingly influential role in the world economy and therefore, attaining an important position within the G20 economies.

The Gulf economies serve as an important model for others in the Middle East. They may be using oil wealth to create new employment opportunities and future development not based exclusively on energy. Through strong sovereign wealth funds (SWFs),[27] the Gulf economies have become net investors both in the developed and emerging economies, including Asia. The Gulf also provides employment for millions of South Asians including those from India, becoming a cosmopolitan area within the Middle East.

The challenge for emerging economies may be how to measure progress, given the different stages of development that the developed, developing and large emerging economies are in. Even within the large emerging economies, the different macro-regions may also have their own developmental differences. Located at different developmental stages, modernization, postmodernity and transhumanism may represent different paradigms of developmental needs at different stages of development and sometimes they may have conflicting needs. Delineating the boundaries of when one process stops and the other takes over based on staged progression in deterministic linear views of development may be a mindset challenge for planners.

In reality, different aspects of these doctrines and development paradigms may coexist within and among regional economies and sometimes within a large emerging economy that may have different macro-regions as well. The reactions and counter-reactions to different modes of development mindsets and framework may become the push and pull of perceptions of progress within and between the large emerging economies and developed ones. It may also become a debate of universalism versus particularism as the universalistic appeal of developmental models/precedents either complements or clashes with the particularistic needs of individual economies.

The tensions between universalistic prescriptions of development and particularistic needs may then be manifested in different developmental priorities. These clashes in priorities may be seen in resource use versus sustainability of its use and the environmental impact that resource use may bring about. These may also be dilemmas in consumption by rising middle classes aspiring to have better living standards while mitigating the excesses of consumption. At play here may be the state priorities of maintenance of social cohesion, harmony and socio-economic equity in development.

Perhaps, rather than differentiating between developed/advanced, large emerging and developing economies, it may be possible to characterize the overall development that is taking place within Asia as a large chunk of humanity emerging out of poverty in concert with the economic exchanges, assistance, loans, aids and technology transfer from the developed and advanced economies. This may be conceptualized as an overall progress in tandem with the needs of different categories of economies within the region.

The intricate and delicate balance of developmental roles and interests among the developed, large emerging and developing economies may also indicate the element of interdependency in existence between them. Here, functionalist and constructivist perspectives see the cooperative element between different economies and also the permeability of the lessons of development through the array of developmental models available in the region as possible examples and test cases for other developing economies.

Given that development has followed a certain trajectory, infrastructure construction, the language of development and the common trans-boundary challenges faced, there appears to be the emergence of a common language that may facilitate communications and also exchange of ideas. Common language may also facilitate the transmission of ideas quickly, for example the benefits of energy conservation, green technologies and environmentally friendly initiatives are all incorporated into the common language of development, the mainstream narrative that appear to focus on no-detriments elements.

Japan, in this case, serves as an important model of development, given that it is the first to develop within Asia and a contributive force in influencing development in other areas. Japan as a developmental model and its role in the transfer of technology in East Asia is also well known. Good educational systems, infrastructure developments and disciplined workforce may all be considered as hallmarks of Japanese success that have been transmitted and adapted by other Asian economies.

The role of Japan and its state-led development and its role in coordinating development and trade may now be familiar. It has been perceived as a recipe for fast growth through the adoption of right policies. The Japanese model with its transnational production networking and also its export-led growth may have also played a role in convincing others in the region of the benefits of tapping into globalization and reaching out to new markets. India and China may be potential beneficiaries of this model.

Japan as a model may be all the more remarkable because Japan is resource-scarce and its rapid growth depended on the availability of energy with nearby sources and, more importantly, with the Middle East. Japan was the first East Asian nation to establish a comprehensive relationship with the Middle Eastern region. The 1970s oil crisis provided Japan with the opportunity to initiate resource diplomacy in which Japan skilfully established a stronger presence in the Middle East.

Japan is a major oil consumer and also natural gas importer from the region. After the 1970s oil crisis which affected Japan and impacted on its economy,

Japan also offered loans and aids to the Middle East as part of this resource diplomacy. In a pattern that appears to be similar to Japan, other North-East Asian economies have also appear to have started their own resource diplomatic efforts to link up with the Middle East. Japan works closely with the US in the region and is also a strong supporter of the peace process.

Non-oil trade export from Japan has also helped Japan balance its oil trade with the Middle East as an importer. With the rise of oil revenues in the Gulf, Japan and the Gulf region are also increasingly engaged in investments. Japan's business association lobbied hard for the Japanese government to engage in a free trade agreement with the region that included energy amid overall expansion of non-energy economic trade and exchanges. Like all other North-East Asian economies, Japan is also working hard to diversify its energy sources and other aspects of reducing reliance on the Middle East for energy.

Given that there are developmental challenges in the availability of resources, Japan's resource-scarce makeup and its advanced development despite this shortcoming serves as a case study for demographically large emerging economies with similar situations of resource-scarcity arising from the depletion of their resources, placing them in similar situation with the Japanese. Japan's contributions as a model for other developing economies and the indirect effect of lifting the peoples of those economies from poverty into economic development phases (particularly the large emerging economies) makes an indirect contribution to lifting a large mass of humanity from developmental challenges as well.

Now that a common motivation for economic development appears to have emerged, perhaps the next stage of development may require conduits, interfaces, media and platforms for understanding developmental needs in different economic settings. Patience, foresight and long-term mindsets may be needed as developed, developing and large emerging economies tackle their own specific, idiosyncratic and unique challenges in the near future. The same elements may also be needed to reduce tensions and differences in developmental needs. This is not as simple to implement as it appears in theory, given the differing geopolitical, economic and national interests of economies in the region. But it may be possible to begin with the common trans-boundary challenges first, given that the instincts for cooperation may be comparatively and relatively stronger there.

Whether a common motivation for economic development has emerged, or if contradictions of development have been resolved, or if there is coexistence of differing levels of recognitions of developmental challenges and poverty reduction, progress seems to be centred on trade. It may be possible that there is a separation of the contradictions of development from trade. Trade may be positively perceived to be beneficial for economic development. It drives prosperity, employment and development. Trade also appears to enhance the interdependency element as it increases economic contact and then branches off to other forms of interaction as well.

In terms of energy relationships, like Japan, other North-East Asian energy consumers and India have developed their own resource diplomacy with the region. China increased its oil import contact with the Middle East after its oil sufficiency era ended in the early 1990s. China's oil use transformation may be considered dramatic. From the 1970s, when it was a net exporter of oil to Japan (after the outbreak of the 1970s oil crises), Chinese economic development moved at such speeds that, by the early 1990s, it became a major importer of Middle Eastern crude oil and, by the first half of the twenty-first century, China overtook Japan as North-East Asia's largest consumer of oil.

Like Japan, China is keen to diversify its energy resources, including examining alternative energy, other non-Middle Eastern locations for crude oil resources, non-oil fossil fuels like natural gas and non-fossil fuels like nuclear. China may also be interested to develop its own gas reserves. Russia probably represents the closest non-Middle Eastern source of oil and gas. Another energy resource-rich region may be Central Asia. Despite all these diversification efforts, some of these solutions may need a long-term perspective while others may not be sufficient to meet domestic needs entirely, therefore importation of Middle Eastern oil remains important not just for China but for the three largest North-East Asian economies, as well.

Even in the oil trade, the range of items covered may not just be on crude oil delivery alone, investments may move into energy-related sectors. Refining capacity appears to be a major limiting factor on China's ability to process its imported oil. Outside just merely supplying oil, Middle Eastern oil producers are therefore keen to move into energy infrastructure investments. The Middle East is interested in building refineries in China as part of the energy relationship to diversify outside just natural energy resource trade. Middle Eastern investors are also keen on other North-East Asian investments for the same purpose. It appears both regions are embedding energy as part of a bigger package of bilateral trade relationship. Like other North-East Asian economies, China is also including crude oil as part of an overall bilateral package of trade items to broaden its relationship with the Middle East.

There is also a possibility of natural gas becoming a major feature of Middle East–China economic relations. The region is the home of some of the world's largest gas reserves, with Iran holding the world's second largest at 993 trillion cubic feet (tcf), Qatar with the third largest at 895 tcf, Saudi Arabia the fourth largest at 250 tcf, and the UAE the fifth largest reserve holder at 214 tcf.[28] Given its environmentally cleaner image, natural gas may represent the future of North-East Asian energy consumption and its interactions with the Middle East. Natural gas may provide even more opportunities for infrastructure exchanges, given that gas delivery and infrastructure construction may be nego-tiated as part of gas supply packages. Given the complexities of such deals, it may be possible that the state will continue to be involved in shaping the outcome and implementations of negotiations.

It may not be possible to discuss the links between North-East Asia and the Middle East without discussing the role of India. India is the major entity in South Asia and it sits as a conduit between North-East Asia and the Middle East via land and water (Indian Ocean). Its strategic position will be of utmost important in trade and energy transmission between the two regions of North-East Asia and the Middle East. India is by itself an emerging economy and enjoys good relationships with many other major economies, and as a democratic coun-try, it speaks a common language with the US and other democratic entities in Asia and the Middle East.

India itself will also become a major top-ranking energy consumer in the world and its strategic position, usage, demographic growth and dominance of space over which these resources are transmitted means that India will be increasingly important. India's rising middle classes, transition to manufacturing sectors, its manpower presence in the Gulf area, emerging economy and popular cultural soft power may be additional extensions of its influence overseas. Indian energy companies have been competing as well as cooperating with energy com-panies from other major North-East Asian economies.

Given its increasing energy use, Indian trade with the Middle East will also become increasingly important. Initially sufficient in energy, Indian energy needs are unleashed by its economic reforms and growth that followed. Indian domestic needs have not met up with its demand and is moving up the ranks in terms of energy import from the Middle East. To diversify its relationship with the region, India has moved on to non-energy trade with the Middle East, including the service sectors, e.g. hotel, hospitality and leisure sectors.

While natural gas may have been identified as a growth area in North-East Asian and Indian interactions with the Middle East, diversification into non-energy trade with the Gulf energy producers may be important because there are also signs that the Gulf economies may need increasing amounts of natu-ral gas for their own economic development. In the Gulf, the lack of energy to meet demand also has the effect of halting or even reversing years of growth.[29] While power consumption in the Gulf states is projected to increase by 50 per cent before 2014, regional power generation will likely meet only 30 per cent of demand.[30] Given the tremendous pressures on the region's natural gas produc-tion, there is much uncertainty as to the source for additional power output.[31]

Within the Gulf itself, there are also plans to create regional networks of energy linkages. Of great importance among the regional energy projects in the Gulf is the $10 billion Dolphin natural gas pipeline that started exporting natural gas from Qatar's vast North Field to the UAE and Oman in 2007.[32] The UAE and Oman for example imported natural gas from Qatar in the multibillion dollar Dolphin natural gas pipeline, and also by the planned $ 1.6 billion multinational power grid.[33] The Gulf Cooperation Council (GCC) also constructed the Interconnection Project across the GCC to harmonize energy production and minimize redundancies in the power sector and this mission is all the more significant in view of the GCC's sizeable power shortages, which was inclusive of Oman, the UAE, Kuwait and Saudi Arabia. In fact, each nation urgently required natural gas (Qatar has an abundant supply) to fuel their power sectors.[34]

To forestall the inevitable rise in prices, many Gulf countries are contemplating everything from nuclear power to extensive solar power arrays as Saudi Arabia's government-sponsored vision statement outlines the steps to become a major producer and possible regional exporter of solar power in the coming decades.[35] Given that the Gulf economies may also need natural gas resources to sustain their rapid economic growth, it may be possible that the nature of relationships and exchanges between the Gulf and Asia may be different. One possible trend spotted may be their mutual interests in the agricultural sectors of East Asia and this area's ability to feed the growing populations in the Middle East.

Having discussed North-East Asia and the Middle East and the South Asian passageway of India and the Indian Ocean, at the centre of the discussion is the role of the US. US support is crucial for any initiatives, events or development cited within this publication. The US is a determinant of whether the role for a particular area or aspect of exchange is constructive. American innovation and technologies are also driving important changes within the areas covered. In other words, its role is indispensible to any energy technological initiative. The US's constant innovation and rethink serves as inspiration for the rest of the Asian economies as they tap into the US's universalist developmental thinking and view it as a model for their own development and adaptations.

The reactive, adaptive and fast-changing US model of development and its ability to cope with multiple challenges gives it a central position in the global economy, therefore the discussion of its central position may be unavoidable. In its re-engineering efforts, the US also influences the rest of the world in development. In this way it has universalistic tendencies, and when it copes with changes and emerges stronger thereafter from the experience, the US inspires emulation, imitation and learning instincts from economies within Asia. The US developmental model's contribution to humanity cannot be underestimated.

Given its central position, therefore, it may be possible to imagine the US as the central hub to which the North-East Asian and Gulf economies may plug into for technology, investments, loans and aids and perhaps most importantly, ideas and inspirations. Being an open economy and firmly embedded into globalization, the US seeks partnerships with other major economies and powers for stabilizing the world system. US involvement in the Middle East is on an inter-regional basis as it envisions a US–Middle East partnership. It plays a global role for North-East Asia and the Gulf by leading the guarantee of stable, secure and safe supplies of energy from the Gulf region to North-East Asia.

Bilaterally, the US is equally important for India, China, Japan, South Korea and the Gulf economies. US importation of Indian-originated information technology enables India to develop into a major service provider, becoming the services workshop for the world as it is known today. Its normalization of relations with China in the 1970s also opened China to market reforms and reintegration into the world economy. US is also a close partner of Japan. US is also a receiving hub of the successful elements of Hindu, Confucian and Middle Eastern models of development that were inspired in the first place by the technologies, globalization plugs, management expertise and development assistance that the US offered.

It may be important to note that the US presence in the Middle East is dominant. By comparison, the North-East Asian presence is relatively recent and less comprehensive comparatively speaking. The US is engaged in both North-East Asian and Middle Eastern regions comprehensively in academic, scholarly, intellectual, military, geopolitical, technological, economic, non-governmental, aid provision, capacity-building, environmental and energy exchanges. It is multifaceted and multidimensional, covering many fronts.

Compared to the US, emerging economies in Asia may be relatively insular as they continue to tackle the internal contradictions of their development. Large emerging economies may continue to resolve issues that are most important to their socio-economic stability before venturing into broader areas to exercise their influence. The exercise of their influence may be incidental and related to the primary task of securing resources within the existing geopolitical order with minimal use of resources to meet the needs of their growing middle classes.

Such inward-looking work is all-consuming and likely to attract energy and resources from the state. Even if diplomacy becomes active, it may be prioritized from peripheral outreach to neighboring states rather than across vast regions. Therefore the impetus and motivation of ties between North-East Asia and the Middle East may still likely be based on trade utilitarianism first. Given these priorities in Asian economies, the US may be the most important entity in the global energy system, underpinning its global energy supply and distribution, perhaps in concert with the energy needs of other major economies.

Having discussed the development, roles and features of the JUICE entities, an argument is made that energy consumption and importation by the JUICE entities may determine the future shape and supply of the global energy industry.

There may be a pattern of energy transition for the JUICE economies from the use of coal to oil to natural gas and in the near future, perhaps to nuclear energy and renewables. This development appears to mirror the evolving concern with environmentalism and atmospheric release of carbon.

The historical process in which the transition from coal to oil energy takes place is covered in the volume. Coal energy was perceived as a resource for earlier stages of economic development when financial resources are not as strong. It is also perceived as a more polluting resource. Externally, the early post-war affordability of oil was also a competitive factor in declining use of coal. The increasing use of technologies, including those by the middle classes of large emerging economies, may also contribute to the increasing use of coal since automobile technologies may still be primarily based on oil.

But coal is not about to go away. Extraction of coal has been perceived to be dangerous and associated with accidents. Coal continues to enjoy one advantage over oil for major North-East Asian economies. Coal resources are nearer to North-East Asia. At least three North-East Asian locations including one nearby, Russia, China and India, have large domestic coal resources. Because of this, there may be more bargaining power for these economies when it comes to importing coal, compared to oil from the Middle East.

Coal remains an important resource in Japan, China and India even today. Imports are continuing, in many cases, increasing. Even domestic sources of North-East Asian coal may not be enough or it may be more affordable, based on market forces and cost-effectiveness of extraction, for some parts of North-East Asia to import coal rather than ship their own domestic coal resources across vast distances.

Quality may be another criteria for importing. Australia, Indonesia and Russia in the future may become important sources of coal exports for North-East Asia. Some optimistic views about coal energy may see it as another possibility for rallying cooperation on a regional basis, particularly in developing new technologies to reduce its polluting feature. Besides developing better technologies in utilizing coal, removing the transnational effects of the by-products of coal-burning may be an additional potential cooperative venture.

The JUICE entities are made up of very different energy importers. Some are large emerging economies while others are mature highly developed advanced economies. Their transition to fossil fuels involved energy sufficiency during the phase of the pre-market reform eras of the large emerging economies while oil crises in the 1970s have spurred some advanced JUICE economies like Japan to become energy-efficient and yet others to go on diversification exercises in periods of oil shortages and supply challenges.

It also appears the JUICE entities are making efforts at energy conservation, developing new environmentally friendly, energy-saving technologies and looking at renewable sources of energy. Within the JUICE constituents, cooperation between some members may be stronger than others but the commonality is that all are major consumers of global energy supply. Market-driven cooperation based on mutualistic complementarity and benefits may be an avenue for the major JUICE constituents to leverage their tremendous resources, technologies, manpower and consumers to make a difference in global energy supply and demand.

Compared to the energy trade, non-energy trade has had a long history in the economic exchanges between North-East Asia and the Middle East. History, customs and traditions may have thus fuelled the imaginations of scholars who imagine a revival of the 'Silk Road' trade. In reality, the world has changed much since then as the Silk Road declined in importance in favor of maritime time trade through which most of the world's trade is now conducted. The global conditions have changed greatly since the Silk Road days and the types and sophistication of the goods traded have also changed.

Inter-regional trade may be complicated by economic complementarity, geopolitical concerns, issues of sovereignty, market forces, etc. These may be the same factors that determine the success and failures of inter-regional institutional initiatives. Given that such challenges are real and difficult to reach compromises over or achieve consensus, the idea of pan-North-East Asian and pan-Middle Eastern blocs may prove to be unworkable.

Ultimately, it may just be considered along with other instruments of exchanges between economies. Even without such institutionalized form of contact, economic exchanges continue to take place according to market forces and the needs of demand and supply. Gulf-Asia trade continues unabated, diversifying from energy into consumer goods, service industries, investment services, hospitality, infrastructure construction and leisure industries.

The focus on consumer goods may not be surprising given North-East Asia's perceived reputation as a global manufacturing centre. North-East Asian economic growth had been based on outward looking and open export-led development. The region had also been busy breaking down trade barriers for just-in-time production and timely delivery of parts for assembly. Industrialization was also made possible by technological transfers, first pioneered by Japan's own technological transfer to other Asian economies.

Given the range of manufactured goods for exports, North-East Asian-originated products like cars may be popularly sighted in the Middle East. Exporting such products to the Middle East may possibly allow North-East Asian economies to offset their energy import trade from the Middle East. The next phase of manufacturing industrialization in North-East Asia may ironically see a lessened dependence on energy imports from the Middle East as North-East Asia embarks on a green technological revolution. However, this is likely to take a long time and is a long-term vision rather than something immediate. The long time needed for the green technological transformation to reach fruition in North-East Asia may provide time for both regions to diversity into non-energy economic exchanges.

While exporting manufactured products to the Middle East, North-East Asian economies also benefit from the import of non-energy-related processed products from the Middle East based on comparative advantages. North-East Asian economies are also interested in investment opportunities in growth industries in the Middle East, including hotel construction, for example. In return, the Middle Eastern economies are also interested in investing in future growth prospects in Asia, capturing potential profitability from the growth of the middle class in Asia through provision of their service needs (e.g. airline services).

The SWFs from both sides appear to be reaching into each other's economies. Financial integration within the Gulf region for example appears to be creating new international investors. A 'spillover' advantage of a strong GCC market will be an enhanced position for regional banks in intra-GCC multibillion dollars oil and gas investments that have almost been the sole purview of Western (or Japanese) financial institutions.[36]

Sometimes these non-energy exchanges may be based on comparative strengths, for example the utilization of East Asian manufacturing platforms by the Gulf economies for production purposes. Simultaneously, there appears to be increasing people-to-people contact in various fields, such as, in the field of education (tertiary education), cultural exchanges, art shows and exhibitions. Asian cultural influences also appear to extend into the Middle East, for example, Indian popular culture like Bollywood movies. All these exchanges indicated above may provide additional avenues for mutual understanding and may also help to diversify the relationship beyond energy. In the future, to reflect the different inter-regional interests and exchanges, it may be possible for energy and trade missions from North-East Asia to the Middle East to be composed of a collection of ministries, government agencies and departments covering a wide area of interests and topics.

Stockpiling, energy conservation, green technological development, energy efficiency technologies, renewable sources of energy, nuclear power development are all possibilities for North-East Asia to diversify away from fossil fuel imports from the Middle East. But they may take time to develop and the time needed may allow other forms of economic and people-to-people exchange to redefine a new relationship between the two regions. It has been argued along the constructivist and functionalist lines for the US to work together with other major Asian entities to develop new ways of determining and shaping the global energy and trade sectors.

Limitations

In conceptualizing the volume as a historiographical and historical study of the conceptualization of energy in Middle Eastern–North-East Asian exchanges, interpretive work may not be as effective as field work. This is a limitation of the volume. It helps to conceptualize and visualize how practitioners and scholars engage in the topic through discourses, narratives and arguments but may not reflect the actual day-to-day realities of energy understanding by the ordinary consumers or producers in both regions.

While the aim of the volume is to be inter-regional in perspective, it may not fully capture the global implications of the inter-regional exchange between the two complex regions. Inter-regional exchanges often have global implications and global events often have impact on inter-regional exchanges. Simulations based on complex theories may be useful in further conceptualizing the quantitative aspect of the subject-matter with complex simulations of oil supply and demand. This exercise may also quantitatively calculate the permutations of various factors on energy demand and supply while making projections for the future.

There are other perspectives not mentioned in this volume. Alternative sources of energy may also refer to competitive instincts for resources in the Arctic circle, the oil sands of Alberta or oil shale (all at points claimed by some to be the next frontier of oil energy) and a wide variety of discourses, studies and narratives on alternative renewable energies, but they are not covered in the volume and perhaps deprivileged in the volume's emphasis on oil, gas and non-energy trade.

The scholarly interpretations of alternative sources of energy are often intertwined with important discourses and narratives on environmentalism and climate change, both of which deserve separate detailed coverage and have been mostly left out of this volume's focus on inter-regional ties between North-East Asia and the Middle East. Such perspectives add value and have important consequences related to the lives and natural environment of the two regions. For example, Helen Caldicott points out that the World Wide Fund for Nature classified the Gulf as an important stop for millions of waterbirds facing the possibility of extinction or in danger of it from man-made energy ventures and the accidents (e.g. slicks and spills).[37] How ecology affects the food chain, product safety, sustainable lifestyles, ethical consumption, corporate social responsibilities, trade standards and many other issues are vital and equally important to the subject matter.

Given enough resources, it may be possible to consider future companion volumes on these two subjects. Other perspectives that may be equally important and may include the views of middle and small powers in the inter-regional trade between the Middle East and North-East Asia. Middle powers like South Korea are equally important in the ecology of inter-regional trade between the two regions of North-East Asia and the Middle East. Readers interested in an accessible and important publication on the history of the position and importance of Korea in the North-East Asian and global context may read Bruce Cumings' *Korea's Place in the Sun: A Modern History*.[38] In this important account, one may detect the inseparable bond between US and Korean modernity and modernization as well as contemporary development within the context of North-East Asia. It is a good example of America's entrenched and essential interests among middle power/state/entities in the North-East Asian sector.

The edited volume by Charles K Armstrong, Gilbert Rozman, Samuel S. Kim and Stephen Kotkin *Korea at the Center Dynamics of Regionalism in North-East Asia* is an important work that takes a Korea-centred approach in analysing North-East Asian development and is a valuable resource to detect how Korea, despite its medium power/economy/state status, remains an important intermediary between entities in the North-East Asian regions and extra-regional stakeholders.[39] Due to the focus on the larger energy consumers – JUICE entities, smaller-sized economies may be deprivileged in this historiography and history of inter-regionalism between the two regions. In the flora and fauna of inter-regional exchange between the Middle East and North-East Asia, the core dominant consumers and producers may make important and far-reaching decisions but the collective decisions and preferences of middle and minor powers determine the path of least resistance for major power decision-making processes.

And then there were uncertainties and new developments, in the midst of writing this volume, Japan's Fukushima nuclear crisis and the Arab 'spring' broke out, adding on to the challenges of interpretations of the role of energy in Middle Eastern–North-East Asian relations. Such political-economic developments may potentially change parts or substantial components of the energy map in the exchanges between the Middle East and North-East Asia. These developments are rather early in occurrence and may potentially have unpredictable results that may give rise to new narratives, discourses and viewpoints about the inter-regional exchanges. For one thing, the events appear to highlight once again the important and crucial balancing and tilting role of the US in the Middle Eastern region.

Bearing in mind the limitations, in writing this historiography and literature review, the following elements appear to be influential in determining the shape, extent and outcome of inter-regional trade and energy exchange between the Middle East and North-East Asia.

Anxiety

Narratives (many of them) are built on anxiety of energy scarcity and the limited nature of energy commodities. Sometimes, the anxiety becomes a form of tangible reality as when 1970s Japanese consumers scrambled for household supplies amid perceptions of shortages. Anxiety is associated with an energy crisis in this case. Anxiety is also built upon the discourse realm of the rise of middle classes in large emerging economies in turn based on the premise of the unproblematic rises of these large economies. Anxiety may also be built upon different interpretations of progress. The different understandings and interpretations of progress and its benchmarks may result in tensions and anxiety directed or misdirected at one particular highlighted and exceptionalized factor. Resource-scarcity drives anxiety but it can also drive innovation in the case of Japan when it sharpened energy conservation practices and motivated new energy saving technologies consequential to the 1970s oil crisis.

Associated with oil crisis is the narrative of dependence and overdependence on foreign sources of energy. This anxiety-driven narrative of dependence motivates economies and states to undertake diplomatic, economic and energy initiatives that are often resource-intensive (e.g. energy diplomacy in dispensing economic capacity-building), technology-driven (e.g. green energy-conserving technologies) and/or requiring of patience (alternative energy development).

History

History provides the precedents for speculating the outcome, shape and actions of inter-regional trade. Narratives of the inter-regional trade may be found at both the imaginative level as well as grounded empirically. It is at the imaginative when narratives include romanticized ideas of Silk Road revivalism, given its very real historical superseding by maritime routes. Yet symbolically, narratives and discourses may be referring to a revived Silk Road as a cultural and historical concept facilitating the development of further ties which may then lead to great trade and energy exchange rather than an actual physical reformation of the ancient trade route. This volume argues that any such conceptual Silk Road takes place in concert with other factors like technology (an internet Silk Road may also be built upon the same cultural and historical symbolism) and also the important and facilitating presence of the US which may not be represented in ancient pre-modern historical terms but whose support is crucial for any contemporary inter-regional trade and energy exchange initiatives to work.

The contemporary global benchmark for trade and energy sectors is probably the US whose innovation and ideas are intermediated through successful regional nodes like Japan or the Gulf states and then transmitted to the rest of the region. Historical emulation and adaptation results in recognizable but locally adapted features such as developmental infrastructure, trade interfaces with the global system and production systems for export-orientation or raw materials/commodities processing for exports in the cases of the Middle East and North-East Asia.

Historical precedents also present important role models for learning and adaptation. Japan is an example of a developmental model for other North-East Asian entities, having been the early industrializer in Asia and also actively transferring its technological and management knowhow to other economies. Japan's state-led model became a de facto model of development for East Asia and to India to a certain limited extent.

As for energy, a dominant historical narrative appears to hint at the evolutionary nature of coal to oil to natural gas/nuclear and finally to renewable energy transition. This evolutionary trail is complex and sometimes based on explanations of environmental friendliness whereby each progressive fuel is more environmentally friendly than the one before it. It may also be based on anxiety about supply as each progressive fuel is seen as more abundant and/or affordable than the one before it. The renewable transition is probably one of the most contentious, given that there is a number of unknowns about how fast renewable resources can be used to replace fossil fuels and the debate also focuses on how long it will take. Narratives about fuel use are complex and sometimes dialectic, for example, coal's abundance and affordability is often contrasted with its polluting and risky extraction process.

Cultural Exchange

While there are narratives binding energy and non-energy trade together between North-East Asia and the Middle East, there is an increasingly prominent cultural component featuring popular culture such as Bollywood and other forms of cultural exchanges (such as those initiated by Japan to the Middle East) in such exchanges. Deliberately or haphazardly, the two regions have developed ties that are value-adding and make exchanges more balanced without predominantly centring on trade and energy. The same concept applies to educational exchanges and students travelling overseas for tertiary studies. Very often, in such exchanges, the globally preferred entity is still the US as an attractor of students from both the Middle Eastern and North-East Asian regions. US popular culture is also globalized, while other alternative forms of popular culture be they Bollywood, K-Pop (Korean popular culture) or J-pop (Japanese popular culture) may be popularized in particularistic realms e.g. inter-regionally and regionally *comparatively speaking and relative* to the global US popular culture.

Emotive Response

Emotive response drives the optimism behind the narratives and discourses on the rise of Asia, India, China and the Gulf states. Emotive responses in narratives may deprivilege the internal contradictions of economic growth faced by large emerging or fast-emerging economies such as pollution, crowded urban conditions, uneven distribution of wealth, etc. Emotive responses may also drive critical narratives of emerging economies and their problems without acknowledging their very important achievements in economic growth, development and increasing prosperity. The resulting power, influence and dominance of these economies are a derivative of both achievements and contradictions and emotional narratives may not fully incorporate both of these elements.

Consumption and Supply

The narrative of consumption and supply is driven by size. Large-sized suppliers like Saudi Arabia (the Ghawar oilfield keeps appearing in such narratives) dominate the supply side of energy narratives. On the consumption side, the concept of size applies to large emerging economies and their large middle classes. The narrative of size sometimes drives anxiety, particularly when it comes to supply availability and the magnitude of the problem but it also drives optimism in certain cases, narratives about the large coal reserves of China, Russia, US, the large natural gas deposits of some of the Gulf states, the sizeable oil sands of Canada, etc. Narratives on consumption sometimes break the hold of determinism in characterizing consumers and suppliers. The Gulf which is a promising natural gas supplier underwent a paradigm shift in which it became increasingly in need of its own energy reserves due to rapid development. Common to the consumption narratives of the large emerging markets is the importance of US consumption driving those economies in the past, present and probably future.

The narrative of consumption also applies to the rising middle classes of India, China and the Gulf states. The narrative of India is also transforming from a service sector subcontracting dominant node to emerging patterns of consumption among its middle class. For China, the narrative has gradually shifted through various agencies like trade publications, global popular media and/or scholarly perspectives from China as a production site and 'world factory' to a consumption site where middle classes are (both perceived and empirically proven) to have greater purchasing power for imported goods such as those from Japan and the developed markets. The narrative of Gulf prosperity based on energy revenues and emerging financial prominence is modifying the narrative of its energy-linked development and shifting towards a balanced development based on infrastructure development, service and finance sectors.

Narratives about inter-regional trade also appear to be shifting away from familiar patterns as the emerging markets in the Middle East and North-East Asia prosper. Instead of solely energy products, the Middle East is also becoming competitive in energy-related products like aluminium for North-East Asian buyers. The Gulf economies are also important consumption outlets for North-East Asian products like automobiles, electronics and other popular consumer items.

The Gulf economies are also interested in infrastructure construction projects in North-East Asia while some North-East Asian economies are interested in service-related hospitality projects in the Middle East. Energy is not necessarily the centre of such inter-regional trade links. Sometimes, the energy shortages in emerging large economies like China are attributed to bottlenecks caused by infrastructural inability to process oil supply (e.g. high-sulphur crude oil) rather than the shortage of the fossil fuel itself. Therefore, supply narratives may also be related to infrastructure development and cooperation.

Given that an era of prosperity, progress and development can be detected in narratives about India, China and the Gulf, there are other narratives that appear to focus less on exchanges with high industrial and technological and more on basic resources for sustenance and subsistence like food. Because of development and prosperity in the Gulf, for example, demand has arisen for agricultural products, in other words, consumption may not necessarily be about hi-tech sophisticated consumer products but can also apply to Maslow hierarchical needs like food items which the Gulf economies are currently searching for in East Asia.

Universalism and Particularism

A relationship exists between universal operating norms and worldviews shaped and pioneered by the US in global trade and energy exchanges. The US global system is universal and accepted as operating norms by stakeholders. At the same time, these operating norms and worldviews are interpreted according to indigenous lenses, national priorities, local needs and regional pulses. They are adapted and fitted to local and regional conditions. These principles are attractive, add value to developmentalism and accepted as conducive to trade and commerce, subject to local adaptations. This volume therefore argues that the US system is universal, and that inter-regional trade between the Middle East and North-East Asia is a particularistic aspect of the US universal global system. Trade and energy exchanges are intermediated through both the US global system as well as the hub system interlinking the two regions. The US is either preferred or indirectly relied on (free-riding) to keep the sea-lanes open for trade and energy mobility and exchanges for the rest of the inter-regional and global trading communities.

The US also plays an important balancing and tilting function. It balances between different interests in the regions within the inter-regional trade and also intermediates the inter-regional trade itself. Its tilting function is either sought or expected (directly or indirectly) by other entities in the region and the direction towards which the US tilts is crucial for any important initiatives and decision-making process to attain success. The US is also a generator of ideas, concepts and innovative thinking which is emulated or referenced by other entities in the inter-regional trade and Middle East/North-East Asian region. These ideas are then particularized, adapted to fit local conditions with modifications.

Time and Space

Time and space is probably the most underestimated element of influence. Patience and impatience often drives energy narratives. Patience is indirectly demanded of long-term solutions such as renewable energies, nuclear power and gas infrastructure development. Impatience drives the spirit of innovation to come up with energy conserving technologies or alternatives fuels that can make a near or medium-term impact on energy consumption rather than having to wait a long time for it.

Time and space related to the theme of sojourning may also be found in inter-regional narratives between the Middle East and Asia, as South Asia (particularly India) and other East Asian entities supply manpower to the Middle East for their construction and service sectors. Demographically, it is a massive spatial shift as large numbers of South Asians have become so intimately and deeply integrated into the Middle Eastern economies that they are essentially needed for its functioning and cannot be easily separated.

Coexistence and Interdependence

The contemporary discourse about inter-regional economic and energy relations between the Middle East and North-East Asia incorporates the narrative that energy is increasingly bundled with non-energy trade as a whole package. This package in turn promotes interdependence in the inter-regional economic/energy relationship between the two regions. Historically, there had been non-energy trade such as Japanese cotton transacted through the Gulf and onto the destination market of India. But, in terms of amount and product categories, they had been limited. Increasingly, electronics and automobiles make up the consumer products trade emanating from North-East Asia to the Middle East.

This publication argues that this inter-regional relationship is intermediated through the US which is the important hub that connects the interrelated exchanges in energy and trade between the two regions which plug into the hub as spokes. It also argues that India is an important feeder to this system, given its central location, important consumer market and physical transit position for energy pipelines and trade routes. Complementarity supports coexistence and interdependence given that common needs and priorities in energy often necessitate cooperation, e.g. transnational pipelines that traverse large spans of territories, prevention of price fluctuations and developing hard to reach resources.

Intra-regionally, the mutually reinforcing initiatives for cooperation, functionalism, regionalism, integration and constructivism often interact with complex forces that pull regional entities apart, whether in issues of history, differing cultural norms, political/geopolitical frictions, differential perceptions and misperceptions and/or contesting and competitive rivalries and alliances. Energy stockpiling, greater information exchanges and cooperation between state companies are all part of this narrative. Many of these instruments of cooperation require the consent and/or non-obstruction of dominant regional entities and the important tilting consent of the US.

Diversity

Instead of traders and states, there is a greater diversity of stakeholders in this inter-regional trade in the form of non-state entities like multinational or transnational energy firms and trading companies, state-owned enterprises, sovereign wealth funds, city-states and consumers. Diversity also pertains to the availability of alternative options such as renewable energy, alternative sources of energy, non-oil fossil fuels, affordable and plentiful alternatives like nuclear power. Diversity in the form of the acknowledgement of the presence of large numbers of stakeholders portrays the complex picture of the energy supply and consumption system, but diversity in the form of narratives of alternatives to oil is built upon hope, advocacy, the de-emphasis on oil as the endangering limit to growth but is also the subject of counter-narratives centred upon accusations of falsities of claim, false hopes and less utilitarian long-term solutions ungrounded in current realities.

There is also an element of competition in the narrative on diversification. Russia, for example, represents an alternative form of energy supply for North-East Asia. There are some competitive instincts between the Middle Eastern energy suppliers and the rising role of Russia as a supplier. Diversification from the North-East Asian perspective is seen as an insurance policy against overdependence on the Middle East, particularly for energy-scarce Japan and rising energy needs of India and China. Historically, there had been other instances where alternatives had been sought in the policy of diversification but none of them have been able to permanently and completely displace the importance of the Middle East as an energy supplying region, for example Japan's attempt to turn to Chinese supplies in the 1970s in Chinese oil for Japanese steel deal. The narrative about geographical alternatives continues today for North-East Asia, focusing on the regions of Central Asia, Australia, Russia and Africa as alternative regions of energy supply.

Besides energy supply, the Gulf economies and North-East Asia also present narratives of mutual investments in each others economies, given the former's oil revenues and the latter's trade surplus. But the relationship is not bilaterally inter-regionally, rather it is triangular whereby the US plays a part in continuing to be an investor in both regions, a partner for projects and/or a facilitator in financing, technology provision or management knowhow.

Table 1.1 Summary and table of various narratives and their elements

The Narratives	Elements of the Narrative
Anxiety	Energy scarcity and the limited nature of energy commodities
	Rise of middle classes in large emerging economies
	Innovation in the case of Japan when it motivated energy conservation practices and energy saving technologies
	Dependence and overdependence on foreign sources of energy
History	Romanticized ideas of Silk Road revivalism
	Role models for learning and adaptation
	Evolutionary nature of energy transition
Cultural Exchange	Popular culture such as Bollywood
	Are value-adding and makes exchanges more balanced without predominantly centring on trade and energy
	US as an attractor of students from both the Middle East and North-East Asia
	Globalized US popular culture
	Bollywood, K-Pop (Korean popular culture) or J-pop (Japanese popular culture)
Emotive Response	Drives optimism on the rise of Asia, India, China and the Gulf states
	Deprivilege the internal contradictions of economic growth in large emerging economies
	Critical narratives of emerging economies and their problems without acknowledging their very important achievements in economic growth, development and increasing prosperity
Consumption and Supply	Narrative of consumption and supply is driven by size
	Large suppliers like Saudi Arabia (the Ghawar oilfield keeps appearing in such narratives)
	Narrative of size sometimes drives anxiety when it comes to supply availability and the magnitude of the problem
	Drives optimism in certain cases, narratives about the large coal reserves of China, Russia, US, the large natural gas deposits of some of the Gulf states, the sizeable oil sands of Canada, etc.
	Narrative of consumption applies to the rising middle classes of India, China and the Gulf states
	Narrative of India transforming from service sector to emerging patterns of consumption
	China, the narrative from China as a production site and 'world factory' to a consumption site
	Gulf prosperity based on energy revenues shifting towards a balanced development based on infrastructure development, service and finance sectors

Universalism and Particularism	US global system universal and accepted as operating norms by stakeholders
	Operating norms and worldviews are interpreted according to indigenous lenses, national priorities, local needs and regional pulses
	Inter-regional trade between the Middle East and North-East Asia a particularistic aspect of the US universal global system
	Trade and energy exchanges are intermediated through both the US global system as well as the hub system interlinking the two regions
	US is preferred or indirectly relied on (free-riding) to keep the sea-lanes open for trade and energy
	US plays an important balancing and tilting function
	US as a generator of ideas, concepts and innovative thinking emulated by other entities
Time and Space	Most underestimated element of influence
	Patience and impatience often drives energy narratives
	Patience is indirectly demanded of long-term solutions such as renewable energies, nuclear power and gas infrastructure development
	Impatience drives the spirit of innovation to come up with energy conserving technologies or alternative fuels
	Time and space related to the theme of sojourning found in inter-regional narratives between the Middle East and Asia as South Asia (particularly India) and other East Asian entities supply manpower to the Middle East
Coexistence and Interdependence	Energy is increasingly bundled with non-energy trade as a whole package
	US important hub that connects the interrelated exchanges in energy
	India important feeder to this system given its central location, important consumer market and physical transit position for energy pipelines and trade routes
	Complementarity supports coexistence and interdependence given that common needs and priorities in energy often necessitate cooperation
	Mutually reinforcing initiatives for cooperation, functionalism, regionalism, integration and constructivism often interacts with complex forces that pull regional entities apart
	Instruments of cooperation require the support of dominant regional entities and the important tilting function of the US

Diversity	Greater diversity of stakeholders in this inter-regional trade in the form of non-state entities like multinational or transnational energy firms and trading companies, state-owned enterprises, sovereign wealth funds, city-states and consumers
	Diversity pertains to the availability of alternative options such as renewable energy, alternative sources of energy, non-oil fossil fuels, affordable and plentiful alternatives like nuclear power
	Diversity in the form of the acknowledgement of the presence of large numbers of stakeholders portray the complex picture of the energy supply and consumption system
	Diversity in the form of narratives of alternatives to oil is built upon hope, advocacy, the de-emphasis on oil as the endangering limit to growth
	Element of competition in the narrative on diversification. Russia for example represents an alternative form of energy supply for North-East Asia

2 PROGRESS AND DEVELOPMENT

Significant interdependency between national economies in the global economy is a neoliberal construct. In forgoing conflicts and tensions, the liberal interpretation argues there is an expected dividend from anticipated trade. The assumption is also based on the rationality of economic entities that in the cost-benefit analysis, benefits from trade will outweigh the costs from conflicts. Economic and trade interdependency is also promoted and advocated to potentially convert adversarial relationships into economically productive ones. Economic expansion of ties enables the stakeholders to create shared values and norms that can mutually enhance interdependency.

Constructivist ideals build upon these economic and often political ties to expand trade bilateralism into a complex and complicated interwoven set of linkages and connections. In such a complex interwoven structures, there may also be a potential for economies to learn from each other, particularly, as models of development for spurring economic improvements and regional upgrading of production structures.

In addition, when economies learn from each other, they may resemble each other more in terms of infrastructural features, such as ports, airports and other transportation facilities. After this bout of development, the infrastructural works in Asia, the Gulf and the US may resemble more of each other as they begin to serve the same purposes, facilitate the mobility and movement of goods, services and people. Therefore, there is an infrastructural common language and terminology that emerges, both in terms of constructed and built physical facilities as well as mental constructs and worldviews of how economic development should take place, according the needs of a globalized economy.

Interconnections and interwoven interests also enhance the potential of regional resilience against external shocks, such as economic crisis, speculation attacks, sudden shortfall of supplies and natural disasters. Due to economies of scale and the collective strength of shared resources, interdependent economies may be able to stave off unwelcome crises better than individual economies.

According to a seminal study by Bo Meng and Satoshi Inomata in 1985, major intra-regional trade flows in the international context consisted of

Chinese imports from Japan, Japanese importation from the US and US importation of industrial goods and electronics from Taiwan and Japan[1] made possible by decreasing trade barriers to flow of goods.

Interdependency may express itself in many different ways, as Asia benefits from American and Japanese job creation, the expansion of their markets also serve as demand markets for US products. It is an interdependent relationship as Asia depends upon US demand for poverty reduction and the US looks to Asia's potential for consumer demand. The US remains as a leading export market for many Asian economies.

Interdependency is also sought after in the area of environmentalism. Transboundary pollution and environmental damage requires the collective resources and collaboration of national economies to mitigate, handle and manage these externalities. The sharing of resources decreases the costs of developing coping mechanisms and also promotes information-sharing. Information-sharing may be crucial in the development of highly interconnected urban areas linked by information superhighways, people movements and economic exchange.

In the near to mid-term, environmental compliance may not only be the issue of one an individual but it may involve the collective efforts of global cities as they become sustainable entities, constantly emulating and learning from each other in terms of best practices and leading benchmarks. Cities can only learn from each other if they become effective global resources that can be depended upon by each other constantly comparing and collaborating with best practices.

Interdependency may also be important for another resource – human talents and manpower. The porous interpenetration of research, training, educational resources and sharing of knowledge and information may facilitate mutual understanding and also provide opportunities for social mobility, particularly in economies that require urgent poverty reduction. Education may be one of the few strategies effective in equipping individuals and societies with the skillsets needed to pull their economies out of economic inertia caused by the lack of access to knowledge.

Interdependency may not necessarily be incompatible with competitiveness. The very nature of a global economy impedes the ability of any entity participating in the global economy from insulating itself from competition. Interdependency may ensure that competition among advanced economies generate best practices and leading benchmarks for emerging economies to follow and emulate.

The US role may have been significant in this area as it fostered, encouraged and enhanced global access to information and technology which were honed by its competitive economy and then transmitted to the developing economies for them to participate fully in the global economy. The US was thereafter joined by other economies such as the Gulf states and Asian economies like Japan, India and China that benefited tremendously from selected features of the US developmental model which had inspired Asian economic development.

Not complacent, the US consistently revises its benchmarks for excellence and sets new standards for other economies to be aware of and improve upon their existing infrastructure. Such continual improvements have been applied in some areas to great success by other Asian economies, including those serving as case studies in this book.

Japan, India and China have all made vast improvements in their standards of education, technical training and human infrastructure and, in some cases, have become global benchmarks themselves, particularly in the essential fields of science, technological and mathematics. Such aspects of education may often be related to patent generation, advanced technological development and quantity of scientific papers crucial for economic competitiveness.

Robust educational infrastructure and training may also facilitate the possibilities of economic leapfrogging, allowing developing economies to bypass stages of economic development and directly access the most advanced technological sectors for their national economic development. In turn, existing and future transitional economies that are rapidly developing may learn from positives aspects of development and growth in the Gulf states, India and China, in accordance with their national priorities and conditions.

In order for interdependency to work, continued engagement by all major participants in Asia may be essential, including the US as well as other Asian economies like the Gulf states, Japan, China and India. Interdependency requires proactive and intricate coordination by all these parties and a cooperative climate that elicits collaboration and exchange.

Another condition for interdependency to work is the presence of all national stakeholders, individuals and organizations, private and public sectors, governments and non-governmental entities, and their commitment to continued conversations and engagements. In order to resolve outstanding issues, they may also be required to interact and communicate with each other on a regular and preferably institutionalized basis. The mode of engagement and interaction appear to modify and adapt to the external environment.

Global issues may require sleek adaptation so that the level and type of engagement in interdependent relationships may remain relevant in constantly mutating global economic environments. Instruments and tools for interdependent engagement may include options like high-level dialogues, forums, working groups, discussions, conversations, institutionalized cooperation, inter-agency coordination and partnerships, among others.

Important elements that may often be neglected in conceptualizations of interdependency include patience and foresight. Patience may be needed for changes, reforms, education, resolution, outcomes and other long-term goals to become manifest. Asia and the US share the commonality of diversity and this inherent makeup inevitably gives rise to different needs, priorities, changes and responses.

Modernity and modernization evolved according to the dialectical forces of localization/adaptation as well as globalization/uniformity in both Asia and the US. The two concepts are constantly searching for a multilaterally and mutually acceptable equilibrium in defining modernity and modernization or progress within the context of globalized universalism. Even like-minded systems (e.g. democracies) require such equilibrium to be reached.

Foresight may also be needed for continuity and longevity of interdependency in Asia. Foresight may encourage longer-term perspectives that may be compatible with Asian economies that appear to be normatively characterized as having large populations, widespread developmental priorities, internal contradictions and dilemmas and constant negotiations between traditionalism and modernity. The most vulnerable groups may have to be readily identified in order to prioritize their developmental needs to assist in national development.

Foresight and patience may be extremely important elements in future management, mitigation and handling of resource-scarcity. Water, energy and other natural resources may move up to the top of the list when it comes to cooperation, collaboration and interdependency. In the name of progress, a global understanding may be negotiated between the stakeholders in accordance with global interests.

In the midst of recognizing innovative ways to cope with inequities, shortages and dis-equilibrium, foresight may be needed to recognize new stakeholders constantly affected by global distribution of resources. Then patience may be needed to negotiate and incorporate their interests into the collective priorities of the global community. The responsibilities will be awesome as the world becomes more interconnected and interdependent, and as more developing economies join global development, it may be expected that the number of stakeholders can only increase both in quantity and diversity.

Finally, greater economic interdependence increases collective consciousness of the impact of actions and decisions, Alessandro Vespignani's study indicates the vulnerabilities of an interdependent system. He highlights infrastructure weaknesses in response to natural disasters, man-made causes, mechanical or human failures in infrastructure management as possible vulnerable points in interdependency because localized challenges may snowball into other problems[2] and reach into other locations and areas of infection.

In addition, Aysegul Aydin's study reminds readers that trade/economic interdependency does not necessarily lead to cooperation among stakeholders. According to Aydin, even states engaged in mutual trade may continue to have conflicts with each other as competitive trade may influence their decision-making process, compelling them to take sides in conflicts that sometimes involve third parties.[3]

Despite the challenges brought about by interdependence, Joe Smith, Nigel Clark and Kathryn Yusoff argue that interdependence may have the potential to become a powerful epistemological concept that can manage global interdependence in many spheres in the world by creating a structure for advanced knowledge-sharing, debate forums and sophisticated conceptual processes.[4]

The project appears to incorporate as many stakeholders as possible as well as interactional fields and subject areas that have to do with participative communications and research functions to gauge the awesome responsibilities of human decisions to both humans and the ecological world alike.[5] This may be an ambitious project characterized by its conflict resolution and ecological sensitivity that may serve to counterbalance realist and modernization perspectives on human progress and achievements.

Ultimately both sides of the coin are equally important. Without conflicts and tensions, there may be no motivation for conflict resolution or neoliberal interdependency. Without interdependence, realists may not be able to consistently probe at the weaknesses and vulnerabilities of interdependent existence. Both may represent the permeability of human existence in that trade and conflict, environmental damage and progress, poverty reduction and development connect and influence each other in an increasingly interconnected world.

Given the context of an interdependent world, it may be necessary to examine the concept of progress and what indeed may potentially account for reasons a country may successfully 'emerge' as a force in the economic and geopolitical sense. A popular theory for progress may be modernization theory, as articulated by the likes of scholars such as Samuel Huntington and Walt Rostow.[6] For many, particularly in the developing world, it may represent a desire to catch up to what they consider the 'modern' societies of the West, while coping with internal contradictions of development.

Modernization itself, however, is inherently a dialectic process that is constantly seeking consensus between resistance and compliance, a consensus that can never be reached fully. If, ideologically and philosophically, consensus can never be reached, then, quantitatively, some studies attempt to register and track progress through material gains. In his study of the 'non-western world', Wolfgang Zapf illustrates the material and social progress made by the Arab world since 1950 vis-a-vis Eastern Europe, Africa and the OECD economies.[7]

There are also counter-reactions to the notions of modernization theory. Peter Johannessen critiqued Samuel Huntington's assumptions about modernization progress in the areas of political reforms, economic liberalization and social tolerance and highlighted several case studies in Asia, including India and the Middle East, to demonstrate this.[8] Counter-reactions may only be expected since any ideology, thinking or worldview with a deterministic trajectory may likely encounter resistance and counter-reactions.

Postmodernity as a counter-reaction prefers to view modernity as an antithesis of progress and rationality. It faults modernity with a host of the negative consequences of development including the irrationality of genocides, mass destruction, wars, destructive economic competition rationalized by modernity's emphasis on the maintenance of order and progress.[9] The intangibility of postmodernity, however, becomes a subject of counter-reactions.

Bran Nicol argues that postmodernity appears to exist by making modernity the 'other', portraying the postmodern age as one that is consumption-based, virtual instead of tangible reality, and a highly developed state of science and technology.[10] It may appear as a culmination of information, technical advancements and digital sensations that permeate human feeling, existence and cognitive functions.[11] The intangible nature of postmodernism may be continually understood, felt and observed while modernity with its material progress may be comparatively more observable and measurable.

With its consumption-based culture, postmodernity elicited a backlash from coalitions against material enrichment, the culture of conspicuous consumption, and against uniformity and the standardization of popular, mass culture. It potentially becomes an anti-progress counter-reaction against modernization and modernity, but such sensations may not be universally felt. Consumer culture characterizes both its advocates and aspirants in developed and developing societies. Both postmodern and modernist lifestyles and worldviews appear to have their own advocates and detractors in both developed and developing economies.

In this sense, both rationality and irrationality are merely different sides of the same coin in the currency of progress. If the 'rise' of something (e.g. Asia for example) is taken in this context, both rationality and irrationality, modernity and postmodernity, have their own advocates and detractors in the Gulf and Asian regions. Again, the rise may be in tandem for both worldviews, or least differential rates for segmented aspects of the two worldviews, wherein lies the usefulness of judging progress in modern or postmodernist terms. Another possibility may be to seek an alternative and push rationality to its highest possible realm and see if progress can be examined from a higher plane of progress.

Other than counter-reactions to modernization, alternatives have been suggested. Transhumanism, for example, is a technologist perspective that examines and perhaps advocates the utilization of technologies to augment existing capabilities and abilities to create a post-human future that is safe, future-oriented and progressive.[12] Even this alternative has its own promoters and detractors because, while transhumanism offers a rational, optimistic and safe methodology for risk minimization, its detractors argue that it may lead to self-destruction and an apocalyptic post-human future.

Transhumanism is both antithetical and complementary to modernization because it may be perceived to represent the highest level of rationality, with the futuristic optimization of technology, but simultaneously completely redefines modernization and social progress by taking its primary participants into a post-human future.

Given the universalistic appeal of modernization, resistance against universalism and other alternatives in between, would it be possible to be reductionist and focus instead on simple progress – an acknowledgement of the complex nature of human progress, with its internal contradictions and dilemmas? How can one simultaneously benchmark progress using comparative indicators while acknowledging individual achievements and regional development and take into account the different regional and local context for development as well as the cyclical nature of progress itself? How can one assess the benchmarks for an economically and geopolitically 'rising' Asia?

While comparative benchmarks may be useful as indicators, world systems theory whether it is in the form of Immanuel Wallerstein's self-contained world system organism, Joseph Schumpeter's world economy and business cycles as well as other influential thinkers on world systems[13] may question how these benchmarks work in a highly interdependent world that may be considered as one political/social/economic system rather than separate units? If indeed world history may be characterized as biorhythms with its own cyclical changes (including business and economic cycles), progress may be circular instead of linear, rendering benchmarks less useful in the long run. This begs the question on the appropriate metrics to use to measure progress, particularly if it is based on long-term empirical studies.

Instead of a comparative or a deterministic process, may it be possible to imagine progress measured in tandem? That all major economies (including the US, China, Japan, India and the Gulf states) are progressing along with the rest of the world? Each of these economies has to continually deal with internal contradictions and dilemmas (some more than others) in the form of rising income inequality, resource distribution, poverty reduction, demographic shifts and transboundary environmental challenges.

But, perhaps, even differential rates and levels of development and developmental contradictions may tend to be evened out, balanced or compensated by progress in some areas and challenges in others in each individual setting. In the aggregate commonalities may appear to be more universalistic than competitive progress. If progress and its internal contradictions are universalistic rather than particularistic, then it may be possible to argue that the world in general is 'rising' in tandem.

Instead of conceptions of particularistic progress, could universal access be a new measure of progress in an interdependent world with its interconnected stakeholders? Universal access to health care, education, anti-poverty measures, technology, resources and environment may be a possible benchmark of progress. Taken in this context, the remarkable achievements made by world entities such as the Gulf states, India, China, Japan, the Gulf, South and North-East Asia, along with the important contributions of the US and other developed economies, may then be conceptualized as universal progress.

Such a holistic approach may transcend and/or incorporate features of modernization/modernity, postmodernity and transhumanism for a universalistic definition of progress. It may be possible that trade and energy distribution are not only trackable, observable and interpretable through the lens of benchmarked quantitative measures but also celebrated for their contributions to anti-poverty measures, educational opportunities and basic capacity-building features such as infrastructural provision.

Can it help to diminish the idea of alternative existences and foster the idea of a single interdependent socio-economic existence of global economies collectively? This aspect is unclear because there are arguments and resistance against a relativistic view of progress. Relativism is based on cultural values, individual subjectivity, moral arguments, religious interpretations and other context-specific angles. Anti-relativism advocates highlight the universalistic nature of rationality, progress and human advancement.

Relativism may be found in all reactions and counter-reactions of human progress, whether in the realms of modernists, postmodernists or transhumanists. They highlight the difficulties in any universalistic claims to progress. Instead of relying on one interpretation, would it be possible to cease from striving for universalism or particularism and recognize eclectic coexistence in understanding human progress? Progress may be characterized by relativism, universalism, modernity, postmodernity, rationality, irrationality all at the same time and in the future, assume a post-human form. This publication examines only two particularistic aspects of trade and energy distribution and their contributions to 'progress'. Given the immense difficulties and challenges in defining progress, it may not argue that there is 'progress' involved in these two areas in the context of the Gulf states, China, India and Japan (or the Gulf, North-East and South Asia). Positive aspects of trade and energy distribution may include greater interconnectivity, increased contact and economic mutualism while maintaining an equilibrium between universalistic development coexisting with different views of progress itself.

The role of the US is just as important as the progress made together or independently in tandem with the Gulf states, India, China and Japan, given the traditional and contemporary centrality it plays in the global economy.

Additionally, given also the concomitant centring of G-20 member economies (which also includes the US, Japan, China, India and members from the Gulf) in the global economy, it may be possible that the interdependency of these important economies coexist with the collective or selective progress that they make in trade and energy resource distribution.

The economic and trade decision-making process of these economies are probably a culmination of modernist, postmodernist and transhumanist impulses of their societies and the interests they represent. It may probably be an aggregate representation of the eclectic instincts for rationality and irrationality, modernization and postmodernity and relativist and uniform understanding of the idiosyncratic, regional and global needs of their economies.

The centrality of the US economy to the global system is widely acknowledged and the importance and global weights of the Gulf states, India, China and Japan are also recognized. India and China are important and large fast-growing economies growing in tandem with resource and investment potential and contributions of the Gulf states along with the continued technological contributions and innovations of Japan. Together with the rest of the world these entities under study forge links and collaborations in the fields of energy and trade that may have impacts at all levels.

Their cooperation and collaboration, whether regional or individual, may represent an outgrowth for more rational distribution of trade and energy within their own regions, a rationalistic sharing of resources to meet common challenges, postmodernist instincts for energy collaboration to lessen environmental impacts and a transhumanist approach towards interconnective technologies for more efficient communications, infrastructural efficiency and productive distribution of resources, while in the process coping with their own internal contradictions and developmental dilemmas.

The issue then becomes how one can define the concept of progress and development. 'Progress' in emerging economies is often characterized by development. There are, however, a number of schools of thought about development. Tatyana P. Soubbotina, consultant at the World Bank Institute, appears to place a premium on quality of life defined by elements such as access to educational opportunities, job availability, clean environment and personal safety, among others.[14] In terms of environmentally conscious perspectives, development may have to be coupled with sustainability. According to the International Institute for Sustainable Development (IISD), development should meet the needs of businesses, industries and other stakeholders while ensuring that resources are used responsibly so that future generations can continue to use them.[15]

According to the United Nations (UN) Millennium Development Goals, development may be considered an innovation-centred priority, empowered by infrastructure development, human talent cultivation, gender non-discrimination, environmental well-being, resource access and technological progress, for example.[16] Within the rubric of universal development, there are also initiatives with explicit agendas in their contributions to development, for example, specific areas that may require special attention at particular temporal junctures may be the subject of studies and prescription of development tailored to local conditions.[17]

Some studies have attempted to quantify development through indicators. Robert W. Kates, Thomas M. Parris and Anthony A. Leiserowitz listed out various indicator initiatives in their article *What is Sustainable Development*.[18] It details historically and contemporarily the concepts of development as human basic need, seeing access to economic growth and the inter-related issue of environmental sustainability as a consequence of conscious human decision-making and actions.[19]

Therefore, there appears to be two main categories of 'development': one that is understood as goal-setting, setting the ideal standards to be reached and the other category is setting the definitional standards and benchmarks necessarily for discourses and action plans. These are all valid and important definitions of development. It may also indicate that development is an all-encompassing concept with broad applications that can signify different priorities from various perspectives.

While development remains highly important as a priority for the majority of the economies in the world, the universal aim is met with localized challenges specific to each region. Despite indigenous conditions that may exist in different world regions necessitating differing tailor-made solutions, there appears to be some commonalities in developmental challenges as well for humankind. It is these common challenges which may carry the potential for different economies to work together and collaborate based on their own priorities and national interests for a better common outcome.

Yeganeh Eghbalnia studies the correlation between resource wealth and development in *Natural Resource Curse: Special Experience of the Persian Gulf States*.[20] In his study, there appears to be the presence of the usual contemporary indicators of development such as education, individual state of health and sustainable development.[21] More importantly, his study appears to indicate the indigenous and localized interpretation and application of growth. For example, sensitivity to and stabilizing resource prices may be a developmental priority in the region. Natural resources prices have a direct impact on the viability of industrial sectors especially in less developed countries (LDCs) and economies since natural resources are needed for production; and because less developed economies tend to have lower productivity levels than their advanced counterparts in manufacturing output, higher resources prices make it more expensive and less profitable for LDCs to manufacture goods for export, affecting industrial development in those economies.[22]

Other than suppliers, this appears to be a feature in oil-scarce economies as well. Because many net oil consumers are not significant oil producers (most are oil-scarce), therefore, they are not in a position to stabilize resources prices by influencing global supplies, instead they may try to regulate their consumption patterns. Motoyuki Suzuki argues that, to have productive use of resources like energy and to reduce wastage, it may be possible to locate the optimal balance and equilibrium in the three equities: 'equity among regions, especially between North and South', 'equity among living species' and 'equity throughout generations'.[23] In other words, this is an attempt at fair distribution, taking into account development goals of emerging economies, the needs of both human and non-human living organisms in the ecological system and also the sustainable use of resources.

Other studies advocate diplomatic solutions, increasing exposure to contacts between oil producers and consumers in order to promote better understanding that can stabilize both supply and consumption. Diplomatic initiatives may also be related to the process of seeking alternative sources of energy or diversification of sources. Such diversification exercises may refer to diversification in terms of location, by searching and exploring new geographical locations of energy resources through collaboration with local stakeholders and the owners of those resources.

Diversification may also refer to the types of resources. It may mean lessening dependence on traditional fossil fuels by seeking alternative sources of naturally replenishable energy that may include solar, hydropower, etc. It may also mean non-fossil fuel alternatives that may be perceived to be cleaner than carbon-based fuel sources, including nuclear power, geothermal, biofuels, etc. For others, it may mean less reliance on one particular source of fossil fuel by diversifying into other fossil fuels besides oil, such as natural gas, oil sands, clean coal, etc.

It may also mean a delicately balanced ratio or proportion of the above. Whatever ingredients are involved in the diversification exercise, the net outcome desired may be for less reliance on a single source of energy, comparatively more stable prices, less supply shocks and prevention of disruption to consumption (industrial or household).

A future-oriented prescription on energy conservation and efficiency may be based on the technologist argument, which, if taken to its natural conclusion, may be related to transhumanism. Technology may be viewed by its advocates as a possible solution to both reducing energy use as well as locating sources of alternative energies. It is a highly progressive, material-based proposal that appears to have a track record, particularly in the increasingly mechanized and digitized modes of production.

The collaboration of people and technologies have been able to dig deeper into oilfields, minimize wastage in the mines, explore more efficiently potential energy sources, develop safe and cleaner sources of energy, making those technologies user-friendly and enhance the reliability of supply, etc. Older sources of energy like coal may have a chance at being brought back into existence for example if clean coal technologies can be developed. Emphasis may be placed on optimization of previously discounted energy resources.

Given that there have been leaps and bounds in technological development and innovation, future innovations may only be bounded and limited by human imagination. Transhumanism may therefore increasingly diminish the autonomous nature of human inputs in the decision-making and development process and replace it with highly productive post-human technology-based allocation of resources for greater equity and fairness in distribution.

Other than technologists and transhumanist arguments, advocates of ethical use of resources may be equally important. Ethical arguments may focus on sustainable use that starts at the individual level, promoting lifestyles that are consciously eco-friendly with self-controlled efficient consumption. Ethical use arguments may also reject profit maximization principles as the sole rationale for resource use, instead tampering it with the needs for consciousness of preservation for future use, ethical exploitation and moderation. It may be related to postmodernist conceptions that may view conspicuous consumption as irrational and damaging outcomes of modernity.

It may be possible to take an eclectic approach and reconcile both technologist/transhumanist and ethical use arguments by highlighting the compatibility between the two. In fact, it may be possible to use the analogy of needing both hands to clap. Technologies by themselves, unless history has shifted entirely in a post-human world, may not be able to resolve the issue if consumption cannot be moderated. It may take time and resources to develop technologies that feature a revolutionary change in energy use. Moderation of consumption may still be needed to maximize technological contributions, particularly for emerging economies that may not be able to utilize newly developed experimental technologies within the short term due to limitations in capital, trained manpower and infrastructural capabilities.

Similarly, ethical use of resource and conscious sustainable consumption may not be as effective without technological accompaniments. Like technological innovations, ethical use and sustainable consumption may require time for lifestyle changes and awareness education. In this sense, both are long-term measures that may go in tandem with each other for maximum impact. At different stages of economic development and in different setting, they may have differential impacts and outcomes.

Energy consumption and supply also appear to be increasingly linked to environmental sensitivities and sustainable use for future generations, both of which appear to be points of commonalities in universal interpretations of developmental goals, particularly by international organizations (IOs). Therefore, energy use, environmental sustainability and development have become an interrelated 'iron triangle'.

At one end of the triangle is energy use that is needed for powering urban infrastructures, production activities and household lifestyle needs, all of which may be needed to sustain developmental goals both at the individual and national economic levels. Without energy, the basic needs of the individual cannot be met as health and safety may be adversely affected. Without industrial development and/or manufacturing activities, another developmental priority of job supply and employment to feed the population cannot be sustained and may also affect social cohesion and stability. Without powering infrastructure, both individual and economic developmental needs may be affected since infrastructures such as ports, airports, highways and rails must be powered by energy so that trade and production output can be effectively transported.

Another leg of the triangle is environmental sustainability. Resource use is eminently useful for powering economic activities but long-term exploitation of resources without careful planning may result in environmental challenges. In Asia, this may often be dramatically demonstrated by unmitigated fast economic growth and in the West, by excesses of consumption. Besides immediate physical and material damage to the environment, unmitigated use of resources may also be a challenge for future generations. Resources that are consumed unproductively and inefficiently may reduce the amount of resources available for future use and that may affect future potential wealth and abilities of future generations to meet their own developmental goals. Thus, the environmental leg of the iron triangle projects present use into the future to highlight the need for responsibility and accountability in current resource use.

These two legs of the iron triangle, energy and sustainability, appear to feed into the third leg which is development. Development may therefore have two temporal components of present use and future sustainability. Its temporal dimensions are extended by the two components, making the triangle effectively three-dimensional in nature if time is taken into account. The iron triangle is intricately and delicately connected. If one leg or one side of the triangle fragments, the other two legs cannot hold.

The developmental leg of the triangle may probably be the most broad-based of the three since it has been discussed that there is no single universal interpretation of development although there are points of commonalities in many different interpretations, particularly in the contemporary globalized and interconnective context.

In Asia's case, the future is often highlighted as crucial in determining developmental priorities and goals because of the factors of demographics, economic fast growth, scale of development and late industrializing economies (therefore able to learn from the demonstration effect), all affecting the pace, extent and mode of development in the regions that it encompasses.

India and China have been discussed within the context of a 'rising Asia' thesis. There have been many worldviews, theories and arguments about 'rising' Asia which appear to view this phenomenon through different perspectives. For example, some reports prefer to focus on quantitative indicators of a rising Asia, such as the National Science Foundation's *Asia's Rising Science and Technology Strength: Comparative Indicators for Asia, the European Union, and the United States* which focused on benchmarks for technology education, workforce capabilities and research and development expenditures.[24]

Education in science and technology appear to be a favorite topic when it comes to discussions about the ingredients or recipe for rising Asia's (particularly East Asia) current or future successes.[25] One example is Richard Levin's speech on *The Rise of Asia's Universities* that details the investments and resources which Asian universities put into their tertiary institutions.[26]

Just as prolific, the popular and trade presses also feature the phenomenon of rising Asia. Due to Asian demographics and rising incomes, popular media have portrayed Asia's rising middle class and its consumption prowess with awe tinged with fright.[27] Paul McCulley and Ramin Toloui for example detail the recovery of Asia after the 1997 Asian financial crisis in their article *Asia Rising*.[28] Future-oriented speeches also urged stakeholders in the global economy, such as the EU to enhance better economic contact with Asia.[29] Even more optimistic reports highlight Asia's lead in new-generation green technologies generated particularly by North-East Asian economies.[30] Such technological progress may be made possible by articles that highlight increasing importance of innovation in Asia.[31]

In many of these accounts, a common feature is the importance of US engagement with rising Asia. US engagement with Asia has been crucial and historically important. For example, the importance of US technical assistance to the Asian educational sector was highlighted by Ronald Anderson as early as 1957.[32] The importance of US aid for Asian education is mirrored by the contemporary growing importance of Asian studies in North America, according to Dr Gi-Wook Shin, Director of the Walter H. Shorenstein Asia-Pacific Research Center (APARC) at Stanford University.[33]

America's continual engagement is often cited in contemporary writings against the backdrop of the perception of rising Asia. Munir Majid, for example, critically examines this role in his piece *US Diplomacy in Rising Asia: Through the Glass Darkly* highlighting what he views as priorities in US engagement with

Asia.[34] Institutionally, Christopher Martin argues that US support for any Asian regionalism initiative may be crucial and important.[35] This is particularly true for the school of thinkers that detect an interdependent economic connection between the US and Asia.[36]

In terms of future-oriented thinking, various US Presidents and their retinue's trips to Asia coincide with the thinking of continual engagement in Asia.[37] There are also calls for the US to engage with the future generation of leaders in Asia and understand their policy directions and initiatives.[38] Perhaps, one of the most important areas of future-oriented US–Asia engagement may be the formulation of trade policies. Marcus Noland argues that US trade policies and interactions with Asia may be an important factor in the future shape of the global economic system.[39] And Michael Schuman points out that the interactive process may be two-way as the US will also attempt to draw lessons from Asian progress, such as the importance of free trade, export-led economies and the manufacturing private sector,[40] all of which were features of American and East Asian successes in the past and most likely for the future as well.

America may welcome a constructive role for large regional economies in Asia, including India, Japan and China. Lawrence Summers and other like-minded Americans appreciate the enormous contributions made by developing economies such as India and China, for example, the elevation of living standards that have doubled within a decade or so.[41] The US and India are two large economies based on democratic traditions with a convergence of ideas about prosperity, international cooperation and integration.[42] The US and Japan together make up more than 40 per cent of international domestic products, a sizable component of global trade in goods and services and global investments.[43] In 2009 in Tokyo, the US leader, President Obama, welcomed the role of China even if there may not be complete agreement in all issues.[44]

Aside from writings on the importance of a sustained US role in Asia, other writings explore the question whether Asia is truly rising and the benchmarks involved in judging its 'rise'. It may also be possible to respond to questions about the possibilities of Asia's rise by examining some of the dilemmas and internal contradictions that Asia faces.

While demographics may be a source of strength in some aspects of Asian development, Milan Brahmbhatt and Luc Christiaensen point out that it can be a challenge, particularly in terms of food supply and especially at times of rising global food prices.[45] Asia still has the largest number of people living in poverty.[46] US along with other responsible stakeholders in the community were instrumental in pressuring developed economies to do more for regions such as South Asia.[47] Aside from traditional poverty issues, new challenges have emerged such as rising inequality for the past three decades.[48]

Besides food supply for the impoverished, Asia also faces the challenge of supplies of other resources. The European Commission's report *Rising Asia and Socio-Ecological Transition* appears to focus on 'socio-ecological transition' of an 'emerging' Asia with chapter contents providing details on natural resources and demographic changes as a result of this transition.[49] North-East Asia is already the biggest liquefied natural gas (LNG) importing region and is also a globally significant oil consumer[50] and its domestic supplies will not be able to sustain continued increases in energy use in the region.

On top of resources scarcity, Asia also faces environmental challenges. Fast economic growth, which has been typically cited as a feature of rising Asia, has also generated environmental challenges for the people of Asia. The transboundary Asian air pollution study by David L. Alles is an example of the challenges that Asia faces in the process of rapid industrialization.[51] World Health Organization (WHO) studies indicated that twelve out of fifteen cities with the most particulate matter and six out of fifteen with the highest sulphur dioxide in the air are located in Asia.[52]

Other challenges include the proliferation of diseases, including the spread of HIV/AIDS in East Asia.[53] One example of an important role in this aspect played by the US government in managing the spread of severe acute respiratory syndrome (SARS) was to increase transparency with regards to information about the disease to all stakeholders in order to contain its spread.[54] Older and more traditional diseases like tuberculosis (TB) are also making a comeback in parts of Asia with India, China, Indonesia and Pakistan witnessing 5 million patients yearly, nearly 50 per cent of the global total.[55] The Asia Business Council highlights the unique vulnerabilities of Asia to epidemics and pandemics due to economic development and the growth of mass transportation, internal attributes like dense populations and urbanization, climatic changes and infrastructural factors like underprepared health-care systems.[56]

Ultimately, in the field of trade and technology, the US continues to drive global innovation and is an important factor for demand in the global economy.[57] It may also be an important guarantor of global access to markets worldwide through its influence in free-trade negotiations.[58] Even with rising competition in the areas of innovation, education, technologies, global competitiveness and research and development, the Task Force on the Future of American Innovation made up of leading private sector members and business associations concludes that the US still leads in research and innovation.[59]

Having pointed out the numerous challenges that Asia faces, however, it does not mean that Asia is definitely not rising. Rather than exceptionalizing the seductive phrase of rising and applying it solely to Asia, perhaps it may be possible to characterize Asia as 'progressing' in tandem with America's own historical and future development and contributions.

Lawrence Lau and Jungsoo Park illustrated that East Asia's developing economies[60] overall have expanded at nearly 8 per cent yearly since the 1960s.[61] Progress made by East Asian economies began to be characterized as a 'miracle', especially after the 1993 World Bank policy research report *The East Asian Miracle*'s study of eight Asian economies with robust economic performance and growth between 1960 and 1990.[62]

In the progress made by Asia, it may also be possible to acknowledge the important contributions made by all its stakeholders, including China, the Gulf states, India and Japan (in alphabetical order) among others. For example, with its young demographics, oil wealth and increasing foreign direct investments into the region,[63] the Gulf States are also progressing in tandem with the South Asian and North-East Asian region. Interdependency between the Gulf states and the US as well as the global economy has grown as the region's investments transition towards both developed, such as the EU and US, and fast-growing economies, such as the BRICM economies (Brazil, Russia, India, China and Mexico).[64]

The Gulf region together with North-East Asia, the US and India are specially highlighted in this book. It does not imply the deprecation of other Asian economies. Rather, in the interests of coverage, they present interesting contrasts (in terms of energy consumption and trade) as case studies and are often cited in contemporary academic literature and the popular media as the major energy suppliers and consumers in the world.

3 CHALLENGES – CONTRADICTIONS OF DEVELOPMENT?

Inherent in any type of economic or industrial development, there appears to be various contradictions in emerging economies. Such contradictions and challenges may be exacerbated by the scale of emerging economies' developmental needs, particularly in countries with large populations such as India and China. These challenges and problems may be divided into the following categories: economic/trade-related challenges; demographics-related factors and resource-use challenges.

The three categories are interrelated because demographic factors may affect the scale and magnitude of resource use and consumption while both demographics and resource use are related to economic development. Sustainable development and adequate allocation of resources, particularly for consumption and economic expansion in demographically large countries, is a potential contradiction and dilemma faced by large developing economics.

Jared Diamond's publication *Collapse* indicates dramatically the problems and challenges that arise when ecological and natural resources are overused and overexploited, causing societies, cities and even civilizations to collapse and fail. Two conventional approaches to resolving natural resource use and/or shortage are to refer it to state management for allocation (e.g. nationalization) or to the private sector (privatization). The basic quest in carrying out these approaches is to restrict the depletion and overuse of natural resources which include energy resources. But Elinor Ostrom argues that neither of these approaches have unmitigated success in maintaining the sustainable long-term use of natural resources.[1]

At the heart of strategies in managing resources are also the elements of rationality and self-motivation and interest in the use of resources. In maximizing the rational self-interest element, stakeholders engage in natural resource allocation may also have to balance between behavioral tendencies for individuals to contribute to collective joint benefits as opposed to free-riding.[2] Even regional schemes, much less global ones, require tremendous resources and political will for materializing. For example, the Japan's Hiranuma Initiative was launched with the idea of stabilizing energy supply in Asia whose tenets were agreed upon by energy ministers from North-East Asia (Japan, Korea and China) and South-east Asia to enhance promotion in natural gas, exchange data and information and cooperate in negotiations with oil producers.[3]

Ostrom also proposes practising a diversity of approaches in devising local resource management to prevent one-size-fits-all solutions that are insensitive to local conditions.[4] But while Ostrom's theories have been applied to deplet-able natural resources like fisheries, they may not be similarly applicable to or intended for strategic resources like energy, and therefore it is unclear if the same rules for common pool resources (CPRs) are applicable here. For Ostrom's CPR allocation to work, the users have to be clearly defined. While it is not an issue for identifying energy consumers clearly, as the resources are almost certainly universally needed, the state may likely step in for ownership because it is a stra-tegic resource with national security implications while local community or users' concerns may be less important than that of national priorities. In the same vein, locally sanctioned fines against misuse of resource may be less effective and important than those of national ones. Ostrom suggests that punishments or fines should be graduated to distinguish occasional or accidental mistakes from repeated offenders.[5]

Therefore, for Ostrom's principles of common use resources to work, one may have to elevate individuals to states and locally tailored rules to internation-ally/globally designed rules and principles. States may only commit themselves to global rules if other states in a similar situation do likewise, and if long-term advantages outweigh short-term disadvantages. Sharing resources through coop-eration may be easier for some economies or states than others.

It may be possible that global resource-sharing may even be more conten-tious than world trade cooperation and liberalization. For example, even in the arena of trade, trade cooperation and liberalization may have different results for different economies and states. Gabriel Sahlgren noted in his report that Gon-zalo Salinas and Ataman Aksoy argued that trade liberalization enabled some developing countries that are not former socialist transitional economies, politi-cally stable and not reliant only one resource (in particular oil) to experience significant improvements in GDP per capita income (between 1.2 and 2.6 per cent).[6] Such unevenness and conditional benefits from global trade is likely to be experienced in global energy-sharing initiatives as well, given the different attrib-utes, needs and priorities of global energy producers and consumers.

The resource attributes of different economies and states can exhibit a sharp contrast. According to Kent Calder, Japan, a major energy importer, has only 59 million barrels of proven oil reserves (mostly in Niigata Prefecture), roughly equivalent to approximately ten days of supply at the rates of consumption at the 2007 levels.[7] In contrast, its next-door neighbor China, also a major energy importer, has one of the two largest coal deposits globally, and was internationally the sixth largest oil producer in 2007 from the large Daqing oilfield that has rapidly lowered levels of output.[8] Russia, on the other hand, does not face acute shortage and is keen to supply Eastern Siberian energy resources to North-East Asia.[9] Given the large disparity between these economies and oil consumers, their priorities and motivation for cooperation and energy-sharing are likely to be different.

Given that energy is such a strategic resource and that it is essential for economies to function, such commitments are likely to take a long time and a tremendous amount of effort and political consensus and will to even materialize, perhaps even more than global trade liberalization and cooperation. It may also require a respected watchdog to enforce the rules, but such developments are likely to be contentious and require universal agreement to achieve, something that may be difficult under current global geopolitical conditions.

The element of success in such possible energy CPRs is dependent on whether individuals are willing to reach a consensus and voluntarily follow the rules while monitoring others in doing so. If individual states or the most important energy consumer in the most similar situation of energy shortage or needs are willing to observe and following global rules on use of energy resources, then the scheme is more likely to succeed. But this is far easier said than done.

Diamond points out that part of the difficulties lie in detecting depletion itself, given some resources appear to be in plentiful supply initially or that long-term depletion and overuse is confused with inherent cyclical changes in resource supply amounts lasting for fixed intervals as well as the difficulties in getting people to share resources.[10] Long-term patience and foresight may be elements needed for any proposed energy CPRs which may not be emphasized to the same extent by Ostrom. And the pool of resources under consideration must be effective, that is, enlarged and expanded to a global scale with the world conceptualized as one community, again practically difficult to implement and requiring a tremendous amount of time, resources, political will, etc.

For now, the world may have to rely on more incremental improvements of energy resource use as one possible measure. Such measures include efficiency in the use of energy resources as well as investments in new and alternative sources of energy. Fadhil Chalabi's (Executive Director, Center for Global Energy Studies) 2004 study that showed developed economies within the OECD lessened reliance on Middle Eastern energy supply, particularly between durations of oil shortages between 1973 and 2002 (down to 10 per cent from 41 per cent in Western European economies and 38 per cent from 63 per cent in Japan) through improved energy efficiency and investments in energy sources.[11] There may also be possibilities for North-East Asia to turn to emerging energy producers in the world, such as Russian gas.

Another incremental and pragmatic conventional may be focused on energy conservation, efficiency and productivity are improvements in infrastructure to deliver hydrocarbons to users and households in energy consumption centres.[12] Kent Calder appears to agree with this view in the case of China as he argues and points out that the challenge for China's energy sector is not reserve availability but infrastructure improvements in the form of hydrocarbon transportation and delivery.[13] From the incremental perspective, it may thus be possible to first look at cooperation and sharing of funding, resources, technical knowhow and personnel to upgrade these facilities, before looking at more ambitious schemes and initiatives of global energy-sharing.

Another alternative that has emerged for North-East Asia is looking at the possibility of non-hydrocarbon based fuels. Some North-East Asian economies are pursuing nuclear energy for example as an alternative to oil shortage and dependence. Such schemes are typically associated with safety concerns and also geopolitical requirements that need to be overcome before nuclear fuels are available for purchase.

Ultimately, the options that North-East Asia chooses must invariably bring into cooperation the US as both Japan and China are dependent on energy imports which is currently stabilized and guaranteed by the US. The US–Japan–China triangle which has been relevant for determining energy supply and consumption may still be equally relevant today with little change. According to the varying geopolitical schools of thought, including commentators like George Friedman, the US may have to facilitate more direct communication between China and Japan and allow the two North-East Asia states to reach a certain equilibrium,[14] given that the internal and external contradictions of this bilateral relationship will certainly need the US to mediate and balance for years to come.

Essentially, the US is crucial to resolving any common challenges and issues like energy supply for North-East Asia. Friedman's geopolitical thinking also foresees the possibility that the US may start extending its relationship to both Japan and China for mutual cooperation, perhaps against common perceived challenges.[15] This may be applicable to South Asia as well as Friedman sees continued US presence in the Indian Ocean as being crucial.[16]

Upgrading infrastructure to make them more energy efficient and environmentally friendly may also be another contributing factor in better resource use and management but infrastructure constructions may possibly be one of the most important challenges faced by emerging economies. As the Gulf states, China and India attempt to cope with rapid economic and industrial growth, their infrastructure construction may also need to catch up with the speed of growth. Infrastructure development may not only be a priority for the emerging economies alone, even Japan and the US may need to rebuild and renovate their existing infrastructure to keep up with younger economies that have implemented newer systems of transportation, communication and information technology infrastructure.

The internal contradiction may lie in the fact that while the emerging economies need world-class infrastructure, they may not necessarily have the resources or the expertise to construct them and may be reliant on overseas developmental aid and loan for their construction. The main challenge is that, regardless of whether it is the emerging or advanced economies' infrastructure in question, all infrastructural systems require constant renewal.

Thus, older working systems in mature economies may have to be upgraded to the same benchmarks and standards as those newly constructed facilities in emerging economies. Within emerging economies, basic infrastructure is needed to stimulate economic activities to develop local and regional economies. Even emerging economies with a certain level of indigenous infrastructure construction capabilities may need to continually upgrade those facilities to make them more environmentally friendly (they may require green technological inputs from advanced nations for example), more information technology (IT) compatibility (equipped with the latest hardware and software for example) or upgrading to higher safety standards.

In this context, many emerging economies, including those characterized as 'rising' may have more space to develop and improve before they can meet the track records of the best practices of developed economies or their technological offerings. On the other hand, the developed economies may be able to learn from successful cases and examples of infrastructure construction and implementation from their emerging counterparts. Such horizontal mutualistic learning may support the argument that both fast emerging economies and developed ones may be progressing in tandem, rather than to characterize some as 'rising' as a way to distinguish them from others. All economies, whether emerging or developed, may have to resolve the contradiction of their own infrastructure needs in order to progress economically.

Infrastructure construction may also be related to demographics because emerging economies with large populations may need rapid infrastructure construction in order to cope with larger influxes of people through migration from less developed areas to comparatively more economically vibrant sections of Asian economies (either within the same country or from outside national boundaries). This has become one of the major challenges of development. Such demographic shifts are also related to the ability of cities and their environments, infrastructure and resource supply to cope with the influx of large numbers of people.

Not all researches have an equally pessimistic view of migration. Piyasiri Wickramasekera's study attempted to dispel the argument of incompatibility of migrant workers with host destinations by highlighting the contributions made by migrant communities to their host countries and lack of evidence to show that migrant workers disrupt the social fabric of hosts' societies or contribute to crime rates; indications that migrant workers fill in jobs usually shunned by locals and the fact that some migrant workers (especially highly skilled individuals) do stay on to contribute to their host societies.[17]

Somik V. Lall, Harris Selod and Zmarak Shalizi's study of rural-urban migration indicated that internal mobility of economic migrants are often deterred between rural and urban sections within the same national boundaries through policies, but the most effective way to manage and mitigate the influx of migrants to urban areas may be through rural redevelopment so that there are less incentives for economic migrants to enter cities and urban areas.[18]

Given that emerging economies are hosting ever-expanding megalopolises growing at a historically unprecedented rate, more equitable development of rural and urban areas may also be needed to relieve the pressures off those cities to host, feed and accommodate the large influx of economic migration. This may be another typical contradiction in development, as urban cities in emerging economies feed their expanding economy and production activities, pushing those cities to the limit, resulting in issues and challenges like urban poverty, environmental pollution, resource shortage, etc.

Developing rural areas may also help to lessen the demands of resource use in urban megacities and areas. Resource use and demographics are therefore linked in this sense. Many emerging economies are faced with what may be perceived as contesting needs of development and environmental sustainability. Resources are drawn from the environment and, in the course of exploitation, there may be side effects on the environment from extracting those resources. Development may therefore now pair up with sustainability to minimize the possibility of severe shortages of resources.

There are a number of views about this. First, some like Khalid Saeed argue that the environment may be conceptualized as a commonly shared good.[19] Therefore, economies in the global system may have to trade their rights to the environment in accordance with the outcome of negotiations based on balancing costs and development. Such delicate balancing acts and negotiation process may be found between national economies, sometimes popularly characterized as a divide between advanced and developing nations or within a national economy itself, between different stakeholders.

Other studies equate environment and resource use with conflict resolution. Viewing the issue of environment and resource use from a developed world perspective, Simon Mason and Adrian Muller see a confluence of negative impact of environmental factors, consumption trends and humanitarian needs and the overall peaceful management and resolution of these needs.[20] They are concerned with the minimization of conflict and tensions over the use of limited supplies of resources and the overarching peaceful resolution of disputes resulting from it.

Another perspective is concerned with distribution of resources but from a poverty reduction perspective. This may be an urgent concern of international organizations that do work related to development. Environment and resource use may be important because resources are often extracted and taken from rural areas that may typically be habitats for low-income individuals.[21] According to International Fund for Agricultural Development (IFAD), 75 per cent of the global low-income population reside and work in rural areas therefore natural resource extraction and environmental degradation affect them most.[22]

They are also most vulnerable because they lack the resources to purchase the technologies necessary for environmentally friendly extraction and exploitation. Many of the emerging or 'rising' economies still have a large rural sector that belongs to this category. It is an internal contradiction of development in that they have to resolve or mitigate the needs of this rural sector in addition to the fast-growing urban areas in order to prevent social unrest, inequitable development and ensure poverty eradication.

Another view of resource use and the environment examines the issue from the perspective of health concerns and nutrition. Timothy Johns and Pablo B. Eyzaguirre argue that environmental destruction and degradation and non-optimal resource use may lead to trends in disease proliferation, nutrition value for individuals, biodiversity changes, etc., and argue that the sharing of resources such as technologies and genetic data may be increasingly important to tackle these challenges.[23]

Nutritional diseases may not only be found in emerging societies in instances of degraded environment but they can also be found in developed economies where there is an overabundant supply of food or supersized processed food, resulting in lifestyle diseases. Such lifestyle diseases have also emerged in the first tier cities and among individuals in the middle classes in the emerging economies. In this way, the nutritional dimension of resource use and environment challenges may be conceptualized as a universal one.

Whether the dilemma posed by environmental degradation or resource use is viewed through the paradigms of the nutritional, poverty reduction, conflict resolution, distributional or any other perspectives, they may be reconcilable through the fact that there is a delicate balance between resource/environment use with development, demographics and economic growth.

Another commonality among these features is the globalized nature of the challenge, necessitating all stakeholders to be involved and engaged in this area. Therefore whether development as a concept is goal-setting or definitional, technologist or ethical, future-oriented or sustainable, it may have to be universal in coverage and particularistic in application, eclectic and not dogmatic in the definitional sense and possess foresight and patience to manage such a multitude of contradictions and dilemmas at the same time.

One way perhaps to achieve this may be to imagine development as progressing in tandem rather than at comparative paces, a continual improvement process rather than deterministic, requiring the collective efforts of emerging and developed economies without the distinction of rising versus non-rising economies.

The dilemma and contradictions posed by economic development and growth, resource use and environment degradation/conservation as well as demographic needs (economic migration and rural development) may not be easily resolvable, particularly for emerging economies. A reductionist view appears to narrow this equation down to development versus conservation. But in actual reality, the situation is far more complicated since all these features are interlinked and affect each other both in the short term and the long run.

Unless large human population units resolve basic needs, it may be difficult for them to achieve the social cohesion needed to foster growth, but growth is dependent on economic expansion, which may extract resources from the environment that may in turn impinge on the basic needs of the human individual. Given that such internal contradictions exist, it may be difficult to characterize any economy as 'rising' since such problems continually evolve into different forms both in developing and developed economies requiring continuous attention.

Nevertheless, progress has been made and may continue to tackle emerging challenges and therefore the contributions of India, China and the Gulf states may be celebrated and recognized for their efforts made in dealing with the inherent contradictions and dilemmas of development. The US and Japan are equally important in serving as central actors and models of development for the world and the emerging economies of India, China and the Gulf states. If global development is taken as one unit of analysis, regions and economies of the world may be 'progressing' in tandem if the net result is advancement in poverty alleviation for the world.

Trade appears to be an important factor in spreading economic wealth and prosperity. One of the factors that drove economic development and prosperity in developed economies such as the US and Japan, as well as large emerging economies as India, China and the Gulf, is international trade. There are many perspectives about the importance of trade. There is space here for only some of these interpretations and views.

From the perspective of proponents of increased global trading, the idea is that international trade may have the potential to prevent conflicts. The notion had its roots in the post-World War Two philosophy that was behind the creation of the Bretton Woods system and the European Steel and Coal Community, which promoted the idea that increased economic interdependence would mitigate the threat of war between trading partners. Conflicts typically result in significant opportunity costs such as the disruption of normal trading relationships which in itself becomes a form of motivation to prevent states from engaging in conflictual relationships.[24] Trade therefore is a mutually beneficial activity that is considered to lead to the economic well-being for all parties engaged in it.[25]

However, not all agree that trading nations would not have conflicts, tensions or wars with each other. The view that trade leads to economic interdependence and mitigation of conflict is countered by realists who view trade as another competitive arena where states further their core national interests and priorities. According to this view, as nations work to secure favorable trade balances it could lead to conflict as they increasingly view the outcome in zero-sum terms. One realist interpretation may also argue that third parties have the potential to join in bilateral trade disputes when it is in their interest to do so.[26]

It may also be possible for yet another interpretation to adopt an eclectic view of these two contrasting views by arguing that, under different contexts (such as trade between two democratic nations or regional trade between hierarchically structured economies with differential levels of economic development), trade may foster interdependence while in other cases, it may exacerbate conflicts, tensions and even wars (military and/or trade wars).

Another political economic interpretation of trade and investments is the so-called state-led Japanese model of economic development. By now, the familiar role that the Japanese Ministry of International Trade and Industry (MITI) played in the 1950s and 1960s of sieving out selectively foreign interest in providing capital and technology as investments for Japan is well known.[27]

This bureaucratic selection of foreign investors compels foreign firms to transfer technological knowledge and licences to Japanese companies at highly affordable prices, conventionally believed to have contributed to Japanese economic development and technological innovation, although Lawrence Lau and Jungsoo Park's study argues that Japanese indigenous innovation, was the main initiator of the Japanese economic miracle.[28]

Regardless of the which interpretation one takes, the net result is that the Japanese success in attracting trade and foreign direct investments as well as its indigenous innovation and economic development became a model for many East Asian economies (and later also selectively studied by South Asian ones) in building up their manufacturing capabilities and attraction of foreign capital and investments to become net exporters to developed economies, creating high rates of economic growth in East Asia, later characterized as a 'miracle'.

In other opinions about global trade away from the international relations (IR) and political economic (PE) paradigms, the green perspective on trade argues that many Asian export-led economies may be compelled to incorporate environmentally friendly technologies, become more responsive towards environmental concerns, competitively conserving energy and minimizing pollution due to the openness of global free trade and the lowering of obstacles to trade.[29] The net result is that open and free trade may compel the transnational private sector to follow global standards on environmental protection and energy conservation.

Taking into account the diversity of views on trade, there is a tendency in this publication to veer towards the view that international trade is an overall beneficial activity to its participants, particularly in the economic and developmental sense even as it confronts challenges and obstacles in its implementation. Some interpretations in support of this view may be briefly discussed here. Denis Fred Simon and Cong Cao emphasized that, while large emerging economies like China have been export-driven, after they have reached a certain economic size and income level, they become significant importers.[30]

Trade in this sense may not be unidirectional as development eventually benefits both sides of the trading relationship (e.g. trading entities that encourage Indian, Gulf and Chinese development may reap the benefits as these markets grow in demand for imported goods and services). As the Indian, Chinese and Gulf economies grow, they have also become investors in other developing and developed economies and regions.

International and regional trade may also have positive side effects. Trade and infrastructure constructions are interrelated and have an intimate and coexistential relationship.[31] Trade stimulates infrastructure construction and vice versa. Infrastructure construction is especially crucial for developing economies, particularly at their early stages of development because the basic facilities have to be in place before economic growth can take place. Basic infrastructures typically include those that promote the extraction of primary commodities and raw materials for export destinations that process them.

There may also be a ripple effect at play because, as large emerging economies like India and China take off and gain experience in managing and building their own infrastructure, they may then transfer such technologies and technical knowhow to other developing economies located at lower levels of development and capacity, as Japan and the US have served as economic models in the past and continue to do so. When this happens regionally, an entire region may collectively benefit.

Besides infrastructure development, technological transfers may be equally important. The UN Millennium Project makes the argument that developing economies may need to engage international trade as a means of upgrading themselves technologically by instituting industrial policies that are tailor-made to the specific needs of each development economy with their differential levels of economic development.[32]

In terms of adjusting trade according to differential regional conditions and national makeup, for example, in their study of the Gulf Cooperation Council Region, Simon Gray and Mario I. Blejer recommended that there is potential for engaging in entrepôt trade in the Gulf either in terms of material goods such as gold (e.g. the Dubai gold market) or as a service hub for example for airlines, and in the process luring traders, merchants and entrepreneurs from other locations to participate in this trade.[33]

For this to happen, Gray and Blejer argue that there has to be technological and infrastructural development necessary, for constructing a world-class airport and to develop the necessary trained manpower with the appropriate skill-sets for managing the airport, as well as competitive airlines that may be able to effectively vie for such business in the global arena.[34] Trade in this sense may be an avenue for transfer of such skills, technical knowhow, management knowhow and technological capabilities.

Skill-sets, knowledge transfers, training and technological upgrading may be important to move up in the value chain of products. Andrew B. Bernard, J. Bradford Jensen, Stephen J. Redding and Peter K. Schott touched on production quality as a factor in international trade since developed/wealthy economies tend to emphasize quality,[35] therefore products manufactured in developing economies have to conform to the same quality standards whether made for export or domestic markets, acting as a form of impetus for those economies to upgrade their capabilities.

Besides the importance of local conditions and quality standards, trade may also take the form of highly coordinated, regionally or globally involved trading networks. A large section of global trade may also take the form of highly specialized parts and components traded either within an industry or firm or between firms as part of production networking and division of labor according to global comparative advantages and the trend of outsourcing.[36]

Non-state actors have been crucial to the international trade system, especially the multinational companies and transnational firms. Trade by non-state multinational private sector actors may also have its own set of benefits for the economies in which they are located. Wolfgang Keller and Stephen R. Yeaple's study indicates that multinational companies (MNCs) play a role in research and development activities of the host country comparative to domestic firms and contribute to knowledge transfer from the main to affiliated branches of foreign companies and that may eventually trickle down to the host country's firms.[37]

Another way in which knowledge transfer may take place could be through domestic companies attracting and employing staff members of the local branches of multinational companies.[38] Concurring with this view, the UN Millennium Project in fact argues that global trade engagement may result in developing economies employing and educating more workers in host countries of multinational corporations, resulting in the dissemination of technologies, skill-sets and knowhow.[39]

Within the private sector, the UN Millennium Project argues that small and medium-sized enterprises (SMEs) have a part to play in: supporting technological dissemination including IT application; organizing conventions and fairs to stimulate trade; marketing and advertising awareness of trade and business opportunities in order to contribute to poverty reduction; and helping local community development and sustainability.[40]

In the future weightless world, with globalization and the enhancement of IT technologies, international trade may assume a non-tangible, non-physical form. For example, the Gulf region has opened up with wide access to electronic data with potential investors able to trade online on a global scale.[41] Such transactions may necessitate a different type of infrastructural development (e.g. cyberspace access, online terminals, wireless communications, etc.), and new forms of knowledge transfers (new training formats to bridge the digital gap), and it may be possible that greater transparency and flow of information may help to diminish economic shocks, tensions, misunderstandings and conflicts.

What does the future of international trade look like? The European Commission Directorate-General for Research Socio-Economic Sciences and Humanities report, *The World in 2025: Rising Asia and Socio-Ecological Transition*, contains some interesting observations and projections as part of one interpretation of the future. The 2025 volume of trade may double compared to 2005 with more exports from the South (over 30 per cent compared with 20 per cent in 2005).[42] Secondly, English may likely be the major working language for global trade.[43]

It is unclear if these predictions and projects will materialize, but one possible trend that may be more certain is the greater need for global poverty reduction. In terms of poverty reduction, Machiko Nissanke and Erick Thorbecke highlight the importance of 'pro-poor globalization' that maximizes benefits for development and economic growth in less wealthy parts of the world with special attention given to the unskilled or poorly skilled by mitigating pure market forces to protect them from global economic shocks and instabilities[44] and ease their transition into the global economy during the developmental phases.

Systemically, they suggested the conceptual balance between equity and efficiency for growth output as a conscious policy choice[45] by the international community. This may be one of the many proposals and views that may arise to reorientate trade towards global sectors of the world engaged in poverty-reduction in the near future. Whatever measures the international community implements to combat poverty, they are unlikely to exclude the ingredients of dissemination of skills, technology upgrading, training, technical knowhow, infrastructure, education, environmental sustainability, elements that have proven their value in contemporary global development.

4 IMPORTANT ADVANCED ECONOMIES: US AND JAPAN AS DEVELOPMENT MODELS

The US model of development is characterized by its adept ability to evolve, adapt and react to external conditions, for example after perceptions of economic decline in the late 1980s, its structural reform and transformation into a high-technology economy during the period of the information technology (IT) economic boom that started in the 1990s stands as testimony to its historically adaptable strength and resilience. This may be just one example of many which has historically led US out of cyclical recessions into prosperity time and again.

The US economy is also based on free competition, ensuring its industries are not sheltered from innovation and improvements from foreign competitors. Risk-averse culture may free up innovation, encourage leaps in product and technological development and inspire people to reach new heights in human achievements. The US economy has also demonstrated innovation in systemic innovation, churning out new ideas for management systems and seeking out growth opportunities whenever possible. The deregulation processes of the 1980s, implemented by the Reagan administration, and then broadened in the 1990s by Clinton freed up the service industries (for e.g. telecommunications) and made them highly competitive in the context of the US and then subsequently global economy. Later, this partly inspired innovation revolutions in information, communication and technology in other economies, which was an important factor in making globalization possible and shrinking the size of the world, facilitating global trade.

The US restructured its economy during the 1980s and 1990s by outsourcing services which required competitive rates, merging and acquiring companies in the corporate sector, downsizing large unwieldy firms and re-engineering and streamlining corporate organizational structures and research and development sectors to emerge as a highly competitive, globalized economic entity that surged forth in high-technology sectors like IT in the later 1990s and 2000s.[1]

Such developments were embodied by the hi–tech centre of Silicon Valley. Similarly, for the sub-prime economic recession of 2008, Sherle R. Schwenninger argues that the US was able to act swiftly with a massive US$787 billion recovery plan to stimulate vibrant recovery after the crisis.[2] He also questions the merits of work-linked social welfarism in the US.[3] While such solutions are still evolving to cope with changing external situation, they are indicative of the ability of the US economy to adapt to external shocks, including severe ones.

Americans may also be regarded as comparatively generous in charitable causes. Alberto Alesina, Edward Glaeser and Bruce Sacerdote illustrate the large number of Americans that donate (privately generated charity welfare) despite the fact that they are offered only standard deduction, implying that contributions are not merely motivated by tax deductions.[4] There appears to be a spectrum of civic non-governmental organizations (NGOs) that provide assistance to members and what they perceive as 'target groups' on a national level, which Alesina, Glaeser and Sacerdote attribute to non-state dependence in the American philosophical worldview.[5] Traditionally, it may also be attributed partly to the American Calvinistic protestant ethics as well as Puritanism that emphasize hard-working ethics and due rewards in return.

American individualism may also be counterbalanced with the US governmental role in its economy. The strength of the US system lies in this constant search for equilibrium between rugged individualism and American governmental help for its people. In November 2008, US President-elect Barack Obama publically announced the strategy to create employment for 2.5 million job-seekers by installing a massive public investment scheme in the first two years of his four-year term.[6] The American model of development has also shown the importance of infrastructure development. In the postwar years of development between 1950 and 1979, public investments in infrastructure areas such as transportation networks, resource management like water systems and power provision like electricity grew at an average yearly rate of 4 per cent.[7]

Well-developed infrastructure was the basis for American pre-eminence and served as an exemplary model to the developing and emerging economies that badly needed to update their infrastructure for economic growth. In the past, the construction of transport infrastructure, highways, buses, rail, air transport, water-supply systems, educational facilities and electricity grids provided the US with jobs and support for a vibrant economy but future investments in infrastructure may give the US a competitive edge in environmentally friendly infrastructure (so-called green technology) for future sustainable economic growth.[8]

People or human resources may be just as important for US economic strength. Overall, in the near future, it is possible that US demographics may be considered comparatively healthier compared to other aging advanced economies such as Japan. Ian Wyatt and Kathryn Byun predicted that US growth from 2008 to 2018 may be based on demographic factors such as expanding population at 1 per cent yearly in that time period, expanding from 305 to 335.4 million people.[9]

Elizabeth Parker and Teresita Shaffer argue that the US has an important stake in the stability of Asia and views China, Japan and India as important elements of peace and security for trade and engagement rather than confrontation as the basis for interactions in the region.[10] As a global economic entity, not solely restricted to India or China, the US is likely to play the role of a hub for spoke-like trade connection and interaction with Brazil, Russia, India, China, South Africa (BRICS) and other G-20 nations, including the Gulf economies.

The US is deeply engaged in bilateral trade and commerce with each economy in North-East Asia and the Gulf. In the Gulf region, for example, Christopher Candland notes that the US is actively and strongly involved in the Middle East through the Middle East Partnership Initiative (MEPI) based on four pillars composed of economics, education, politics and women[11] and in the economic sphere, and the Middle East Entrepreneurship invites individuals from the Middle East engaged in private sector business to the US for management courses.[12]

Candland argues that bilateral trade outside energy and arms between the US and the Gulf economies is mainly in oil, cars, civil engineering and telecommunications equipment, with increasing interest for acquiring US agricultural products.[13] While exchanges between Gulf economies and Asia have grown and expanded tremendously, Gulf Cooperation Council (GCC)–US trade remains concentrated on value-added products. According to Aysu Insel and Mahmut Tekce, the GCC economies' trading relationship is still focused mainly on developed economies such as the US, importing hi-tech items such as aviation component parts, cars, machinery, engines, turbines and power transmission equipment from the US.[14]

Most importantly, perhaps, the US role in the Gulf appears to be a global one when it comes to maintenance and provision of energy supply and trade. The US provides a global guarantee that crude oil and petroleum continues to be supplied from the Gulf to feed the needs of the international economy and trade as part of its international responsibility even though Amy Myers Jaffe argues that the US is able to meet its energy requirements by providing a security blanket over energy resources nearer its shores, such as those in Canada, Mexico, South America, the North Sea and the African continent.[15] Its priorities are to maintain the stability of the global energy system and its pricing to prevent any energy impact and fallout from affecting the global economic and trading systems.[16]

The US provides the security umbrella which enabled Japan and other allies in North-East Asia to experience postwar economic recovery and economic development. Historically, US acquisitions contributed to Japan's postwar economic recovery through special procurements from 1950 to 1955 valued at US$3.55 billion, making up 44 per cent of the foreign currency into Japan as payment for exported products.[17] Its technologies and technical knowhow were also instrumental in helping Japan recover from the devastation associated with the war. The US worked closely with Japan through economic exchanges and capacity-building programs, while contributing to regional trade and development.

The US as a trading partner is also crucial to India's economy. According to Parker and Shaffer, US importation of India-originated IT services contributes to its total bilateral trade with India valued at US$50 billion.[18] In 2005, according to Christopher Rusko and Karthika Sasikumar, both the US and China were India's top consumer markets, taking in 18 per cent and 19 per cent of Indian exported goods respectively while the same two economies made up 7 per cent (China) and 6 per cent (US) of India's imports.[19]

Similarly, the US role in China's economic development was of the utmost importance. China's establishment of official relations with the US after Nixon's visit in 1972 and Chinese economic reforms saw a growth of Chinese exports to the US as a percentage of overall US imports from 7.7 per cent to 20.9 per cent between 1987 and 2000.[20] Given the interconnectedness of North-East Asia and the Gulf to the US economy, there may be some avenues for the major economies in the Asia region to cooperate with the US, for e.g. energy representatives from South Korea, India, China, Japan and the US met to discuss sustainability, energy and collective work in clean-coal and nuclear energy developments in December 2006 in Beijing but such initiatives require tremendous political consensus and strategic compromise to move forward.[21]

There are also growing trade exchanges between the spokes. Between China, India and the Gulf economies, there have also been exchanges, including energy, investments, infrastructure construction and food. For example, John Calabrese pointed out that Dubai International capital (DIC) combined with Chinese First Eastern Investment Group to set up a new fund known as China Dubai Capital to invest in Chinese firms.[22] Infrastructure development appears to be another major focus, for example, Dubai Ports World (DPW) and Tianjin port Group Company Ltd combined to construct a container facility in Tianjin in 2006 in addition to six existing container facilities at six Chinese ports.[23]

Indian energy supply also originates from the Gulf, and it is on the way to take over South Korea's fourth position as the largest user of Gulf energy after the US, China and Japan.[24] In terms of trade with individual economies, according to Insel and Tekce, India has arisen to attain the position of the most significant trading entity for Kuwait from 2003 onward.[25]

Agriculture may also emerge as a growth area in economic exchanges between the Gulf and Asia since the GCC members source most of their food externally and such needs may grow in accordance with demographic expansion, lack of agricultural space, less than optimal amounts of hydro-resources and rapid economic growth. Because of these factors, Calabrese indicated that bilateral trade in agricultural and manufactured food between India and the Gulf economies expanded from US$5.5 billion (2001) to US$48.6 billion (end of 2006).[26] There are also labour exchanges between the Gulf economies and Asia as less-skilled and skilled workers take up jobs and occupations in the Gulf, making up 13 million out of 35 million people in the GCC states.[27]

Between the two fast-growing emerging economies, trade exchanges have also expanded. Bilateral trade between India and China attained the mark of US$38 billion in 2007 and China became India's largest trading partner for merchandise trade, according to Parker and Shaffer.[28] The question remains if the two largest newly emerging economies are able to work with each other based on economic complementarity. Overall, however, it may be significant to note that India is a comparatively small trading entity with China, making up only 2 per cent of China's total trade.[29]

There remains numerous push and pull factors in close trade relations between India and China. While both are crucial entities and participants of the global trading world, they appear to be engaged in both competition and cooperation at the same time, perhaps something inevitable given their size and importance to the global trading community. For example, while there may be historic plans to open up the 'Silk Route' between India and China through Sikkim and Tibet and other initiatives to regionalize growth through encouraging trade between south-west China, north-eastern India, north Myanmar and Bangladesh;[30] such plans are likely to take a long time to materialize and need to surmount competitive instincts among those involved.

It is highly likely that US may increase engagement with the newly emerging economies of India and China as they move up the technological and value-added ladder and as their economic and trading systems develop indigenous features. Both India and China have penetrated higher value-added production and services in some aspects. For example, by 2003, India was already a leading outsourcing centre for ten years with approximately 50 per cent of the globally biggest top 500 private sector firms and state entities subcontracting their IT and business processes to India.[31] As for China, according to Arvind Panagariya, China's exports have also moved up the value chain with office-use and data processing technologies; telecommunications devices and sound-recording machines and electrical machinery and appliances as three of the four highest-ranking exports from China.[32]

Like the precedent that Japan has set, India and China will likely continue evolving and adapting their systems of development, trade, commerce and economic development for integration with the global economy. Literature on development, particularly those written in the 1960s posit a similar pattern that most developing economies may follow, including the rise of a middle class in the course of economic development.[33] Such standardized patterns of development may not be fully accepted by some scholars who highlight the possibility of indigenous models of development, including large newly emerging economies. For example, A. H. Somjee argues that both India and China are highly complex entities and, due to their entrenched and 'multilayered' societies, sometimes external influence does not fully penetrate the different strata of their societies,[34] leaving behind incomplete or semi-developed systems and patterns of trade that may not fully emulate Western models of development.

Scholars such as Howard J. Wiarda characterizes these models of development and trade as the 'Confucian' or a 'Hindu' theories of development based on non-Western native traditionalism and sociocultural factors,[35] but he also cautions against underemphasizing the importance of strong global forces, advocating more similarities and uniformities between world regions.[36] Wiarda argues that there is almost an inevitable preference for Western popular cultural exports, including American-style consumerism, and other universalistic values[37] or soft power influence.

The tussle between universalism (tendency towards strong global forces) and particularism (indigenous systems of development and adaptation to the global system) is likely to continue to adapt and cope with the changing global climate. The achievements of both India and China must be recognized, given that they have reduced poverty rates in their societies after the 1980s and also experienced GDP per capita growth. It may be quite likely that India and China will adapt selective positive features of Western trading systems and developmental model for their own indigenous development and use.

Challenges remain in the Chinese and Indian economies and their development, including income disparity and unevenness of growth between regions. For both economies, the ability to sustain economic growth into the future may be crucial for social stability and to mitigate other challenges. India and China's emerging economies are also viewed as both competitive challenges and engines of growth by the rest of the world. Mahvash Saeed Qureshi and Guanghua Wan pointed out that India and China present opportunities for some regions of the world while posing a challenge for others, for example, Lesotho is challenged by increasing imports of textiles and clothes from both India and China.[38] To resolve such contradictions, it may be necessary for the major components of the global economy to engage more intensely with each other.

Japan as a model of development is renowned in East Asia and has been emulated by many successful economies since then, including the four tiger economies and other emerging economies in the region. The model of development exerted so much influence that, during the period of the 1980s, Japan was seen as an alternative to the US model of development or even surpassing it in terms of productivity, efficiency and effectiveness.

Japan's traditional strength lies in group harmony at the workplace, harmonious working relationships, state-led development, export-led development, lifetime employment (LTE) and job security, interlinked conglomerates through the keiretsu system and continual improvements in production processes. In the socio-economic aspect, the ability of Japan to prioritize the collective above the individual is a powerful force that may reassert itself, particularly in situations of crisis, reform and exigency.

The Japanese model also became responsible for what later became known as the East Asian miracle as successful features of Japanese economic development were implemented by other East Asian economies, resulting in fast growth of the region, economic expansion and the setting up of an intra-regional production network that is perceived to become a regional factory workspace for the rest of the world.

The Japan model has also met past challenges through indigenous adaptation of Western technologies and knowhow to transition from a pre-modern economy into a modern one, during the Meiji Restoration of 1868, and effectively re-engineered itself from a heavy industrial economy into an energy-efficient economy after the oil crisis of 1973, and thereafter has become a leading global advocate of environmentally friendly green technologies in the contemporary setting.

Both economies have also demonstrated foresight and patience, often foreseeing economic and developmental challenges before they occur and taking long-term approaches to problem-solving and innovation. Having gone through many modern and contemporary economic and business cycles, they also have track records of success and innovation. Consequently, emerging and developing economies continue to look towards the two examples for inspiration along with newer models of development, selecting features that best suit their needs and local conditions.

Given the historical developmental inspiration that the US and Japan have provided for emerging economies, they continue to play a central role in global economic development. The US model may be considered as comparatively more universalistic than the Japanese model, given that it has a longer history of development and inspired Japanese economic growth both during the late pre-modern period with Commodore Perry's visit as well as during the postwar years of 1945–52 under Allied occupation.

The US also played a central role in globalization with its desire for open sea lanes, free trade access, technological innovations that revolutionized transportation and travel and its information technology-driven connectivity as well as established global leadership in many international economic and developmental organizations. In many cases, the US brought these technologies and technical knowhow to the rest of the world, closing the gap between developing and developed economies and tackling new disparities such as the digital gap by generously offering assistance to set up training and facilities to those who need it.

The Japanese model of development may be considered as comparatively particularistic compared to the US universal model since Japan was most influential in East Asia first before it was exported to the rest of the world. The fact that it may be comparatively particularistic does not take away from the merit of this model as it has lifted a large percentage of humanity from poverty by being a model that inspired the East Asian economic miracle. The Japanese model of development was disseminated to the rest of East Asia through individual 'Look East' policies as economies in East Asia and later South Asia instituted programmes learning from Japan.

Given Japan's geographical and geological resource-scarce make-up, the Japanese model is highly important in its own right because of its lean production formats and systems, energy-saving technologies and environmentally friendly development – something it has taught and led the world in since its own developmental challenges in the 1960s and 1970s from its own economic high-growth period when pollution caused incidents of the itai-itai and Minamata diseases.

For economies like Japan's which has no natural resources, it must depend on trade and economic competitiveness to generate economic development and growth. East Asia's early commodities trade structure was designed to provide Japan's postwar industrialization with raw materials in exchange for foreign direct investments (FDIs), official development assistance (ODA), loans, capital, technology and manufactured goods from Japan. Technology transfers also took place in a Japanese–Middle Eastern trade relationship. Japan has, in fact, been the major supplier to that region of technologies, including consumer electronics and automobiles, since the 1970s and 1980s.[39]

Besides sales of technology through consumer goods and products, as Japan moved up the value-added ladder, it also transferred lower value-added manufacturing activities further down the regional economic structure – from the four tiger economies to the rest of Asia and finally to the formerly socialist economies in East Asia.

As part of its efforts to secure global trade, Japan, like a number of other advanced countries, incorporated into its 1960s strategies a self-styled 'mission' that encouraged export and trade and coordinated its ODA project's activities with the activities of emerging economies.[40]

Japan's rapid postwar growth in the twentieth century demanded a stable and voluminous supply of energy resources. Logically, some historical features of Japan's regional trade may have been partially shaped or stimulated by energy exchange. In the case of Japan's trade with its largest neighbor, the oil crisis or shocks as they are called in Japan during the 1970s partly motivated Japan to trade with China after the resumption of official ties and also after the inking of the 1978 Long Term Trade Agreement (LTTA).

Besides turning to China for oil, Japan maintained a carefully balanced strategy with different factional groups in the Middle East. It successfully persuaded Middle Eastern oil suppliers to relabel Japan as a non-hostile nation during the 1970s oil crisis to assure a constant flow of oil.

While nearby energy suppliers in East Asia remain important, Japan's energy trade (like many other North-East Asian economies) greatly depends on Middle Eastern sources. Therefore, a long relationship between Japan and that region may not be surprising. Japan increased contact with Middle Eastern economies after the 1952 San Francisco (SF) Treaty that marked its reintegration into the international community after the war. It was the first state to establish official relations with Israel in 1952.[41]

Actually, Japan established official relationships successively, as follows: with Egypt in December 1952, Saudi Arabia in 1954, Iraq in 1955, Iran in 1956, Libya in 1957, Kuwait in 1961 and Algeria in 1962. It also based envoys in Oman, Bahrain, Qatar and the United Arab Emirates (UAE) from 1971 onwards.[42] Following the 1956 Japanese Arabian Oil Company's initiation of survey and exploitation of Saudi oil resources in 1960, Saudi royal family members Prince Sultan bin Abdul-Aziz Al-Saud and the King Faisal bin Abdul-Aziz Al-Saud visited Japan's capital city in 1960 and 1971 respectively.[43] Japan, in fact, has a comprehensive relationship with the Middle East as a region.

The decade that coined the term 'oil shocks' was treated as a period of 'resource diplomacy' in Japan, where trade interests integrated with political policy and geographical priorities. This merger of policies justified Japan's decision to advance aid worth US$3 billion to the Middle East in December 1973.

It also justified Japan's widening use of developmental aid and loans beyond East Asia and onto a global platform for close alignment with diplomatic and raw commodities requirements.[44] With this reprioritization of its economic policies, Japan became the world's largest ODA provider and between 1980 and 1995 (other than the first Gulf war period). In fact, Japan's ODA to the Middle East made up 10 per cent of the total amount of aid.[45]

Along with dispensing aids and loans, marketing products and engaging technological transfers to the Middle East, Japan also became a major global customer for energy, including natural gas, of which the Gulf states are major suppliers. In the early twenty-first century, Japan will likely remain a leading natural gas customer, probably making up approximately 60 per cent more demand than did the Atlantic Basin in 2002.[46] But, for the near future, Devin Stewart points out that, even though Japan had a head-start in the global LNG trade, keen competition reduced its world market share to only 50 per cent of world demand.[47] India and China will likely be important sources of demand for global gas supply.

The Middle East–Japan relationship is so comprehensive that it also affects other non-energy related products. In terms of non-oil trade, growth often occurs in various sectors. For example, Japan is an important customer for Gulf-originated aluminium that enjoys advantages of affordable labour costs, close proximity to major clientele in Asia and big gas reserves.[48]

In the non-energy sectors, the GCC member economies' share of imports from Japan stands at 7 per cent.[49] An early form of non-oil trade consisted of the cotton commodity. Dubai middlemen acquired sasooni cotton from Nichibo mills, cotton latha from Nishinbo Three Peaces and Toyobo Flying Dragon mills from Japan, before reselling them to Indian customers, who made traditional sari textiles. This Dubai trade was subsequently upgraded by value-addition into the lucrative trade in Japanese consumer electronics that the late 1970s witnessed.[50]

Such non-oil trade with the Middle East is crucial, to the extent that it helps Japan offset trade deficits with the region that result from the voluminous energy resources that Japan imports.[51] Such trends in non-oil sector trade growth are likely to be integral to the trade between North-East Asia and the Gulf regions for the foreseeable future. By way of overview, non-oil regional importation from North-East Asia into the Gulf economies may be valued at US$32 billion annually, boosted by emerging customer needs for automobiles, machines and other forms of raw materials associated with the Gulf's robust construction and building sectors.[52]

In addition to export-import trade, investments are undergoing increasing exchanges. Historically, investments had emanated from Japan to the Middle East, for example, in the mid-1980s, Japanese investments in the Middle Eastern hi-tech industry, such as the telecommunications industry, was strong enough to capture a sizeable market share in that region.[53] Given the rise of the Gulf economy and also healthy energy prices, investments now head both ways, from Japan to the Middle East and *vice versa*.

According to Minister Mustapha Al-Shamali, Gulf investment agencies, like the Kuwait Investment Authority (KIA), want to increase investments in Japan to US$48 billion, and to simultaneously expand investments in Japan's neighbors, such as South Korea.[54] In another example, the private sector in other Gulf economies, like Saudi Aramco, participated in Japan's downstream sector, and acquired a 15 per cent stake in Showa-Shell Oil Company.[55]

During the lobbying efforts for increased trade exchanges with the Gulf and the Middle East, the Japanese trade federation Keidanren was the dominant motivator that persuaded the Japanese government to discuss free trade agreements with the GCC. In September 2005, Keidanren released a document entitled, 'Call for Early Launch of Negotiations for Japan-GCC Economic Partnership Agreement' that advocated the inclusion of energy and better business conditions in future bilateral exchanges. More specifically, the report capitalized on the track record of good economic relations and exchanges that Japan established in the Middle East.[56]

In addition to trade agreements, there were strategies to guarantee the security and maintenance of energy transactions, including sea lanes and maritime space. Because clusters of industries and consumers in North-East Asia in Japan, Korea and Taiwan are generally found near the coastlines, secure maritime transportation rather than pipelines are crucial.[57] This means that Japan requires cooperation with other stakeholders in the region for secure energy supplies, including the US for stability and security in maritime waters.

Even as Japan is traditionally aligned with its allies' security umbrella, it focuses on trade and commerce as the main forms of interactions and exchange with the Middle East. Not only is Japan dependent on a stable Middle East, it also benefits from exporting goods and products to that region. As the Middle East is a newly emerging regional market, Japan is an ardent supporter of the Middle East peace process.[58]

Because of supply vulnerabilities, the foreseeable future will likely witness Japan's ongoing attempts to reduce her dependence on Gulf and Middle East fossil fuels. Because of previous oil crises, Japan has built up crude oil stockpiles. For example, by July 2004 Japan had attained a reserve volume sufficient for 162 days of consumption. Of this total, governmental supplies comprised an eighty-eight day reserve and the private sector, a seventy-four day reserve.[59]

In the process of paring down reliance on Middle Eastern oil supplies that totalled, for example, 86.5 per cent in FY2003, Japan is keen to participate in Russia's energy resources survey. It also wants to utilize the Russian oil supply as a suitable supply buffer in case of regional instability impacts Middle Eastern oil supplies.[60] Shoichi Itoh (Researcher, Research Division, Economic Research Institute for Northeast Asia ERINA), however, presented several arguments that downplayed Russian oil as a credible alternative to Middle Eastern crude oil. First, as he pointed out, Japan has not yet experienced a sharp reduction in her ability to import Middle Eastern oil; second, Russia may likely seek high profits for her oil supply; third, Russian investment and business conditions and business laws may not be complementary to Japan's private sector expectations.[61]

Past attempts to lessen Japan's overdependence on crude oil were not necessarily restricted to locating alternative sources of fossil fuels. By way of illustration, Japan's long-dominant Liberal Democratic Party (LDP) – which ruled Japan (with the exception of a short period of a few months in the early 1990s and 2010) from 1955 to 2009 – advocated greater use of nuclear energy by 1990.[62] A White Paper was released in Japan in 1987 revealed that Nuclear Energy comprised 28 per cent of the overall Japanese energy sector,[63] a percentage that seems likely to grow.

The MITI now known as Ministry of Economy, Trade and Industry (METI) established an institution to develop alternative, and non-nuclear, fuel sources.[64] The traditional state-organized trade promotional role remains strong. In the past, Japan has worked to align its diplomacy, economic initiatives and bureaucratic priorities together, given that its economic profile is substantially more pronounced than its political profile. This dilemma continues today. At least since 2008, Japan has entrusted to a single ministry – METI – those functions that involve establishing alternative energy agencies, coordinating trade investments and coordinating market promotions.[65]

Like the US, Japan has also been a major distributor of ODA, loans, training, infrastructure assistance and other capacity-building measures for the world. Japan has also assisted in the growth of large emerging economies such as Indonesia and China, two entities that have become developmental models for other economies in their own right. Its economic role in the region is also coupled with soft influence through its pacifist stance and environmentally friendly approaches to development after the 1970s. Like India's Bollywood and other entertainment soft influences, Japan's developmental inspiration may continue to inspire non-growth oriented indicators associated with developmental peace, sustainability and moderation.

The American and Japanese middle classes as well as their lifestyles and consumption patterns inspire emulation and inspiration for the rest of the world. This may be visible in the emerging economies like India, China and the Gulf region where evidence may be detected through popular culture, entertainment, material acquisitions, branding, new and traditional media and consumption patterns. The growth of a transnational middle class may bring about its own benefits as well as its own set of challenges. The diversity of opinions that may arise from both large emerging and established economies may add more options to the common marketplace of ideas and this may be utilized for the overall benefit of all if equilibrium may be reached between all stakeholders.

Again, it may be important to recognize progress and positivity when it emerges. Together with the US and Japan, the large emerging economies of India, China and the Gulf region are making progress for humanity in tandem. If the world is imagined as one economic and social unit, the net effect of progress is inspiring and may not require exceptionalist 'rising' labels. The nature of problems faced by the large emerging and the developed economies may be similar to different extents but display the commonality of requiring continual adaptation and improvements to tackle ever-increasing new challenges. But when progress is made, whether inspired by established or emerging models, they may be recognized for the contributions made.

It may be possible for the US and Japan themselves to acquire some selected successful features of large emerging economies like India, China and the Gulf region for their own economic development in the future. In this case, equilibrium may be reached between traditional and established developmental priorities and emerging developmental priorities. Such equilibrium may be necessary to manage common problems, particularly those that are transboundary in nature like pollution, resource use and sustainability, for example.

5 EMERGING ECONOMIES: ASIA AND THE GULF

With growing trade and energy links between North-East Asia and the Gulf economies, some observers like Christopher Davidson have argued that a twenty-first century 'Silk Road' connecting the Middle East region with North-East Asia (among other world regions) augmented by popular perceptions of the so-called shift of gravity to Asia-Pacific economies has encouraged an eastward-looking shift among Gulf economies.[1] For example, Davidson argues that the Gulf economies may be physically connected to North-East Asia by an ancient Karakoram Highway although this may be contested by local tribal stakeholders.[2]

While the Silk Road may have been a main trading route for ancient empires, its long disuse may mean considerable efforts to revive it for contemporary transportation of modern goods, products, services and energy. Any revival has to overcome tremendous challenges of geopolitical, economic, security and infrastructural nature. While it has on some occasions been unified and stabilized by ancient empires to make them profitable routes, the contemporary array and variety of important stakeholders as well as the presence of global and regional economies and states in that region means it is challenging to achieve wide-ranging consensus on the (re?)utilization of this route. The complex situation in the Gulf region may be highlighted by the Gulf Research Center (GRC) which has illustrated the importance of the US's role in the Gulf, as well as India's presence that GRC argues is 'more extensive than China's' despite China's growing infrastructure projects in the region.[3] Regardless of such comparisons, it may be clear that all major economies and states have a vested interest in the region.

Just what is the historical origin of the so-called Silk Road? From the North-East Asian perspective, among many other golden eras, there appears to be three examples of North-East Asian–Gulf/Middle Eastern interactions: during the Han Empire, the Chinese Tang dynasty and the Pax Mongolica. Facing incursions from the Xiongnu nomads, the Han Emperor Wudi (141–87 BC) dispatched Zhang Qian to form an alliance with the Yuezhi in 139 BC who themselves faced threats from the Xiongnu.[4]

Zhang Qian travelled for thirteen years before he came to Bactria (in contemporary Afghanistan) to meet the Yuezhi people but was unable to persuade them into an alliance and was instead twice captured by the Xiongnu for eleven years.[5] His efforts were not entirely wasted as Zhang returned with knowledge about the Central Asian region to the Han capital city of Changan.[6] Emperor Wudi dispatched his emissary to purchase Central Asian horses[7] but the emissary was killed in the process by a friend of the Xiongnu, prompting Wudi to exact revenge through counter-attacks led by General Li Guangli in Ferghana in 104 and 102 BC who succeeded on his second attempt.[8] General Li got hold of the best horses in Ferghana for the Han but only after expensive punitive missions that consumed human lives.[9]

Liu Xinru argued that, to facilitate trade access to Central Asia, the Han Chinese state lengthened the Great Wall towards the Jade Gate, west of Dunhuang and guaranteed the security of the route through stationing troops and forming local alliances in the Taklamakan Desert, and that was how fragrances and spices from South Asia, Arabia and East Africa found their way to China.[10] According to Kent Calder, there was an active trade between Han and Persia and Mesopotamia in silk, spices and other products.[11]

Through cultural exchanges, technologies, products and goods also interacted across civilizations. Liu pointed out that Sassanid Persia manufactured polychrome silk textiles that went to China in the sixth century, eventually influencing silk weaving in Tang China.[12] During the time of the Sassanid Empire, many Zoroastrian Persians often traded with Tang China, which established a government department (*Sabao* derived from the Sanskrit *sarthavaha*) to deal with this group of traders, and Zoroastrian places of worship could be found in Chinese trading centres.[13]

The domination of the Silk Road was only achieved when the Mongols took over most of Asia, first among the non-sedentary Inner Asian steppe people and dominated trade lines from Persia to China.[14] Technologies from North-East Asia and the Middle East interacted and were used in integrated forms by the Mongols who mobilized Chinese and Muslim armaments to attack locations with catapults and battering rams continuously.[15]

In terms of communities, the Mongols lived among their subjects in China and Persia behind guarded city walls and eventually integrated with their subjects, to a certain extent, in economic and social spheres.[16] According to Charles Halperin, industrially, Persian silk manufacturers benefited from the Mongol world system as they were able to reach networks and contacts that opened up with China while caravan trade along China, Persia and Central Asia profited because of such open (and safe) trade routes.[17]

Samir Pradhan's materials posit that India has an earlier trading footprint in the Gulf region than the Chinese, given that, since the third millennium

BC, trade items exchanged between India and the Middle East included textiles, spices, dates, pearls and semi-precious gemstones.[18] Given this historical presence, India is often considered a 'bridge' in the so-called Silk Road region, occupying a strategic location for trade and energy both for the overland as well as the maritime routes, a fact that will see many economic and state entities courting it for time to come.

In some ways, certain features of the Silk Road trade appears to have endured. For example, in terms of items traded, according to Jeevika Weerahewa and Karl Meilke, one of China's top five largest exports to India was silk.[19] Geographically, Christopher Rusko and Lartjola Sasikumar argue that, bilaterally, India and China also attempted to provide access to the space that links Sikkim and Tibet in the hope that it can lead to trade in the amount of millions of dollars, subject however to active opposition from India's officialdom raising security concerns.[20]

In effect, any revival of the ancient Silk Road is challenging due to its long disuse. According to Liu, the Silk Road was a Eurasian transmitter of culture and trade before trade though the maritime space overtook it in the eleventh century.[21] Reopening its route remains subjected to the cooperation of local interest groups such as tribes and also contemporary officialdom with strategic concerns and it may be premature or at least early to tell if such challenges may be overcome.

First, for any true contemporary Silk Road project to work, all important stakeholders may have to be involved including the US, India, China, Russia, Central Asia and South Asia as well as their local communities, tribal groups and other local interest groups. For the moment, such wide-ranging consensus across different political and economic systems and interests may not be unambiguously and easily attainable at least in the present circumstances.

Local interests may include organized groups but they can also include different factions within a state. In her writing on the tourism industry in 'The New Silk Road' in Central Asia, Cynthia Werner noted that a wide-ranging group of 'mediators' that include bureaucrats, tour agencies, guides, media and planners shape the tourism industry in that region and their interests are at times not mutually agreeable or complementary.[22] Similar mediating factors are likely to exist in most other industries under consideration for a Silk Road initiative and they need to be convinced of the universal benefit of the project.

The operability of a contemporary Silk Road is also subject to many challenges that require strong political will and economic rationality to overcome. Some studies/reports appear to indicate this – for example, an 'Energy Silk Road' from Central Asia may require strong multilateral consensus from potential financiers, experienced engineers for pipeline construction and also approval from sovereign nations including but not restricted to Russia, Mongolia, China and the Korean Peninsula.[23]

In discussions about the ancient Silk Road, it may also be noted that there had been historically peripheral but engaged actors in the Silk Road trade, such as Japan,[24] but who, with modernity, have since attained a major and central role in economic and trade activities in the Gulf and Central Asia. For example, during the administration of Japanese Prime Minister (PM), Junichiro Koizumi, Jacob Townsend and Amy King indicated that Japan's 'Silk Road Diplomacy' was spurred by high level visits (including those by the PM himself).[25] Therefore, it may be possible that their opinions, involvement and participation also have to be taken into account in any future reconstruction of the Silk Road.

There are also many forces of pull and push that work to exert their influence in this region. At different periods and in different situations under different contexts, there have been forces of pull and push between multilateralism and unilateralism, globalization and regionalization, cooperation and conflict, multipolarity and unipolarity, uncertainties and stability, etc., which makes the existence of an unproblematic, unbroken, continuous Silk Road tenuous. In other words, initiatives in a contemporary Silk Road may be contextually based, subject to prevailing political and economic conditions.

Secondly, intended, proposed or imagined contemporary Silk Road projects may no longer be neatly segregated into overland and maritime routes as both spaces are part of a unitary whole when it comes to aggregation of economic, trade and energy interests. Security and trade access in both spaces, for example, are difficult to separate in this region, given major economic and geopolitical interests. States and economies may likely include possible access to both spaces when it comes to negotiations, bargaining and dealing. It is a multidimensional and multifaceted configuration of different interests.

Thirdly, the nature of goods and products traded in any intended, proposed or imagined contemporary Silk Road spaces (both overland and maritime) has also become complicated. Unlike the barter trade of the ancient times, access to goods, trade and services now have to be negotiated and treated as part of the same package as energy, food and non-economic-related products. A commodity such as energy requires consensual cooperation from all parties involved (from producers to intermediaries to consuming markets), motivated by economic returns and benefits, before it can be transported safely and securely from suppliers to consumers.

In terms of overland trade, goods are no longer carried in caravans or on camel backs for primitive forms of barter exchange. Still, the transportation aspect has its own set of challenges, given advances in transportation technologies since the ancient times. Overland transportation requires robust highway infrastructure that can accommodate vehicles while maritime transportation rely on tankers

and other high-volume container cargo transportation. Both require sophisticated systems of management and port as well as custom clearances that may
need time to develop. For example, some observers cited possible challenges
concerning the efficacy and effectiveness of a revived Silk Road that may need to
be overcome, such as delays at border customs in Central Asia.[26] The complexities of the geographical entities involved and also the wide variety of products
traded may also mean that there is a need to negotiate these items under the
rubric of a free trade agreement (FTA) or other macroeconomic arrangements.

Contemporarily, it may be more useful to discuss inter-regional trade rather
than a cohesive concept of a Silk Road. Inter-regionally, there may be potential
for economic interactions between more industrialized and wealthier components of a particular region and the less-developed units of another region.[27] It
may also take place between a developed economy located in one region and
fast-developing unit or units of another region on the other hand (such inter-
regional interaction could be based on entry into the other party's consumer
market or joint state-private sector engagements in investments and trade for
example).[28]

In the economic realm, each region may also have its own priorities for
interacting with other regions, such as spurring economic growth, or fostering
intra-regional trade.[29] Such diversity in purpose may create valuable opportunities for inter-regional exchanges.[30] For example, a regional framework in one
location that places particular emphasis on trade networks serving the needs of
transnational private sector companies and facilitating cross-border investments
may be attractive for an economic unit from another region keen on investments.[31]

Heiner Hänggi categorizes three different forms of inter-regional arrangements: [32] (a) political-economic relations, connections and links that exist
between regional groupings; (b) bi-regional and transregional cooperative and
integrative arrangements; and (c) hybrid arrangements such as those between
regional groupings and single entities (usually major economies/state entities).[33]
Following Hänggi's argument in the last category, FTAs, bilateral agreements,
and regional trade agreements signed and acceded to with larger economic units
like India, China or Japan may constitute a form of inter-regionalism, at least in
the definitional sense. This may make sense in certain cases since such macro-
state units and economies may generally have delineable or economically active
subunits in the form of macro-regions or smaller units available for business with
other regions.

As an interesting example, Japan, China and India may be considered dominant units for the purposes of inter-regionalism discussions that concern a unit
with impact and influence not just in its own region[34] but with other regions
as well. Each of the above is a highly complex entity with large macro-regions,

local and provincial units. Moving away from the example of inter-regionalism between two large dominant units, another example of inter-regionalism may be between an institutionalized regional grouping and a geographical region.[35]

It may be possible to argue that Asia–Middle East economic, commercial, energy and trade ties and exchanges may satisfy some of the criteria and discussions of economic inter-regionalism above. However, to institutionalize such arrangements will require tremendous amounts of time, political compromises, political will and economic cooperation. Given these tremendous challenges, institutionalized inter-regional ties between Asia and the Middle East may not be immediately (or in the near future) possible in all areas. Neither is the idea of a North-East/South/East Asian trading bloc interacting with a pan-Middle Eastern economic bloc currently feasible, realizable or possible.

Trade need not institutionalize in these areas, given that market forces appear to have worked well in promoting private sector and trade interactions between entities within the two regions. The interaction, which appears open and inclusive, does not lock its participants into arrangements that exclude other parties. Interaction between Asia and the Middle East has also extended beyond energy, into manufacturing, investments and service sectors. In other words, trade appears to show signs of a multidimensional, multi-sectoral relationship.

For example, private sector interactions have been taking place between Asia and the Middle East as both regions reach out to each other in infrastructural, financial and other forms of trade – investments and non-energy trade – in addition to their more established ongoing energy trade. Even if inter-regionalism cannot be formalized due to the host of challenges involved, inter-regionalism or economic exchanges between entities within the two regions may be another addition to an already complex flora of cooperative instruments, often overlapping and coexisting, and inter-regionalism may further enhance the quality and quantity of exchanges between regions and bring mutual benefit.[36] Perhaps the important element of inter-regional trade is that it remains open to other participants and stakeholders, including IOs, the EU and the US and that it facilitates other parties to be involved in accordance with market forces and economic complementarities.

Gulf–Asia trade stands at more than US$300 billion (three times more than the value in 2000), with Asia taking in more than 50 per cent of Gulf exports and the Gulf takes in 33 per cent of its overall imports from Asia.[37] According to a 2006 report by the Institute of International Finance (IIF), there appears to be 'a gradual shift in GCC trade relations', with Asia increasing its share of the Gulf's overall trade.[38] This shift remains private-sector-driven and non-exclusive, often involving other parties that are interested in accordance with market forces and the participants' own priorities. At certain levels, it also takes place at a people-to-people, individualized exchange level. Consider, for example, tertiary academic opportunities for students and manpower/labour movement between the two regions.

Within the trade relationship between entities from the Middle East and the economies and private sector participants of North-East Asia, the transactions between the two regions are expanding from the more established bilateral energy trade to other non-energy sectors. Increasingly, commercial and economic deals appear to be part of a comprehensive package that include both energy and non-energy components.

Perhaps indicative of future practices, future contracts and deals may be concluded and won as part of an overall package that may include both energy-related and non-energy-related components. According to Yoshikazu Kobayashi from the Institute of Energy Economics Japan (IEEJ), the Korean National Oil Corporation (KNOC) led an alliance that successfully obtained Nigerian upstream deals by providing attractive investment packages that were comprehensive and included non-energy infrastructure deals.[39]

Besides bundling construction and infrastructure projects as part of packaged deals that include energy, trade exchanges appear to have also proliferated at the consumption level.

John Calabrese observed the presence of consumer demand for North-East Asian products from brands such as Haier, Huawei, Lenovo, Petronas, Ranbaxy, Samsung and Sterlite Industries.[40] Asian-made automobiles are one example of consumer products found in the Middle East. According to Geoffrey Kemp, Japanese and Korean-made cars and heavy vehicles symbolize this consumer trend.[41] In fact, overall, bilateral trade between the Gulf economies and economies like China are increasing. For example, according to Michael Thorpe and Sumit Mitra, China–Gulf trade increased from US$1.5 billion in 1991, to US$10.1 billion in 2000 and to US$33.8 billion in 2005, growing yearly at approximately 30 per cent and projected to double between the years of 2008 and 2013.[42]

What are some of the usual items traded between the Middle East and Asia? In consumer products, Kemp noted that cars, electronic items, textiles, fashion apparels and fashion accessories made up a sizeable proportion of Asian export trade with the Middle East while energy continue to be the main item coming from the Middle East to Asia.[43]

East Asia has been characterized and perceived by some as the world's manufacturing centre. To a certain extent, this characterization may factor in trade relationships between North-East Asian and Middle East economies. Calabrese gives the example of China–Dubai trade where China is Dubai's second largest trading partner, twelfth largest market for exported goods and makes up about US$180 million of Dubai's approximate US$45 billion non-oil exports, and Dubai imports around US$19 billion in goods from China annually.[44]

In terms of interactions between a region and a large macro-unit, Thorpe and Mitra's study of GCC–China trade relationship notes that the GCC is China's eighth largest export partner and ninth biggest source of imports; China, in turn, receives approximately 6 per cent of GCC exports. This is a substantial amount, since the US and EU both account for slightly more than 10 per cent each and Japan accounts for 19 per cent. Trend-wise, however, Chinese exports to the GCC increased from 4.4 per cent of overall GCC trade in 1997 to 8.0 per cent in 2006, even with changing categories of goods. By comparison, China's exports to the US comprised 8.2 per cent of China's total exports, China's exports to Japan comprised 7 per cent of the total and to the EU approximately 30 per cent of China's total.[45]

Relative to East Asia as a global manufacturing platform, Prince Saud bin Abdullah bin Thinayan Al-Saud, Saudi Basic Industries Corporation (SABIC)'s chairman, explained that 'Asia is a region where SABIC not only wants to supply products, but is also a region that regards as a strategically important location for future manufacturing of its products'.[46] If such thinking is actualized, one possible future trend may be the presence of Middle Eastern companies in East Asia producing goods and products not only for consumers in the two regions but also for the world.

Such arrangements may facilitate Middle Eastern attempts to tap into the affordable labour costs, the highly developed transportation network that facilitate just-in-time production, the consumer markets, the comparatively low intra-regional tariff barriers and the convenience of parts-sourcing found in East Asia that have similarly attracted investors from other regions.

The trend for exchanges in processed goods, not only pertains to Middle Eastern demand for North-East Asian-manufactured consumer goods, but works the other way round, North-East Asian economies have also shown demand for some of the semi-finished products from the Middle East. A part of this trade may be in the form of items needed for North-East Asian industrialization. These items may be sourced at highly competitive prices, when compared to comparable products from the Middle Eastern region.

Calabrese explains that China's desire for energy-intensive phosphate and aluminum encouraged Abu Dhabi's Borouge petrochemicals to send a marketing representative to Shanghai.[47] Borouge, then, teamed up with Vienna's Borealis to construct a polypropylene plant in China, and supply plastics to the car industry.[48] Calabrese also pointed out that Japan and other Asian economies need processed materials, like aluminum made in the Gulf, that is, products that are competitively affordable, because of lower labour and production costs, closeness for delivery to Asia and the Gulf's ample gas reserves.[49]

Because of such complementarities in demand and trade, the figures for bilateral trade between economies in the two regions indicate a rising trend.

According to Kemp, from 2003 to 2007, inter-regional trade between Asia and the Middle East expanded 269 per cent (numerical value from US$141 billion to US$379 billion), with Japan's bilateral trade expanding 195 per cent (US$70 billion to US$137 billion); Chinese bilateral trade increasing by 366 per cent (from US$30 billion to US$109 billion); South Korea's increasing by 243 per cent (US$34 billion to US$82 billion) and India's by 759 per cent (US$7 billion to US$51 billion).[50]

India is to be a growing Asian presence in the Middle East. India is not a new presence in the region, given its established need for crude oil from the Gulf region through the Arabian Sea. It has been importing natural gas from Qatar.[51] India's bilateral trade with the Middle East increased from 9 per cent of its total trade to 23 per cent from 2003 to 2007.[52] Increasingly, Indian economic interactions in the Middle East also reach into the non-energy sector. For example in the hospitality sector, Kemp notes that the Indian Flora Group Hotels started managing its sixth property in Dubai in 2008 and plans three more facilities in the same region.[53] The interest reaches both ways.

Given that India's population is projected to become the largest globally before 2150,[54] some Middle Eastern businesses see opportunities in serving India's rising middle-class and consumer needs. Saudi Air Arabia headquartered in Sharjah is expanding its airline schedules between India and the Gulf. This will increase inaugural flights that were started in March 2005 to more than fifty-five runs per week, at nine locations in India. Flights to India will constitute 25 per cent of Air Arabia's flight schedule.[55]

India's soft power initiated exchange platforms in Bahrain's arts and popular cultural sector. India's cultural soft power needs no introduction as its Bollywood industry reaches out globally through DVDs, movies, television programmes and enjoys fan appeal in Asia in general. India's soft power offers other trade inducements, including its status as a lifestyle trendsetter, its yoga practices, cuisines and long tradition of philosophical intellectualism.

The mutual interests that span between Asia and the Middle East extend beyond energy sectors. According to Calder, North-East Asian economies like China, Japan and Korea may have been selling goods and services to the Middle East to ease the high expenditure of energy trade.[56] Some of these goods and services may include high-value items. For example, Calabrese notes that the GCC economies are interested in looking beyond energy businesses and in utilizing their oil-generated profits for sectors like the physical infrastructure, education, information technology, and financial services.[57]

Among other items, investments are seemingly directed to construction projects for processing crude oil. This function is increasingly in demand because of the increased crude oil imports by large emerging economies like India and China. For example, according to Calabrese, Kuwaiti investors are constructing a US$5 billion refinery in Guangdong province in southern China.[58] But the mutual interests in each other is not restricted only to energy-related infrastructure, there are also property deals and other projects related to the hospitality, residential property and hi-tech specialized infrastructure industries.

By 2010, Asian economies inked agreements valued at US$500 billion for construction and infrastructure work in the Middle East Region, while the Gulf economies came up with US$250 billion for investing in East Asia in similar sectors, including property and construction.[59] Thorpe and Mitra's study indicates that GCC investment in Asia, for the years 2008–13, will approximate US$250 billion. These funds will be spent on long-term energy infrastructure investments, finance, telecommunications, real estate and tourism. China may require a projected US$3.7 trillion in energy delivery infrastructure by 2030, that is a figure estimated to be 18 per cent of the global share.[60]

Like Thorpe and Mitra, Calabrese notes that non-energy categories for Gulf-Asia trade relations applies, among other things, to non-energy related real estate and to the construction sector as well. In November 2007, for example, Emirates Building Systems (subsidiary of Dubai Investments Industries) partnered with China Jingye Construction Engineering Contract Company of China, to construct multistorey buildings, stadia and aircrafts.[61] According to Calder, Korean construction firms experienced a 65 per cent increase in contractual deals in the Middle Eastern region for the first six months of 2005, for a total of US$6.2 billion.[62]

Kemp notes that a number of infrastructural projects in Gulf city states (including Doha, Abu Dhabi, Dubai) are managed by South Korean companies.[63] But it may be possible that Chinese firms are focusing on their own competitive advantages to catch up with more established peers, South Korea and Japan.

Other examples that Calabrese cites include Zhongon Construction Group's collaboration with Fkamber Holdings to invest approx US$100 million in Dubai's property sector while China's Dashang invests at least US$200 million in Dubai's retail industry.[64] Real estate deals and retail outlets may not be the only service sector construction projects that participants and entities in the two regions are interested in.

Tourism is a growing and important industry in both Asia and the Middle East. Calabrese also noted Damac Properties (the biggest real estate firm in the Middle East) went into the Chinese market with a US$2.7 billion development in Tanggu district and the Jumeirah Group managed the hotel HanTang Jumeirah, Shanghai.[65] Other North-East Asian economies are also interested in the Middle East's tourism sector. Kemp points out that, in May 2007, the Japan Airline hotel group, which had the longest experience managing outfits in that region of Japan, inaugurated a 257-room hotel in the UAE and plans to begin additional luxury guest accommodation projects in Dubai and Bahrain in 2011.[66]

US infrastructure and economic help for nation-building in the Middle East is more established compared to North-East Asian initiatives, with a postwar history as early as 1945, according to Michael B. Oren.[67] Therefore, it may be important to contextualize developments initiated by North-East Asian economies as something relatively recent and contemporary.

As for the investments sector, Calabrese provided one example of financial investment by Gulf economies in North-East Asia – the Dubai International Capital (DIC)'s collaboration with First Eastern Investment Group of China to create the China Dubai Capital for investing in China-based/owned companies.[68] Emanating from the other direction, Thorpe and Mitra note that some observers estimate that, as of 2007, China likely invested about US$7 billion in the Gulf region.[69] This appears to be an example of cross-investments between two emerging economic units.

Besides investment firms, specialized outlets associated with each region engage in the inter-regional financial sector. Calabrese points out that Gulf firms have major projects to attract Asian capital through conventional and Islamic bonds.[70] He points out that the growth of Islamic banking in the Gulf and Asia assists this investment project. Standard and Poor report that Islamic banking makes up about US$1 trillion in value worldwide, and that links between Asia and the Gulf are increasing.[71]

As for investments coming from a subregion within the Middle East, Thorpe and Mitra note that, in 2006, GCC investment in China was about US$20 billion and in 2007 approximately US$30 billion.[72] Such investments may be related to the desire of government sovereign funds to diversify into different global regions, including those in the emerging economies. Diversification policies are designed to hedge against risks arising from one particular region vis-a-vis the others. Sovereign funds in the Gulf have expanded due to favorable oil prices that have augmented oil revenues for Gulf economies.

As Gulf-originated SWFs increased to their present value – GCC SWFs currently have a total value of US$1.6 trillion in 2009, Abu Dhabi Investment Authority (ADIA) approximately US$900 billion in 2009 – managers sought to diversify portfolios, expanding their shares in Asia.[73] China's FDIs in Saudi Arabia and the UAE totalled US$240,000 and US$31 million, respectively in 2003.[74] By 2008, China's investment totals increased to US$620 million (Saudi Arabia) and US$375 million (UAE).[75]

Calabrese notes that GCC investment funds, which grew enormously in the twenty-first century, make up 50 per cent of SWF globally in 2009.[76] The government-linked KIA, assets valued at approx US$100 billion, expanded its Asian component of overall investments from 10 per cent to 20 per cent in

2005.[77] Kuwaiti Finance Minister Mustapha Al-Shamali went to eight countries in August 2008 and with the intention for KIA to increase investments in Japan threefold to US$48 billion and expand in South Korean investments.[78]

This trend towards increased investments shows that Gulf fund interests in Asia are not restricted to large emerging economies like India and China, but that they also seek mature and established economies in North-East Asia, such as South Korea and Japan. The interest in Korean investments may be complementary to the expanding bilateral trade between Korea and the Gulf economies. According to Kemp, from 2003 to 2007, South Korea's bilateral trade with the Middle East region expanded from 6 per cent to 11 per cent of its total trade amount.[79]

Gulf investors also appear to be interested in the advanced Asian economies. Japan, for instance, is a mature hi-tech economy that is resource-scarce and oil-dependent. One example of Gulf capital investment in Japan is Aramco (Saudi Arabia)'s 15 per cent investment in Showa-Shell Oil Company's downstream market.[80] Since the 1990s, Saudi Arabia's Aramco discussed with Japanese petroleum firms possible investments in Japanese refineries. These discussions did not bear results, with the exception of Aramco's shares in Japan-based Showa Shell in 2004 and 2005 (the company provides Japan with 300,000 b/d of crude oil).[81]

After purchasing 14.96 per cent in Showa Shell, Saudi-based Aramco's refining capacity, in facilities external to Saudi Arabia itself, reached 695,000 b/d, a figure that exceeds 27.5 per cent of the firm's overall refining capacity.[82]

Japanese investments in Saudi Arabia appear to be comparatively more active. In 2000, Japan's FDIs in Saudi Arabia totalled US$714.53 million and its investment in the UAE totalled US$26.98 million. These figures increased to US$2.56 billion (Saudi Arabia) and US$251.62 million (UAE) in 2007.[83]

One example of Saudi Arabia's domestic investment portfolio is the Aramco partnership with Sumitomo Chemical of Japan, to build a refining petrochemical complex in Rabigh in Saudi Arabia.[84] According to Kobayashi, this deal was symbolic in many respects. Japan's business sector had concluded that Japanese-Saudi economic exchange was on the decline especially since 2000, when Japan lost its stake in the Arabian Oil Company's venture into that portion of the Khafji field located in the former Saudi-Kuwaiti neutral zone.[85]

Tourism and tertiary education sectors may have also benefited from increased exchanges between Asian economies and GCCl member economies. Workers, among other persons, moved to the dynamic economies of the Middle East.[86] This is important because tourism, study opportunities and jobs that require manpower may be the three most people-intensive sectors. Such exchanges take place at a more personalized and individual level, and offer more potential to foster interaction and understanding between societies, in contrast to large infrastructural, investment or trade deals.

Kemp argues that Middle Eastern students may be attracted to the Asian tertiary education sector because locations like India, China and South Korea have enhanced their standards, charge less for tuition fees (sometimes half of established institutions in the West), provide affordable expense scales for daily activities, and offer easier access to student visas, due to the increasing business ties between the two regions.[87]

Intellectually, however, again, it may be important to note these educational exchanges may be considered of recent vintage. The United States and UK remain established, traditional and entrenched destinations for Middle Eastern students.[88] Oren indicates that Middle Eastern studies proliferated in the US in the 1990s, with over 100 tertiary institutions offering subjects in this area, and the Middle East Studies Association (MESA) was established in 1966 in the US now with around 3000 members.[89]

Asian workers not only provide manpower for jobs that may be considered dangerous, dirty and laborious but are also managing GCC service industries in managerial and executive roles. This includes the leisure, tourism and hospitality industries, which are important in both regions and are expected to grow in the near future.

These industries include both traditional (e.g. group packaged tour) and non-traditional forms of tourism and hospitality (e.g. medical tourism, eco-tourism, etc.). India, for example, has increasingly established itself as a global destination for medical tourism, given its lower costs for medical operations and highly skilled medical establishments. These overall innovations are likely to serve the lifestyle, entertainment and leisurely needs of growing middle classes of both regions.

According to Kemp, Asian manpower in the Gulf region numbers 8.5 million (at the point of Kemp's writing in 2010, not including workers and others found there illegally) working in agriculture, the energy sector, banks, tourist establishments, hotels and academic sectors.[90] They are a mixture of recent migrants and multigenerational Gulf inhabitants.[91] Some Asians are welcomed and valued for their industry, their comparatively smaller salaries and others for highly desired specialized skills, including language.[92] India for example is a major provider of manpower to the Gulf. Its workers and skilled labour sustain the economies of the Gulf and make important contributions to their economic development.

These exchanges increase contact at the individual level. They take place according to market forces and happen in the normal course, with other non-Asian entities such as persons with the US, EU and other regional economies with the Middle East.

If open to all, these exchanges will benefit participants in the global economies and will benefit MNCs that have a global presence. Collaborative project-sharing capital and technologies resources may benefit stakeholders, in accordance with market forces and economic complementarity.

There may be new emerging areas for collaboration and cooperation in sectors of mutual interests to both East Asian and Middle Eastern economies. For example, the future may hold possible collaboration, trade or exchanges in green technologies that may be of interest to both East Asia and the Middle East in the near future, if not now.

Because East Asia industrialized and manufactured products for the world, rapid economic development impacted the environment and raised questions of sustainability, and natural resource use. Gulf governments may have to focus greater attention on clean and green or renewable energy technologies, in which Japan and South Korea are perceived as global leaders.[93]

Similarly, Middle Eastern economies, including those in the Gulf that have been developing rapidly, may see the middle classes clamor for higher standards of living and quality of life. Energy-efficient and environmentally friendly technologies developed in resource-scarce North-East Asia may be useful for technological transfers to the Middle East.

This is particularly true, as global resources such as water, energy commodities and food are expected to be in short supply, with rising needs among the world's developed, large emerging and developing economies.

Green technology and environmental preservation may be especially amenable to inter-regionalism but collaboration will require tremendous political consensus, will and geopolitical compromise to be successful. Inter-regionalism may spur regions to come together and to cooperate on common, single-issue, challenges (usually macro in scale and trans-boundary in nature).

Regional systems may develop inter-regional ties to cope with environmental challenges, because such issues tend to be trans-boundary in nature and to require a larger array of resources to manage the problems.[94] These two regions may not view institutionalized ties as something particularly urgent for such cooperation, since each is currently focused on internal priorities, including balance of trade, economic and fiscal issues. Open, non-exclusive economic exchanges seemed to have benefited economic exchanges between participants from the two regions thus far.

It may be possible to focus on broad issue-specific challenges that are common to both regions, through an open and non-exclusive format that welcomes investors, stakeholders and interested parties from IOs, developed economies in the EU and US, NGOs, civil society and private sector entities (MNCs or SMEs) from all geographical regions.

Cross-boundary transnational issues in general may also serve as rallying points for regions to come together to resolve common challenges in those areas (e.g. climate change and infectious diseases).[95] Inter-regional exchanges may arise from more basic forms of exchanges, such as dialogues, conversations and other discussion forms, before moving on to more concrete proposals and initiatives that require formal signatory assent.[96] These non-ambitious forms of exchanges and interactions again should be open and involve the participation of international stakeholders.

Trans-regional cooperative units at the non-state level, in defined cooperative units, may also be important contributors to inter-regionalism.[97] Rather than being broad-based agreements that include economic and political cooperation, non-state trans-regional cooperation tends to be more targeted in the kind of cooperative activities that units advocate.[98] Notwithstanding the smaller scale, cooperation at the non-state level could be an innovative way to develop interdependence and to leverage local strengths and needs.[99]

Private sector deals in both energy and non-energy-related sectors, and in people-to-people exchanges through tertiary study and employment opportunities, provide examples of possible non-state exchanges and interactions for the two regions.

Perhaps this is why many agencies may have to be involved in future deals between the Middle Eastern oil producers and North-East Asian economies. According to Kobayashi, Japan's engagement with the Middle East is a multi-agency, multilayered effort, with a combination of entities, such as the Japan Petroleum Energy Center (JPEC), The Japan External Trade Organization (JETRO), the Japan Cooperation Center for the Middle East (ICCME), and the Information Center for Petroleum Exploration and Production (ICEP) and/or a close relationship fostered through the auspices of Japan's Economic Planning Agency (EPA) or FTA.[100]

Sometimes, Japan's economic, trade and commercial initiatives in the Middle East are initiated and led by important business associations rather than the state. According to Hidetaka Yoshimatsu, Keidanren spearheaded the efforts in April 2006 for initiating FTA negotiations with the GCC through inaugural meetings on this subject organized in Japan's capital city in September of the same year.

These negotiations added to the already intimate connections between the GCC and Japan, given that Japan obtains 75 per cent of its crude oil supply from the GCC.[101] According to Yoshimatsu, the origins of this initiative may partly be found in Keidanren's advocacy in September 2005, with the initiative known as the 'Call for Early Launch of Negotiations for Japan–GCC Economic Partnership Agreement'. The negotiators recognized that the premise of these negotiations was that, 'Japan must actively pursue a comprehensive EPA with the GCC. Such an agreement should include not only elements of an FTA but also cover the energy sector and the improvement of the business environment'.[102]

The multidimensional approach to interactive relations between Japan and the Middle East is also reflected in other ways. Japan has a soft power presence in the Middle East region by virtue of information exchanges, the performing arts and cultural facilities in Cairo and Tehran and, through its Japan Foundation, organized art shows, entertainment and displays throughout the Middle Eastern region.[103] The Japanese capital city of Tokyo also promotes academic and arts exchange programmes.[104]

One could argue that cultural exchange, student exchanges and sister city relationships bypass the tradition obstacles that nation-states have to deal with, such as territorial disputes, historical misunderstandings and ideological differences, and enable people-to-people exchanges.[105]

Perhaps agriculture is one of the most important businesses in the repertoire of exchanges that characterize inter-regional Gulf–Asian economic relations. Kuwait, Saudi Arabia, and the UAE have been interested in agricultural investments in Asia, because of import dependence for food due to expanding populations/urbanization, limited arable land, limited water supply for agriculture, increasing food prices and other challenges.[106]

The pressing importance of the issue is indicated by a Kuwaiti-Bahraini delegation that surveyed Asia for agricultural investments in May 2008. They visited the Philippines and Thailand for rice imports. UAE investors were reportedly interested in the fishery industry, and in grain, fruits, and vegetables farms in Philippines.[107]

The increasing non-oil links between the Middle East and Asia may contribute to continued economic and commercial interactions even as both regions sought to diversify trade partners and to move beyond energy trade. North-East Asian economies, for example appear to be keen to diversity into non-oil energy resources, including nuclear and renewable energy resources. For the foreseeable future, however, non-oil energy technologies require time to develop and implement. For the moment, oil and natural gas will remain important items in this inter-regional trade.

Even though North-East Asia's engagement with the Middle East may be increasing, this arrangement may be considered something more of a contemporary phenomenon in comparison with the US engagement with the Middle East. Oren argues in *Power, Faith, and Fantasy* that the origins of US involvement with the Middle East may be as early as 1776.

Unlike the US engagement with the Middle East, North-East Asia's interactions appear to be mainly trade and energy-focused. They do not contain the same multifaceted elements, like religion, politics, popular culture, military, intellectual exchange, gender relations and other forms of exchange that have made US–Middle Eastern interactions deep, intertwined and, sometimes, volatile. The US will likely remain the dominant trade partner in the Middle East region and – given its working relationships with Japan and South Korea – also in the North-East Asian region.

Further, Asian economies may remain internally focused in comparison with the US which is a global power. Asian economies have to deal with the contradictions of fast economic growth, including tackling socio-economic gaps, environmental issues, inflation and other developmental challenges. Further, both Asia and the Middle East may be reluctant to overcommit themselves beyond economic and cultural exchanges, given pressing domestic priorities and a conscious effort to concentrate on peripheral diplomacy, before wandering to farther regions in non-economic and cultural outreaches of inter-regional significance.

The reason why a now-defunct Silk Road arises in some imaginations and conceptualizations is due to the global emergence of India, China and the Gulf states which may have become familiar stories by now. The success of emerging economies like India, China and the Gulf states are praised for their contributions to economic development and poverty alleviation. Together, these three rapidly growing economies and regions have uplifted millions from poverty and also provided growth for the world economy in times of difficulties. One popularly cited statistic in this aspect is the annual rates of Chinese economic growth averaging out at 9.8 per cent for the past two and a half decades while the equivalent was 5–6 per cent for India.[108]

There are conscious efforts to categorize and understand the economic growth of large emerging economies. For example, Sascha Muller-Kraenner suggests an interesting definition of economies like India, China and the Gulf states by utilizing the German Development Institute's (or Deustches Institut fur Entwicklungspolitik (DIE) in German) interpretation of the 'emerging powers of the South (Anchor countries)' which consists of large developing countries like India and China based on the size and extent of their economies, reach of influence and their ability to affect the international environmental order.[109] It is unclear if this definition can also apply to regional groupings or blocs of smaller 'emerging' or developing economies.

One commonality that appears to characterize almost all North-East Asian (and the East Asian) economies is an emphasis on export-oriented, outward-looking, developmental blueprints for economic development.

Such metaphorical blueprints are generally characterized by criteria to increase international market access, the removal of obstacles to trade and the promotion of politico-economic stability.[110] North-East Asian economies use open and outward-looking trade as a tool for obtaining natural resources, including energy resources, for economic development and growth – items especially relevant for North-East Asian economies that lack natural resources.

Japan is exemplary in this regard. Japan's achievements in trade probably should not be understated, because it has been very efficient and effective in reaching raw commodities, ensuring the entry of Japanese goods and products into non-Japanese markets, enjoying healthy relationships with most parts of the world and maintaining an important and strategic relationship with the US, all done within the existing international economic system.[111]

The energy trade in North-East Asian economies can also take the form of bilateral trade agreements such as the 1978 Sino-Japanese LTTA, which promoted the export of crude oil from China to Japan. This was an early form of economic and trade exchange, in which Chinese energy resources were exchanged for Japanese technical knowhow, technological goods and foreign currencies.

With rapid economic growth and technological development,[112] North-East Asian intra-regional trade shifted from being a raw materials supplier to providing finished products that maximized benefits from intra-regional economic integration and cooperation. For example, even with bilateral trade agreements between North-East Asian economies like Japan and South Korea, there are also attempts at FTAs and the formation of joint energy markets.[113]

These prospective FTAs may capitalize on the geographical complementarities between the two North-East Asian neighbours. In fact, South Korea's port facilities construction was centred mainly on the south-eastern maritime areas that enjoy closeness to Japan and that are used as maritime links with the Middle East, which accounts for the majority of energy commodities from that region.[114]

Likewise, other members of the North-East Asian community also attempted to turn their geographical positions into intra-regional trade advantages. For example, according to G. Enkhtaivan, Mongolia's position – sandwiched, as it were, between the Chinese and Russian economies – gives it a special geographical advantage to benefit from trade between China, Russia and other regional stakeholders.[115] Japan's recent focus on Mongolia's 'rare earth commodities'[116] is likely to be a major factor in bilateral trade agreements with region-wide implication.

Even though the recent past witnessed North-East Asian initiatives to employ trilateral agreements, as a vehicle to increase intra-regional trade, progress has been slow, contentious and cautious, even in regard to energy commodities. In 2002, a flurry of activity took place with regards to energy trade, and according to Xu Xiaojie, the Chinese 'responded to' a Japanese invitation to participate in regional energy dialogues between (North-)East Asia and West Asia.[117]

At about the same time, according to Xu, Japan, China, North and South Korea collaborated with Russia to advance upstream and downstream energy sectoral development in eastern Siberia, in addition to other locations in far-eastern Russia.[118] Because of a host of preliminary challenges that the parties must resolve before the trilateral initiatives can be implemented, it is unlikely that either negotiations or the actual trade arrangements can be implemented anytime soon.

Setting aside the question of intra-regional trade, the North-East Asian economies are important for the Middle East trade even on an individual basis. This importance was demonstrated during the 1997 Asian financial crisis that witnessed a decrease in crude oil importation to Asia, including Japan, which made up 57 per cent of the Middle East's mineral exports in 1996.[119]

China is another of the Gulf states' important trade partners. According to Julian Madsen, the Gulf Cooperation Council has witnessed trade volumes expanding from US$1.5 billion to US$20 billion in 2005, and within the same year, to US$33.8 billion of the overall Arab–China trade (valued at US$36.7 billion); therefore Madsen concluded that the Gulf forms the nucleus of the Arab–Chinese trading relationship.[120] Simplifying this trade into an analogy, Madsen argues that it may be characterized as Chinese textiles for Gulf oil exchange.[121]

This characterization may have to be modified in the near future, as The Yomiuri International Economic Society argues that an important change in China's trade with the rest of the world is underway. While lower value-added and non-industrial agricultural products remain the majority of China's exports, the trade in higher-technological goods are expanding quicker and, in fact, leading the export expansion.[122]

The trend for the near future may be North-East Asian (including, and perhaps especially, Chinese) economic and trade diversification will be channelled into non-energy related trade, particularly with Gulf oil suppliers like Saudi Arabia and Kuwait.[123] According to Zhang Guobao, the crude oil trade as a single item commodity caused China a trade deficit that totalled in excess of US$30 billion in 2004.[124] Therefore, if trade between these regions – and China in particular – experienced diversification into a wider range of trade in goods and services, this trade deficiency could be mitigated.

Trade expansion into goods and items beyond raw materials trade may also be a mutual benefit for some interest groups in the Gulf economies. In some respects, Gulf economies seem to want a more balanced trade and economic relationship with the rest of the world. This would enable Gulf nations to work towards a more evenly balanced economic development beyond only raw materials extraction.

For example, one Gulf economic view – attributed to an unnamed official of the Kuwaiti Central Bank in the 1990s – indicated that the Gulf economies wanted to mitigate the global trade pattern of developed economies supplying manufactured and agricultural goods in exchange for raw materials from the developing economies.[125] If this is the case, opening up trade to include a multitude of products at various levels of value-addition, based on market forces of demand and principles of equitable and free trade, may help. Yet, it remains unclear if this is the dominant view among Gulf trade officials.

There have also been vested interests in inter-regional trade. Calder pointed out that both China and Japan have tried to ink FTAs with the GCC as well.[126] But perhaps the most important inter-regional trade agreement may be between the Middle East and the US. Having briefly discussed North-East Asian–Gulf ties, the main player in the Gulf is unambiguously the US, which has worked with the region to achieve an eventual Middle East Free Trade Agreement (MEFTA) to be completed by 2013.[127]

With a global economic presence and deeply entrenched interests in most macro-regions of the world, the US is a comprehensive economic participant both in the Middle East as well as North-East Asia. In North-East Asia, the US economic presence remains important and fundamental. Not only does the US remain a major export destination for many North-East Asian products and services, but the US retains its position as a high-ranking investor and trade partner for most North-East Asian economies.

According to Maryanne Kelton, South Korea was the seventh largest US export destination.[128] Michael Plummer properly observed that a sizeable proportion of Asian trade is driven by the need for consumer goods in the developed West,[129] including – perhaps particularly – the US consumer market.

The recent rise of newly emerging economies appears to be complementary to and – somewhat dependent on – US interests in free trade. Some North-East Asian watchers argue, like Ron Huisken, that China will work with the US to maintain a global system that provides free and unimpeded access to trade, investment and technological exchanges.[130]

This interdependence may be a motivating factor for the maintenance of global trade *status quo*. The US Commerce Department reveals that trade and commerce between US and China expanded to the point of a 12.7 per cent growth from 2006 to 2007, which capped out at US$386.7 billion.[131] Wang Jisi argues that, although US purpose for interacting with China in trade and economic fields is beneficial to the US, the net effect of this bilateral economic exchange has also benefited China's economic development, wealth and the implementation and availability of technologies.[132]

Given the common benefits derived from keeping trade open and free, the near future may witness increasing calls for free access to the maritime sphere, in order to facilitate unhampered global trade. Sea lanes, including those that link Russia's far-eastern regions with her western provinces, may be crucial for commercially linking both regions, since 50 per cent of this internal trade goes through maritime traffic.[133] Such access applies equally to North-East Asian economic access to the Middle East and the rest of the world and vice versa.

To ensure sea-lane security and assure guarantees against other forms of disruptions, some North-East Asian economies are, in the meantime, trying to lessen dependence on crude oil importation from the Gulf or other locations that they view as being as vulnerable as sea-lane access.

One strategy that North-East Asian economies like China utilize is to improve and increase the technological capabilities of its industries to access hi-tech/low-energy usage sectors. Another is to establish additional, higher value-added service industries, to lessen dependence on energy-guzzling industries and to produce lower-value-added products for export trade or internal consumption.[134] China and other North-East Asian economies may study how Japan's experiences with the 1970s oil shock motivated it to become the market's leading energy-efficient economy.

To lessen dependence on a single source of oil or energy commodities, the North-East Asian economies reach out to other energy producers, and prompt competitive instincts among the Middle Eastern/Gulf suppliers. At times, for example April 2004, some Gulf oil producers like Saudi Arabia considered reduction of energy prices to North-East Asia (Japan, South Korea and China) to outcompete Russia.[135]

Bernard Cole explains that some North-East Asian economies, including China, are also building up stockpiles of oil and other energy commodities (possibly up to 4 million cubic meters, worth US$10 billion) as buffers against supply reduction strategies or Middle Eastern instability.[136] However, diversification to non-Middle Eastern sources by North-East Asian economies may lessen dependence on Gulf oil, but cannot lead to complete non-dependence on Gulf producers.

While North-East Asian economies try to diversify supply sources and lessen overdependence, Gulf and Middle Eastern economies may diversify by increasing the number of customers and serving clientele in other regions with oil products and energy commodities. With the rise of India in the South Asian region, bilateral regional trade may result in a multifaceted growth into non-energy sectors as well.

For example, during 2006, the economic exchange in raw and processed food products between the Gulf and India expanded from US$5.5 billion (2001) to US$48.6 billion.[137] India's consumption of Gulf energy products showed an increase for the same period.

India

As the world's largest democracy and a transparent political-economic system with healthy growth rates since opening up economically (in the 1990s), India has become a central player in the global scene. It is believed by both like-minded members of academia as well as popular journalism that India's democratic system may provide the economy with 'systemic resilience and stable economic growth', that a transparent, liberal and free system may yield economic dividends in the long run.[138] Extending beyond its national boundaries, India plays an important major role in supporting trade and commerce in the Indian Ocean and its diaspora is economically prominent in the Gulf region.

Other Indian strengths include demographically young members of the labour force who can contribute to other economies in addition to India's own. India's labour force consists of both highly skilled (such as English-proficient university graduates) and semi-skilled labour. In the area of highly skilled manpower, India also has a dominant presence in the IT software industry and its software exports have been growing at an annual rate of 30 per cent since 1998 while its large pool of computer programmers and highly skilled IT personnel remain very attractive for technology companies and IT service firms to invest in India or to form partnerships.[139]

Even in terms of hardware, India has the capabilities of maintaining the longevity of computer systems because of low labour costs of Indian computer hardware technicians.[140] Both its expertise in the software and hardware IT sectors as well as the abundant pool of demographically young manpower contribute to India's global leadership in the outsourcing sector. India is a global leader in IT, call centres, back-office business processes and other forms of outsourcing services.[141] Another natural factor facilitating India's emergence as a business processing, back-office operations and call centre for the world is its location which allows India to meet the broad spectrum of time-zone requirements in these industries.[142]

Besides the well-known example of the IT software sector, in other niche industries, India has acquired a dominant presence, for example, production of processed gems and jewellery. Other skill-intensive industries that India has excelled in include project engineering, product design, biotechnology, pharmaceutical, health-related and multimedia products.[143] Through its multimedia entertainment products which include entertainment and movies (Bollywood), India also exerts economic soft influence on consumer markets that enjoy its popular cultural exports. In this sense, India has an all-encompassing economic influence from soft cultural power to hi-tech sectors and as a global centre for outsourcing.

China

China has become symbolic of success in the export-driven manufacturing sector. Dieter Ernst and Barry Naughton highlight the competitive and comparative advantages that China enjoys for its advanced technology sectors such as the IT sector: for example, it has a large consumer market for products and services driving domestic consumption and productive development; China also has a large pool of affordable labour that has demonstrated a track record of being highly trainable in terms of skill sets; China has also placed resources into innovation and it can learn from the past weaknesses as well as strengths of its East Asian neighbours' individual developmental trajectories.[144]

Several labels by the popular media have been utilized to highlight this aspect, for example, 'workshop', 'factory' (as opposed to the label of 'office' for the world in India's case)[145] of the world, etc. Such reductionist labelling indicate the images that China conjures up in the imaginations of the industries, business world and the global community. At the same time as Chinese incomes rise along with economic growth and production activities, China is also providing consumers in other economies with affordable products and goods. In terms of China's domestic consumption, according to the study by Chen Yantian and Dan Jin *Who Benefits from the Emerging China?*, many East Asian economies (including Korea and Taiwan) are benefiting from China's economic growth[146] and its consumption. This may be in addition to Chinese economic outputs driven by Taiwanese and Korean investments.

China has made great contributions and progress to the lives of its people as average incomes quadrupled, alleviating 300 million Chinese citizens from poverty, and transformed its economy into one of the world's largest, producing a significant global share of the world's electronics products output and supply.[147] William Overholt pointed out that by 2007, China produced 38 per cent of the world's steel production.[148]

China has also made progress in human capital development. According to Jayati Ghosh, in rural China, the comparatively equitable allocation of land and the urban provision of residential areas have been considered as offset factors to decrease poverty and overall inequality.[149] Other achievements (in the field of education) were pointed out by Denis Fred Simon and Cong Cao that China churned out approximately 159,000 graduates with masters and PhDs in the fields of technology and science in 2006, in addition to 1.34 million engineering and 197,000 science undergraduates.[150] Simon and Cao also highlighted, statistically, China's quantities of scientific research papers included into the Science Citation Index (SCI) was ranked fifth in 2006 and the country hosts over 1,000 foreign research and development centres.[151]

The Gulf States

While India and China are now considered by the popular media as familiar success stories, there have also been other developmental examples of prominent regional entities that were highlighted both in the news and other forms of popular media. On 26 April 2008, the *Economist* published an article entitled 'The Rise of the Gulf' that highlighted improved wealth management by economies in that region. Interestingly, the article related the Gulf's success and enrichment to economic growth in India and China due to their rapid consumption of energy (especially oil), in turn driving the wealth of the Gulf.[152] In this sense, interestingly, the growth of India and China are interlinked and related to the emergence of the Gulf economies. As major oil producers accounting for 40 per cent of the international oil reserves, the GCC wields tremendous influence in the oil and energy sector.[153]

Kito de Boer and John M. Turner point out that FDIs into the GCC increased from below US$2 billion to US$20 billion in 2005 with almost US$1 trillion worth of infrastructure investments underway by 2007.[154] Saudi Arabia is building six new cities which can hold up to 2.5 million residents that may form the basis of their future economic growth by designing them as intentional attractors for local and foreign investments (the construction of one of the cities alone, King Abdullah Economic City, may create 800,000 jobs).[155] According to de Boer and Turner, the GCC economies have created 55,000 medium and high-skilled jobs annually over the past decade.[156] Some of these jobs have benefited foreign economies as they provide employment for migrant workers from India, the Philippines and other foreign nationals. In this sense, they serve as another link between India and the Gulf economies. For the foreseeable future, the Gulf economies' priorities lie in creating jobs that require skillsets for its younger citizens.

According to Michael Sturm, Jan Strasky, Petra Adolf and Dominik Peschel, because of energy revenues (hydrocarbons), the GCC as a group have almost doubled their yearly nominal GDP since 2003 to approximately US$791 billion in 2007.[157] Gulf states and their economies have also become net investors in other regions including the US and Asia.[158] According to Sturm, Strasky, Adolf and Peschel's study, the GCC region hosts some of the globally largest SWFs, worth an estimated value of US$1–1.5 trillion.[159]

The achievements of India, China and Gulf states appear to have become potential models for the rest of the developing and emerging economies in addition to the established models of development offered by the US and Japan that have benefited and inspired many economies in the global setting. Developing or emerging economies studying these examples (large emerging or established models and patterns of development) may selectively pick out some features from these examples based on what they consider as suitable, applicable and implementable in accordance with their national priorities and conditions.

The achievements by these economies have also not gone unnoticed. As a testimony to their accomplishments, all three entities, India, China and some of the Gulf states, have representation in the G-20 forum, along with the US and Japan. Development in India, China and the Gulf may bring about their own set of challenges and developmental dilemmas and contradictions, as with all other developing or emerging economies, but the achievements may be recognized for what they are, contributing to poverty alleviation, economic growth, increase in living standards and better infrastructure. Such improvements and upgrading may be significant as they affect a large percentage and portion of humanity. Instead of characterizing such improvements as 'rising', it may be seen as progress, progress by these economies to continually meet the challenges of ever-evolving development needs.

6 INDIA AND THE MIDDLE EAST

India is a major South Asian participant in Gulf–North-East Asian energy and economic interactions. Not only is India a growing economy, but also a major energy user with expanding consumption.

Robert Kaplan quoted Admiral Sureesh Mehta[1] as saying that India's economy had been expanding at 9 per cent yearly, with 10 per cent increase in industrial production, and the size of its middle class is anticipated to expand from 200 million to 500 million people by the year 2020.[2] These figures may have implications for India's trade and energy imports from the Middle East. However, Indian economic statistics may not be the only item that underlines India's growing importance for the Middle East.

India's commercially strategic position on the map should experience enhanced importance with increases in its economic status. Energy resources en route from the Middle East to North-East Asia must pass through India or the Indian Ocean. It is, therefore, logical for India to utilize its strategic position to highlight its economic, energy and commercial significance for the Middle East. India's geopolitical concerns, its economic incentives and the stability of its territories may increasingly have a direct impact on energy delivery from the Middle East to North-East Asia. It may also determine the pricing of energy resources.

In its overland territory, India may be viewed as a conduit that enables energy pipelines to branch out and extend into the Indo-Chinese countries like Myanmar, Thailand, into other South Asian entities like Bangladesh, into central Asian areas like Turkmenistan and on to North-East Asia. In many respects, India is a great junction that brings together the interests of many great energy suppliers and Asian consumers. Equally important, India enjoys good relations with many economies in the Middle East. Not only is India categorized as part of the group of democratic nations in Asia, but it has a rapport with a great many nations.

Most importantly, India enjoys cordial relations with the US, the dominant entity in the Indian Ocean and the Middle East. In the past, India had been involved in initiatives to cooperate with other great Asian energy consumers. Highly indicative of this spirit of cooperation, Indian Prime Minister Manmohan Singh visited Japan in December 2006. Once there, he and Japanese Prime

Minister Shinzo Abe launched the Japan–India energy dialogue at the cabinet level. These two great leaders also issued the Joint Statement towards Japan–India Strategic and Global Partnership, as the joint initiative to work together in the various energy-related fields, which included energy-saving resources.[3]

India also enjoys good relations with both Arab and Israeli partners. India allowed the inauguration of an Israeli consulate in Mumbai in 1952, and by 2008, the overall bilateral trade between India and Israel reached more than US$4 billion. India also attained the status of Israel's third largest trade partner, with exchanges and collaborative work in agricultural and technological industries, which is currently inclusive of telecommunications software development and which may in the future include renewable energy.[4]

Relative to its maritime activity, India's sphere may become increasingly important, because – as Kaplan points out – the increased energy needs in the large emerging economies of India and China have caused the Indian Ocean region between the Middle East and the Pacific be become crowded. According to Kaplan, one million vessels go through the Indian Ocean annually.[5] India's role in overseeing the Indian Ocean may become increasingly important.

In addition to India's maritime space, the overland routes, spatial conceptions and geographic layouts may become important aspects of India's energy delivery system. Because these peripheral areas may eventually be covered with gas pipelines, the distances of these vast expanses of land and the barriers in those spaces will affect pricing. Further, because India is a subcontinent, its deep interior and other geographically isolated areas may present challenges for delivery.

Any such considerations may be important because they have the potential of increasing India's consumption of natural gas. According to James Jensen, the 2004 inauguration of Petronet's Daheej terminal, and of Shell's Hazira terminal in Gujerat, marked a renewed period of LNG activity in India.[6] Natural gas, which is believed to be cleaner than oil, and more specifically than coal, seems consistent with India's growing emphasis on environmentalism, its middle-class lifestyles and its commitment to a cleaner environment.

Historically, and particularly in contrast to the West and Japan, India was able to tide over challenges from the 1970s oil crisis in better shape than many of its developed counterparts. Japan, which is resource-scarce, experienced some degree of social unease and panic as toilet paper and other necessities were stocked up in fear of hiked-up oil prices. Amy Jaffe argues that India, at this point, was relatively unaffected in comparison to the West, because of its energy self-sufficiency.[7] However, given the rapid economic development that has since occurred, India may not cope with future oil crises so proficiently. As Anthony Bubalo and Mark P. Thirlwell note, as early as 1980, Indian sufficiency in crude oil had eroded. Because the difference between domestic production and usage was 450,000 barrels daily, India was a net importer of oil barely a decade after the 1970s oil crisis.[8]

India may also be transitioning from its legacy as a service industry to claim a new future in the manufacturing sectors. Indian economic growth, which is predicated on its strong service industry (now well-known through media portrayal of its subcontracting industries and call centres), appears to augment its industrial production as well. Manufacturing industries may become India's major energy consumers in the near future. In 2006, according to Geoffrey Kemp, India consumed 1.43 million barrels of oil from the Middle East daily, and he projects that India's daily needs may strengthen to 4.5 million barrels per day.[9]

Bubalo and Thirlwell explained that in 2003 India globally ranked as the sixth biggest oil user, with 3.1 per cent of the world's total usage. Its need for oil expanded by more than 80 per cent in the decade that preceded 2004.[10] India sources 90 per cent of its oil from the Gulf region. Kaplan argues that by 2010 India's energy consumption will rate it the World's fourth largest consumer of oil alone and engage a sizeable portion of the Indian Ocean's maritime traffic.[11] India projects that its growing middle class will account for this energy consumption.

Demand appears to outstrip supply even as India, which churned out 900,000 barrels daily in 2007, is projected to achieve an output of 1.3 million barrels daily by 2030.[12] Bubalo and Thirlwell project that India may overtake Chinese oil consumption in 2029, when China's percentage of total global use peaks at 16.5 per cent of the overall global consumption.[13]

Perhaps, India's greatest contribution to the Middle East is the estimated 3.5 million strong labour force, employed in the GCC economies, which repatriates US$4 billion yearly back to India.[14] South Asian skilled and unskilled labourers enjoy the reputation of working hard for affordable-level wages offered by Gulf employers. Many also have the advantage of proficiency in English – a major working language in the Gulf region. English may come in useful in the service industries, leisure and hospitality sectors and banking and financial sectors in the Middle East, particularly the Gulf area.

According to Kemp, India's trade with the Middle East expanded by 759 per cent from 2003 to 2007. In currency terms, this means a bump from US$7 billion to US$51 billion, even as India's trade with the Middle East increased from 9 per cent of India's total trade to 23 per cent.[15] With its large, well-trained labour force that is amenable to affordable wages, India may be set to become a major manufacturing platform in the world, with products that are popular in the Middle East.

Currently, more well-known exports from India related to its soft power are Bollywood movies and other forms of popular culture likely to be well-received in the Middle East. The cultural reach is not just one-way. For example, according to Kandel Arielle, India welcomed Israeli arts and cultural performances – and likewise Israel from India – to foster greater contacts between the two societies.[16]

India is also reaching out globally in part to diversify its energy resources. In 2003, ONGC Videsh, a branch of an Indian state firm, purchased a stake in Sudan's Greater Nile Petroleum Operating Company.[17] India's attempts at the acquisition of overseas energy assets may reflect either competitive or cooperative efforts vis-a-vis foreign and domestic business endeavors. In terms of collaboration and cooperation, Xu Xiaojie noted that in May 2001, India's ONGC Videsh Ltd (OVL), Reliance and Algeria's Sonatrach combined efforts to work on the Tuba field between Rumaila and Zubair, and invested US$500–600 million, and in the meanwhile, OVL inked another contract with the Iraqi Oil Exploration Company to survey block number 8 of the Abu Khema site in south Iraq in November 2001.[18]

As for the competitive side, India's Oil and Natural Gas Corporation (ONGC) also tried to acquire PetroKazakhtan and Nations Energy, before it eventually lost out to foreign competition. In other cases, ONGC combined efforts with the same rivals the China National Petroleum Company (CNPC) to obtain shares in the Great Nile Oil Project in Sudan, in the Al Furat oil facility (Syria) and in assets of Omimix of Colombia.[19] Rivals may sometimes end up as partners for Indian oil acquisitions, particularly when there is economic complementarity based on market forces.

Cooperation may not only be restricted to collaboration and joint bids for oilfields. Shoichi Itoh explained that Japan and India convened a discussion on oil and natural gas at the Japan–India Summit in April 2005, held in the Indian capital city of New Delhi. In September 2005, Japanese Minister of Economy, Industry and Trade, Shoichi Nakagawa, and the Indian Petroleum and Natural Gas Minister, Mani Shankar Ayar, announced that Japan and India would encourage bilateral interaction and discussion in six highlighted aspects: exploration and development in third countries, oil stockpiling, joint research on Asian oil markets, methane hydrate, energy conservation and hydrogen fuel.[20]

There are other promising non-Middle Eastern sources of energy that may increasingly interest India in the near future. According to Mehmet Öğütçü and Xin Ma, India's ONGC is also interested in the oil and natural gas industries of Russia, whose own economic and strategic calculations may determine the future shape, scale and viability of such intended acquisitions.[21]

India may also examine and intensify its interests in nuclear power and renewable energy resources. This energy strategy would be consistent with India's increasing environmental awareness and the middle-class clamor on quality of life issues. Given the move away from overdependence on the Middle East for crude oil, India may also broaden its relationship with the Middle East in non-energy areas. For example, India is also seeking a gateway for its investments into the Middle East. According to Mukesh Ambani, Chairman and Managing Director of Reliance Industries, India's largest industrial conglomerate, 'Dubai will be the gateway for our future investment in this part of the world and beyond'.[22]

India may not be the only entity in South Asia keen on connecting with North-East Asia. Given the importance of the littoral states along the Indian Ocean, large emerging economies and developed economies offer aid, loans and funding for infrastructure development. John Calabrese indicates that Pakistan may be another overland connector between the Gulf and North-East Asia. Pakistan's Gwadar port, which was constructed and funded by Chinese conglomerate, became ready for use in March 2008. According to Calabrese, the passage from Gwadar to Saindak that is linked to the RCD Highway (N35) is a shortcut for China to trade with Central Asia.[23]

Despite prospects of rising competition in the Indian Ocean for management of sea routes, a dominant entity already exists in that region. For the foreseeable future, the US will continue to be the major presence in the Indian Ocean, while other emerging, or developed economies locate and define their own places and presence within this maritime space. The US presence may be universally welcomed to keep the sea lanes open for trade.

The US continues to guarantee open access and the safety of navigation through the Indian Ocean. The US and other major energy nations may continue to work with India multilaterally, given India's importance outlined above both as a consumer and conduit of energy.

Jaffe is one such advocate urging the possibility of the US working with the EU, India, China and Japan to reformulate the global conditions and procedures through which energy trade may take place[24] based on new players and new patterns of consumption. Coinciding with Jaffe's views, Itoh also argues that it may be possible for multinational initiatives such as the Five Country Energy Ministers' Meeting (involving Japan, the US, China, India and South Korea) and the East Asia Summit to discuss policies related to energy consumption, even as Japan augments energy relations and cooperation with India bilaterally.[25]

In the non-energy aspects, perceptions of India's strength include its affordable labour, its IT productiveness, its strategic maritime location that overlooks the Indian Ocean, its strategic overland platform for energy pipelines, its rising middle class, with the potential to create a market for massive consumption, etc. Kemp has issued projections that, within three decades, India's economy may surpass that of the US.[26] Consistent with its economic growth, India's energy use and its Middle Eastern engagements are rapidly increasing.

Some early engagements were established between India and the Gulf economies, including Dubai – the main re-export centre for products and goods (including textiles and cotton and later electronics) headed for India in the 1950s and 1960s.[27] The significance of the Gulf and Middle East did not become pronounced even during the global energy crisis of the 1970s. In the 1970s, India remained unscathed because it was self-sufficient to a degree that has since changed dramatically.[28] Tsutomu Toichi attributes the increase in India's energy imports from the Middle East to two factors – 'sudden' industrialization and vehicular use in India.[29]

India's energy usage is likely to rise. For example, India utilized 1.43 million barrels of Middle Eastern crude oil daily in 2006, and will, as Kemp notes, likely consume 4.5 million barrels daily by 2030.[30] India appears to have a projected growing middle class consuming this energy supply. Demand appears to be outstripping supply even as India churned out 900,000 barrels daily in 2007 and may be projected to have an output of 1.3 million barrels daily by the year 2030.[31] India, which also overtook other major Asian energy consumers – including Japan and South Korea – in LNG consumption, exerts important influence in this industry on gas pricing, such as to Asia's heartland (the crossroads of South, Central and East Asia) regions, by virtue of the viability of its overland pipelines,[32] its infrastructure financing, etc.

Indian trade with the Middle East and the Gulf is not confined to energy and natural resources. Aysu Insel and Mahmut Tekce pointed out the rising trend of made-in-India products and machinery equipment in GCC economies between 2000 and 2010.[33] India also has investments in the Gulf's service sector, for example, the Flora Group Hotels that operated the sixth hotel facility in Dubai in 2008 and that presented plans for three more.[34] India and the Middle East both demonstrated an interest in the service industry. Within a mere two and a half years after its humble beginning with flights to Mumbai, Air Arabia plans to offer fifty-five flights per week from the Gulf to India. This, in effect, amounts to one quarter of its overall total flights.[35]

For some Gulf economies, India has become the most important trade counterpart. Consider, after 2003, India attained the position of the most significant trading partner for Kuwait.[36] For other Gulf economies, India ranked among the top positions in trade.[37] According to Kemp, from 2003 to 2007, Indian trade with the Middle East increased by 759 per cent, that is, from US$7 billion to US$51 billion, while the Middle East's share of India's total trade increased from 9 per cent in 2003, to 23 per cent in 2007.[38]

India also provides crucial migrant labour to the Middle East, essentially manpower that sustains the various economies of that region. For a number of reasons, many Indians find the Middle East a destination of choice. Among other things, they are motivated by the Middle East's geographical proximity, the attractiveness of higher wages in the Middle East, the region's need for skills that are valuable to its economies, and the region's need for English-speaking persons, who can contribute to service industries like tourism.[39]

India, in turn, has become a ranking destination for candidates seeking quality higher educational services. A 2005 study of UAE respondents revealed that many were destined for India because its visa applications were less burdensome and it offered much more affordable higher educations.[40]

Further, India remains an important participant in the global energy market.

Observers like Jaffe argue that it would be difficult to reconfigure the global energy industry, without Indian participation.[41] However, India also has its own set of energy priorities. In reducing overdependence on the Middle East, India seeks not only those energy resources in the Middle East, but it also seeks to extend its reach to other regions as well. Syed Fazl-e-Haider, reveals that the Turkmenistan–Afghanistan–Pakistan–India (TAPI) pipeline, based essentially in Central Asia, has Washington's support.[42] More northerly, India's ONGC is also interested in the Russian energy sector.[43] Finally, like other Asian economies, India is committed to finding alternative energy resources and to weigh the prospects of nuclear energy.[44]

Because of its strategic position and the resources it offers to the global economy, India has been courted by Japan, and other major Asian economies. In April 2006, METI of Japan proposed a comprehensive economic partnership agreement among East Asian, India and Oceanic economies.[45] Relative to the field of energy, Japanese delegates attended the Japan–India April 2005 Summit, held in the capital city of New Delhi. India's Mani Shankar Ayar (Petroleum and Natural Gas Minister) and Japan's Shoichi Nakagawa (Minister of Economy, Industry and Trade) used this occasion to discuss the possibility of collaboration in energy.[46]

7 THE ENERGY GIANTS[1]

Justin Dargin, Stephen Nagy and Lim Tai Wei

The JUICE (Japan, US, India, China) energy entities are influential energy consumers in the international system. JUICE may be divided into two main categories, the fast-growing and newly emerging economies, including India and China, and the developed advanced economies, including Japan and the US. It may be possible to discuss the JUICE constituents in a realist framework, if they are described in terms of weaknesses and strengths that they have vis-a-vis each other in energy, other natural resources, their geopolitical reach to these resources and the ability to keep and maintain that reach. That discussion would be useful to establish a descriptive paradigm of the JUICE constituents, which are not only major energy consumers but also influential states in their own right.

It may also be possible to focus on the complementarity qualities each JUICE constituents has and to look, not in terms of weaknesses and strengths, but the inherent contradictions embodied in each of these constituents. It may, thereafter, be useful to examine the complementarity between them in terms of energy, whether in environmental technologies, usage or common needs. Realism promotes a zero-sum perspective that may be reflective of the competitive nature of states and their economies. The principle of 'complementarity' allows us to look at the element of coexistence, and to learn to live with energy giants in the age that inquires as to sustainability. In the process of nurturing coexistence we should expect a fair share of conflicts, tensions, cooperation and accommodation.

Historically, the JUICE entities appear to be similar to each other at various historical time periods. As Vaclav Smil recognized, the basic needs of a nation's citizens cannot be provided for if their yearly primary commercial consumption falls below the equivalent of 100 kg of oil.[2] Large emerging JUICE economies may be preoccupied with this basic needs figure internally, and it may be a consideration if a nation considers the prospect of providing enough energy supply for its rising middle classes.

China and India have been catching up with or surpassed the economically developed Japan and the US in terms of energy utilization. In terms of energy usage, China in 1950 would be equivalent to Western Europe before

1800. Similarly, China of the 1980s, Japan of the 1930s and 1950s and the US between 1870 and 1890 are comparable in terms of energy usage.[3] Both India and China now rank among the top energy consumers in the world and each is still rising in terms of usage.

While oil may be an important energy resource, the Asian JUICE entities transitioned to this source relatively recently. Japan transitioned to oil 15 years after the Pacific War.[4] The importance of oil and other energy resources may have been mitigated by the fact that some of the JUICE constituents produce energy for domestic use. Historically, too, some members of JUICE were more prolific energy producers than others. For example, China exported Daqing oil to Japan after the two economies normalized relations in the 1970s. China's oil exports lasted as late as 1993, when it became a net importer of foreign oil for consumption in domestic economic development and household use. Relative to energy production, Japan's southern island of Kyushu in the prewar and wartime period produced coal for domestic use using foreign labour from the Korean peninsula.

But demand for energy in these JUICE entities soon outstripped their domestic energy resources, some earlier than others. In some cases, certain types of energy resources were outcompeted and out-demanded by other types, for example, domestic Japanese coal was unable to compete with more affordable foreign coal and eventually the availability of Middle Eastern crude oil. At one point or another, some JUICE entities had dabbled with the idea of energy or oil self-sufficiency but failed and had to rely on imports to meet their increasing energy needs. Self-sufficiency may no longer be a realistic or practical option in most JUICE energy policies. However, many nations implement plans to release domestic oil reserves to overcome limited periods of supply shortages. Because JUICE states have different levels of development and different energy requirements, their individual energy coping mechanisms may have differing trajectories.

In reviewing this chapter, Stephen Nagy argues that it is also important to note that both Japan and the United States completed most of their development in an era when there was much less competition for resources and less environmental awareness of the consequences of uncontrolled energy consumption. Therefore, Nagy contends that newly emergent JUICE members face more restrictive acquisition and usage conditions, with regard to newly energy acquisition and usage. In short, he argues that the newly emergent JUICE members are developing in a much more competitive international energy system. Of particular importance, Nagy argues that their development is further complicated by energy consumption standards developed by senior JUICE members and other developed countries.

A good example of reliance on imports may be resource-scarce Japan. In 1968, for example, resources and energy made up 58.1 per cent of Japanese imports.

These same resources and energy, by comparison, made up 18.1 per cent of the US imports. Japan's import reliance of coal resources between 1960 and 1970 increased from 35.8 per cent to 78.5 per cent, and petroleum increased about 100 per cent.[5] At various points, JUICE constituents have expressed concerns about the challenges of reliance on imported energy but have had no choice but to continue to do so, even while they search for ways to cope with it. The resource search situation may also be prompted by the increasingly spent domestic oil-fields in North-East Asia that could formerly provide for and meet the needs of North-East Asian economies like China, with its Shengli and Daqing oilfields.

Of total North-East Asia imports, 80 per cent are from the Middle East.[6] Attempts had been made to diversify sources of energy. There are some energy-rich producers in East Asia, including Indonesia, Brunei, etc. But those sources may be depleting. According to Kent Calder and Min Ye, even some nearby sources of non-Middle Eastern oil like those from Indonesia may also be drying up.[7] This has therefore spurred newly emerging large JUICE economies to undertake a global search for energy resources, something that the developed JUICE economies had been doing since the development of their industrial economies.

Relative to regional resources drying up, Nagy adopts an international relations perspective, in the realist perspective, to emphasize that continuing territorial disputes between East Asian nations hamper development of proven energy resources, such as in the South China Sea, especially the Spratlys, the Natuna Islands, the Paracel Islands, and in North-East Asia, especially the area surrounding the Senkaku Islands or Diaoyu Islands (as they are known to the Japanese and the Chinese respectively)[8] and the Tokdo Islands or Takeshima Islands (as they are known to the Koreans or Japanese respectively) and the Northern Territories or Kurile Islands (as they are known to the Japanese and Russians respectively).

These maritime disputes flare up from time to time and bring maritime energy resources under question, even though such questions remain dormant until these claimant's next assert their sovereignty. At times, however, when prag-matic mindsets prevail, there is some evidence of cooperation. Thus, these island disputes swing between nationalist assertions and swaggering, functionalist intentions in cooperation and dormant silence. Other analyses, however, do not see these issues as energy disputes. Given the perceptions of limited quantities of underwater energy resources, these observers tend to frame these differences as declarations of sovereignty over waters that lay between neighbouring countries.

Energy needs for the JUICE economies are probably much higher today, because they are all sophisticated economies with hi-tech components of production and at least two JUICE countries are, demographically speak-ing, large economies with rising middle classes. For example, China's demand for oil accounted for 40 per cent of worldwide demand growth between 2000 and 2004.[9] The process was also hastened by the advent of more oil-powered technologies since the twentieth century. Not only that, but consumption also accelerated during the early postwar period, when the older JUICE economies – like Japan – first developed the ready availability Middle Eastern oil. In this sense, India and China, with their comparatively recent economies and even later industrialization, are latecomers to the use of global energy resources. China embarked on market reforms in the late 1970s, and India's reformed its economy in the early 1990s.

Nagy raises an important caveat – that the energy needs of JUICE economies are higher, but differentially higher, because their development levels, and each country's respective diversification of energy consumption, implies that they are deriving energy resources from different sources. Nagy argues that this is further complicated when we investigate how energy resources are invested in each JUICE member country. Nagy differentiates the needs of different JUICE energy entities. For instance, the US retains a large, global position for its enormous military that requires energy resources both at home and abroad. China, as a second example, diverts most of its energy requirements to domestic, industrial developments and demand. As a third comparative, Nagy highlights that Japan presents a different case, with a large, highly developed industrial base that consumes energy from a diverse set of resources, but does not have a military presence abroad.

The JUICE energy consumers also appear to be different. Japan is an energy-poor economy, while China and the US have some of the world's largest coal deposits. Such differentials in the availability of domestic energy resources may impose differing levels of urgency on JUICE economies' global search for energy resources. Because Japan is resource-poor, its interests may be more global and far-reaching than other JUICE constituents that are comparatively and relatively better endowed. However, given that all JUICE economies may require energy either for securing their current levels of economic development and lifestyles or to fuel their economic growth and expansion, all JUICE constituents feel a need for effective, global reach in searching and locating energy resources.

Given the size of all JUICE economies, which are among the largest in the world, there is presumably a high likelihood that they might brush up against each other in the global arena. This possibility is likely greatest in resource use and the economic competition for resources. The US has an existing global energy diplomacy profile, and Japan developed such a profile during energy crises in the 1970s. The remaining JUICE nations, China and India, however, are currently in the process of a rapid expansion of their energy diplomatic profile, beginning in the 1990s and the twenty-first century respectively. The JUICE constituents' global energy diplomacy tends to be highly developed, with a combined use of economic incentives, soft power, strong persuasion, diplomatic protocol and exchange, technological exchange, infrastructural help, etc.

Much of such energy search by JUICE economies appears to take place in energy-rich locations. It may be in locations like Africa, Central Asia, South America, maritime areas, etc. Much of the competition in these areas was expressed in the form of economic competition that attempted to avoid mutually damaging, unfriendly conflicts. Avoidance of damaging conflict and competition may be a wise strategy, given the possibility that the larger JUICE nations may be relatively more absorbed with the internal contradictions of development. Having comparatively better developed economies, the smaller or more developed JUICE units may be more dependent on external interests, which, in fact, are well-established globally and well-developed economically. Consequently, with their directions and sights set on differing priorities, for the moment, it may be possible that they appear to be keen on avoiding harmful clashes.

Regardless of large emerging or developed economies, one feature that probably serves as a common JUICE characteristic is the transition to fossil-fuel based economies. The US, as the first JUICE economy to develop, used fossil fuels, such as oils, to transition from a rural, wood-fuel based economy in the 1850s to a major economy.[10] Most of the later JUICE developers that followed suit discovered prosperity, growth and development through similar energy transitions as well. Today, the diversification of energy resources goes beyond the carbon-based coal or oil category into hydropower and nuclear technologies, along with energy conservation measures. The JUICE constituents transition differently, in accordance with their geological makeup, their energy use patterns and their energy policies/strategies.

Among the JUICE entities, China probably used fossil fuels, such as coal, for the longest time period, to fuel a form of proto-industrialization depicted in the seventeenth century manual *Tiangong Kaiwu*. China's transition to oil-powered technologies, however, is of more recent vintage. Demographically larger Asian JUICE units may have been relatively slower to transition to power their proto-industries, and industries, with fossil fuels than the early modernizers because of the ready availability of alternative energy resources, including substantial amounts of manpower and animal strength.

As the first East Asian economy to modernize, Japan depended on coal for its industrialization. By 1936, coal amounted to 51.4 per cent of Japan's overall energy use. Similar to the US, Japan retained a reliance on charcoal and firewood that was used largely for household needs and that totalled 18.6 per cent of Japan's overall energy use.[11] In fact, even as late as the 1950s, the Japanese classified oil as a supporting industry rather than an industry by its own, which was understandable, since Japan was still mainly coal-powered.[12] But in the postwar period, oil had taken over as Japan's major source of energy, largely due to factors of oil's availability of affordability. Before the 1970s, perceptions of oil as more energy-efficient and less environmentally challenging than coal, resulted in an increased application of oil-powered technologies.

Economic narratives and discourses pertaining to coal energy are delicately interwoven with themes or implications of themes of environmentalism, emerging economies, technological advancements, fuel transitions and more abstract ideas about unions and integration. While in the recent past, coal had been perceived as an unclean resource, narratives, discussions and discourses about coal have become far more complicated than that. The possibility of continued utilization of coal is sometimes associated with technological advancements that may utilize coal energy in a more efficient or pollution-free manner.

The initial optimistic transition away from coal seemed to have been relatively unproblematic, linear in development, with ideas of smooth, gradual and systematic transition from less clean to cleaner fuels (e.g. coal – to oil – to natural gas – to renewables). Pollution and problems associated with extraction appear to be the main criticisms levelled at the use of coal energy. But some scholars discovered that certain industries found coal to be indispensible (e.g. the steel industry), and other attributed a return to coal to worries and anxieties about overdependence on single sources (namely, the Middle East).

In consultation for this chapter, Nagy argues that there are still developmentalist scholars, who stress that coal-based energy is the most cost-effective energy source for developing nations without financial resources to invest in greener energy practices. Nagy's arguments for coal's cost efficiency probably reflects an underlying presumption that coal is integral to North-East Asia's overall energy mix, rather than any urgings for its complete elimination as an energy resource.

Adopting an international energy relations perspective, Nagy noted that coal consumption may also reflect developmental levels. Coal resources and those geographical limitations that give rise to arguments as to logistics and cost-effectiveness, create a chokepoint. This is particularly true, if the desired resources must be imported from politically unstable states.

The narrative of readily available energy has resurfaced, because coal is found in Russia and in North-East Asian locations like China. Because few of the smaller North-East Asian economies have the same geological attributes, attention shifts to nearby energy resources. These nearby Asian locations include Indonesia, Australia, etc. Proximity to North-East Asia often governs narratives as to the advantages of coal energy.

Peter Knights and Michael Hood offer a valuable perspective of exports by coal producers to North-East Asia and other consumers. Even if North-East Asian economies, such as Japan, must import coal, it is from a non-Middle Eastern source. This fact alone supports the argument for moving away from (over) reliance/overdependence on Middle Eastern crude oil. According to Kang Wu, Batsaikhan Usukh and Bulganmurun Tsevegjav, North-East Asia has 114.5 billion metric tons of coal reserves which is 13.9 per cent of the world's total reserves (data is dated at 2009).[13]

Although these figures provide statistical dimensions to the domestically available energy, this writer found no statistics as to how long these resources could satisfy the needs of these coal-consuming economies.

Even though China has the largest coal resources in the region, scholars and researchers have not reached a consensus as to how long their coal supplies are estimated to last. Elizabeth Wishnick argues that Chinese coal reserves may be reaching depletion, since the Chinese are acquiring coal from Russia.[14]

Richard Morse and Gang He revealed possible vulnerabilities in the Chinese coal energy system. China's competitive market availability stems from the fact that transportation costs through Pearl River Delta and Yangtze to the production centres in the south may allow foreign coal to possibly gain a foothold in the Chinese market, based purely on competitive pricing.[15]

Knights and Hood argue that Chinese coal reserves are found mainly in the northern part of China and that China's southern economic and industrial centres (particularly south-eastern China[16]) continue to import Australia's thermal coal for generating power.[17]

The aggregate of coal reserves in northern China suggests that these deposits should be reasonably available to the southern coal consuming industries, particularly in the manufacturing centres of those coastal cities that presently import foreign coal. The fact that the southern industries import coal from foreign sources suggests that the northern coal deposits are partially inaccessible, because of China's limited ability to ship this coal from north to south.

According to Morse and He, three northern China locations – Shanxi, Shaanxi and Inner Mongolia – contained approximately 69 per cent of its proven reserves and accounted for 50 per cent of the output in 2009.[18] This geographical variation in China's coal use dispels the image that coal availability and demand are evenly distributed throughout the country.

Perhaps another blunt narrative that dispels the notion of China's coal sufficiency comes from Morse and He, who conclude that China's sufficiency in coal and its status as a producer/exporter ended in 2009, when it imported 126 million tons of foreign coal.[19] This may be a market-driven feature, if one considers, too, that foreign coal prices may be cheaper than shipping domestically available from the north.

But coal may offer one advantage over oil for China. Several studies explain North-East Asian price vulnerability, when it comes to oil, based on the region's inability to leverage against the Middle East crude oil supply that the region depends on. Scholars and researchers are keen to differentiate between oil and coal energy use in North-East Asia. One side may well argue that China has greater bargaining power over coal prices, because it may apply price differentials of acquiring domestic sources of coal versus coal imports, taking into account the quality of coal, shipping charges, and shipping distance. China's coal pricing system is reflected in China's 'Two Markets Two Resources' system, which bases coal acquisition on market forces to decide between overseas and domestic coal resources.[20]

As for other North-East Asian economies that may not be endowed with coal resources, the ability to import coal from nearby sources, such as Indonesia or Australia, may enable them to leverage against distant sources of coal imports. As stated, China, which has its own coal reserves, purchases from nearby sources. Robert Kaplan pointed out that China purchases coal commodities from Kalimantan Indonesia.[21] The nearest sources of coal resources to China are probably Russia, Indonesia and Australia.

Even if the main driver for this discourse on coal is a desire for non-oil diversification, it is a fact that overreliance or overdependence may be equally applicable to coal energy. For example, consider the case of Japan, which had been keen to diversify away from Middle Eastern crude oil. Knights and Hood point out that Australian coal imported into Japan grew at a much quicker speed than shipments from rival producers, which suggests that Japan may be largely reliant on Australia for coal.[22]

However, this Japanese-Australian relationship may also result from favorable Australian coal prices and the long working relationship that Japanese companies, like Mitsui, have with their Australia/American partners in developing Australian mines in the postwar period. The example of China vis-a-vis coal consumption and importation compares, to a substantial extent, with India.

Kaplan explains that, even though India also has sizeable coal reserves, it has to acquire foreign coal from Mozambique, South Africa, Indonesia and Australia to sustain demographic growth.[23] Because India and Japan (along with South Korea and China) are likely sourcing from the same areas in East Asia/ Oceania, it may be possible that future competition may impact pricing.

Aside from an individual state's coal usage, the most ambitious narratives revolve around the possible regional integration of coal communities, using the EU as a model. The idea of an EU developed from its early origins that modelled itself after the European Coal and Steel Community. These are probably long-term projects, even though they may not become functional for some time and would require tremendous political will, determination and compromise. Many such narratives remain ideas and perspectives, perhaps for scholars, academics, think-tanks, researchers and government officials to ponder over.

There is a wide-ranging variety of ideas, studies, narratives and discourses related to coal resources and the use of coal energy in the North-East Asian

region. Most ideas overlap with one another, even though some central arguments may be highlighted to illustrate their possible narratives. By classifying the
ideas rather than categorizing the authors, three main schools of thoughts may
be detected. Each theme, also, depicts variations of the main arguments.

The first school of thought covered in this chapter focuses on domestic
resources. The variations in this loose collection of ideas centre around the availability of coal reserves in North-East Asia (specially referring to China) and in
East Asia/Oceania (inclusive of Indonesia and Australia's availability of coal
resources for exports, particularly to South Korea and Japan). Such ideas may
be embedded by scholars and researchers who project increasing coal imports
into North-East Asian economies in the future (including southern China) into
their text as a current–future scenario for comparative analysis.

The main line may be based on the current emphasis on using domestic coal
resources (e.g. India and China) that may eventually be outstripped by future
demand and necessitate greater imports from established nearby sources like
Indonesia and Australia but also rising global suppliers like Russia. The 'domestic
resource school of thought' may also be highlighted by scholars and researchers
to compare the North-East Asian region's vulnerability to Middle Eastern oil
prices with the ability of some North-East Asian coal users (e.g. China) to leverage the pricing of their domestic supplies with those of foreign supplies.

Japan's example in the 1970s is familiar by now as the oil crises in the 1970s
affected Japan's energy supply stability, later known as the 'oil shocks'. Learning
from this lesson, Japan invested much energy, time and resources to securing
energy resources through resource diplomacy (*shingenko*) that was designed to
balance energy security needs, socio-economic stability and the need for a stable
energy supply, and to carry out energy conservation, even as it developed energy
efficient technologies.

The second school of thought that this chapter covers is the 'functionalist
school', visualizes the coal commodity as a resource to rally other North-East
Asian economies for greater collaboration and cooperation, be it relative to
terms of a regional, bilateral or market-driven format. Some examples include
the Greater Tumen Initiative (GTI) that consists of China, Mongolia, the
Republic of Korea and the Russian Federation, the Northeast Asia Economic
Forum Expert Working Group on Energy Cooperation in Northeast Asia, the
North-East Asia Petroleum Forum, and the Framework for the North-East
Asian Subregional Program of Environmental Cooperation established by sen-
ior officials in September 1996, etc.

The pace and success of these organizations may require time and tremendous
political consensus to bear fruits, even though they serve as useful platforms for
current information exchange. Adopting an international relations perspective
in reviewing this chapter, Nagy argues that there are also many hurdles to over-

come in North-East Asia in terms of cooperation, such as different economic systems, various levels of development, political systems and not to mention territorial disputes entwined with resource complexity.

In accordance with this view, if coal energy appears to either remain one of the energy mixes of developing and advanced economies in North-East Asia with India and China registering rising imports, resource competition may increase.

Adherents of this view may refer to the EU – again, which had its roots in a coal and steel community. Visionary and creative but idealistic and long-term in perspective, this school of thought may focus on a no-detriments policy that tries to resolve challenges common to all stakeholders, but requires tremendous political will, determination and consensus for implementation. Coal energy or the prevention of the emission of its by-products appears to be a central concern here.

The third school of thought may visualize coal as part of an eclectic mix of fuels that can neither be totally replaced nor displaced with other types of fuels. The eclectic school, which may be considered pragmatic, cites the continued use of coal with pricing based on the availability of other fuels and niche industries that need coal for their production activities. The eclectic school visualizes coal as just another component in a national mix of fuels, with proportions that decrease and increase according to the market forces that drives the demand and supply of a combination of other fuels.

Coal utilization may be viewed as in constant jostling with other fuels, and with the successes, failures and advancements of energy-efficiency technologies. Newer variants of this school of thought are technological in nature, because they look at the development of new technologies that can help to mitigate the polluting by-products. This school of thought, which may be highly technical in nature, deserves greater study and research.

Sufficiency of Coal Resources

Coal is probably the resource that North-East Asia may potentially free North-East Asian economies from energy dependence on the Middle East. Two large North-East Asian economies with large energy reserves are Russia, which has is just short of 200 billion short tons of coal, and India, which has slightly more than a 100 billion short tons.[24] Towards the south, Australia and Indonesia, which are also major coal sources, have an established relationship of supplying North-East Asian economies like Japan and South Korea.

Relative to coal transported by maritime means, Rudianto Ekawan, Michel Duchêne and Damien Goetz co-authored a publication which concludes that Japan continues to be the largest destination for China's coal. Japan imported 91.8 million tons in 2002, in comparison with Korea that imported 44.4 million tons, and Chinese Taipei, which imported 42.4 million tons.[25] Japan's volume of imported coal may relate to its lack of domestic resources. This is quite unlike China, which uses imports to complement domestic supplies, and which has inactivated a portion of its domestic coal industry because quantities available for extraction and use are low.

The studies by coal producers in East Asia generally concur that, while Japan is currently the largest importer of foreign coal, emerging economies like India and China are catching up fast. This narrative is often compared with current Chinese use of domestic coal, which still dominates its supplies. The implication is that, if Indian and Chinese economic development continues, domestic sources may find it increasingly difficult to meet future demand. This may be especially true given China's logistical challenges in shipping coal supplies from North to South, vis-a-vis the costs of importing foreign coal into the region.

Ernest Wyciszkiewicz explains that Chinese coal, which is still primarily mined for domestic consumption, constitutes approximately 65 per cent of China's energy use.[26] North-East Asia generally, and China in particular was – from a historical perspective – probably among the first locations to utilize this fuel.

Given its early use in world history, coal may also be associated with antiquated technologies and obsolete methods of extraction. Even in early modern societies, the combination of coal, iron and the machines that run on them, such as ships and trains, were considered an early fuel for industrial technologies. In China's pre-reform history (pre-1979), coal was a mode of exchange for items crucial for industrialization.

In the 1970s, both Chinese coal and oil were exported to Japan and other advanced nations to obtain processed steel products, industrial equipment and technologies in return. As a fuel for development, coal is inefficient, polluting and dangerous compared to cleaner fuels like oil and gas. In fact, gas has replaced coal, in part because gas is a cleaner resource. Despite the emergence of cleaner fuels, coal remains important in China for electricity generation and use in industries like steel-making.

Although Japan, by comparison, is nowhere near coal self-sufficiency, the Ishikari coalfield in Hokkaido is the largest of all domestic Japanese coal mines.[27] Hokkaido is located in Northern Japan. In the south, according to the study by Toyohiko Yamazaki, Kazuo Aso and Jiro Chinju, the coal reserves in Kyushu start from the towns and cities of Ube to Chikuho, Onga, Fukuoka, Karatsu, Miike, Ariake, Hokusho and Sasebo and then go into maritime areas of Takashima, Sakito and Matsushima in Nagasaki.[28] Many of these coal facilities are currently inactive, because Japan relies on imported coal and oil for its energy needs.

South Korea's geological conditions are, generally speaking, similar to Japan's. There are smaller-scale coal facilities near Chugcheong but, according to a volume that Peter and Michael edited, South Korea's output has been decreased from 25 million tonnes to lower than 5 million tonnes annually.[29] Analysts also report that the 335 million tonnes and 135 million tonnes of coal reserves held by Japan and South Korea are currently inactive as work has been stopped on them.[30] Nagy argues that inactivity may be reflective of the fact that it is cheaper for South Korea and Japan to import foreign coal rather than mine it domestically.

Japan's coal mining is of much more recent vintage and dates back to the Meiji period. Japan's coal output in 1900 stood at 7.429 million tons valued at ¥25.294 million.[31] According to Nisaburo Murakushi, the modern development of Japan's coal mining coincided with its introduction to capitalism and its importation of equipment from other advanced economies.[32] The technology associated with coal coincided with late pre-modern and the early industrial age.

The transition away from coal began for most North-East Asian economies in the postwar period. Immediately after 1945, the coal industry faced the first phase of decline due to the dissolution of *zaibatsu* or prewar and wartime Japanese conglomerates (leaving behind only small-scale mines). In his study of female miners in Chikuho, Matthew Allen argues that women were instrumental in keeping these mines alive to provide coal for Japan[33] in the immediate postwar period. Further competition for coal came in 1949 when Japan was allowed to rebuild refineries for crude oil and when full postwar recovery was underway. Japan associated coal energy with economic status and possible emergence as a well-off economy in the international community of nations.[34]

Regional Ideas about Coal

Coal has also given rise to many ideas, fantasies, studies, research, initiatives and imaginations. There have been many ideas about the role of coal in North-East Asia. Niklas Swanstrom, Mikael Weissmann and Emma Bjornehed represent an optimistic functionalist school of thought that sees coal as a possible unifying factor for a future North-East Asian coal and steel community that seeks to minimize conflicts and rivalry.[35] This view resonates with Roland Dannreuther, who made the optimistic argument that coal integration may contribute to transcending political-cultural, and other, barriers.[36]

Other ideas may be far less ambitious. Suh-Yong Chung points to some cases of success, for example, the initiative 'Mitigation of Air Pollution from Coal Powered Plants', which limited or restricted emissions into the air by decreasing coal power facilities funded by the Asian Development Bank (ADB). This facility was established and put into practice by the United Nations Economic and Social Commission for Asia and the Pacific (UNESCAP) together with officials from Japan, China, Mongolia and South Korea between October 1996 and March 1998, as a system to track, interpret and accumulate information about the environment.[37]

Similarly, Stuart Harris pointed out the potential benefits for cooperation among Russia, Japan, China and Korea of North-East Asia if they work together in gas energy to reduce the incidence of acid rain from the fastest-developing economies in the region.[38] Such narratives tend to focus on themes of cooperation, regionalism and integration in the fields of energy and environment. It may also be associated with mutually beneficial policies that do not seem to have obvious downsides given their utility in tackling a common problem. Participant nations – or regions – must overcome similar challenges that facilitate other forms of regional cooperation – including political compromises and conflicting needs of participants.

Chung's study on the North-East Asia Subregional Program for Environment Cooperation (NEASPEC) goes somewhat further in discussing a 'Vision Statement' for the region, including the 'Northeast Asian Training Center for Pollution Reduction in Coal-fired Power Plants'. These policy statements, if implemented through initiative and programs, may take substantial amounts of time.[39] Again, these policy and mission statements offer perspectives and discussion points for stakeholders to consider in accordance with their national and organizational priorities.

Other less ambitious partnerships may also include bilateral cooperation. For example, Wishnick notes that to resolve transboundary acid-rain issues, Japan's METI worked with China on developing desulphurization technology through its ODA. This project specifically involved a Green Aid Plan, centred on clean coal developments and effective energy use.[40]

The most common and practical forms of bilateral exchanges may probably be in commercial collaborations that could potentially yield profits for their participants. Driven by market forces, these projects may be relatively less restricted by sovereignty and contentious geopolitical concerns than state exchanges must confront. Consider the nineteen overseas coal projects that Korea undertook in 2003, with the collaboration of Australian coal facilities.[41] These projects demonstrate that states, while influential in these deals, may not be the only actors involved. Transnational energy firms are likely to play an important role as well.

Decline of Coal?

In the postwar period, particularly after the rise of environmental awareness in North-East Asia, environmentalists not only cast coal in a negative light on account of the pollution it generates, but also supported its classification as an unclean fuel.

Nagy points out that Japan's developmental experience with coal, and its 1970s grassroots activism, laid the groundwork for its environmental awareness. Work in coal mines was also deemed *kiken, kitanai, kitsui* or the three Ks (dangerous, dirty and demanding or the three Ds). Phasing out coal energy or reducing its share of the overall energy mix, it seemed, would enable a natural transition for many economies to shift from coal to oil and, then, onto natural gas. The evolutionary aspect of this is that each stage of energy use was cleaner than the one before.

The drive behind transiting away from coal energy, indeed, seems to be focused on clean and environmentally friendly fuels. Hirofumi Katayama highlights one advantage of transitioning away from coal – the immediate possible effect is a decrease in carbon intensity.[42] This environmental function may be extremely important.

According to Hirofumi Katayama, the overall carbon dioxide emission of Russia, China, Japan and South Korea, that is, North-East Asia, makes up 30 per cent of world carbon emissions.[43] The implications are that collective efforts by the region may make a difference, considering the magnitude of their energy consumption. Nagy, points out that future energy use by these economies may see some subregions pulling ahead of others. This may logically imply that larger consumers may carry a greater burden in the collective efforts.

The selective grouping of North-East Asian economies to depict significant statistical consumption is another way to highlight the severity (actual and projected) of coal usage. Calder advances strong arguments with regard to ruling out coal as the solution to North-East Asian energy needs, particularly in light of its unclean by-products, its largely antiquated status as a fuel for powering vehicles.[44]

Another narrative theme or narrative emerges from the transnational nature of the challenge and problem. As a certainty, the cross-boundary nature of the impact of coal use is often used to demonstrate that a collective response may be needed. One example of this response was the bilateral treaty, signed between China and Japan in March 1994 that obligated these nations to collaborate on the mitigation of acid rain.[45] A pervasive by-product of coal-burning is the transnational acid rain in North-East Asia. Fogs are another by-product of long use of coal resources. Regardless of the form of pollution that it causes, coal-burning creates health problems for people with respiratory issues.

By comparison, nuclear fuel and renewable energy resources are evidently comparatively carbon-free. This feature accentuates the attractiveness of nuclear and renewable energy resources. The safety track record of nuclear, however, is now a matter of debate, particularly, in the wake of the meltdown at the Fukushima nuclear reactor after Japan's tragic 3 March 2011 Earthquake and tsunami.

In a bid to lower pollution, China may be tempted to switch some of its coal-based power plants to natural gas.[46]

Another negative side effect of burning coal may be its effects on urban pollution, more specifically because coal remains an important resource for China's electrical power.[47] Within the framework of the North-East Asia demography, coal consumption for electricity generation is not regionally specific to China.

Knights and Hood note that Japan relies on coal for 26 per cent of its electricity generation, Korea 38 per cent and China 82 per cent and that all use of electrical products is proportionate to lifestyles, life expectancy, economic growth and quality of life.[48] Levels of economic development and aspirations towards middle-class lifestyles may, for the foreseeable future, be important factors in North-East Asian energy use. The tension between economic development and lifestyle upgrades as opposed to reduction of pollution by-products is particularly at issue in coal energy use. Besides pollution potentialities, there appears to be other criticisms against coal energy.

Criticisms to be weighed include human factors and the heightened focus on individual and community plights during the dangerous nature of coal extraction, particularly since the trapping of miners deep in underground caverns conjure up images of claustrophobic darkness. Not only carbon emissions, but the public thinking with regard to coal is challenged in other ways, including images of mine floods that trap and drown unfortunate miners.

Accidents involving explosions and fireballs may be equally dramatic in highlighting the dangers of coal use. According to the study done by Masuyuki Ujihira and Hashimoto, Kiyoshi, an extremely serious accident in Kyushu, Japan that involved coal, resulted in a gas outburst that reached a volume of 100,000 cubic meters, asphyxiated five persons, and caused a spontaneous discharge of 600 tons of coal.[49]

In the immediate postwar period, a factor that helped replace coal with oil power was the price of the latter. Oil, which was affordable for most of the time before 1973, allowed Western economies, including Japan, to recover and pursue postwar reconstruction. Inexpensive oil also facilitated growth and development between 1950s and 1960s. Japanese developmental economic history recognizes the 1960s, for example, as a period that doubled income and enabled fast growth. This period also allowed the more advanced economies to examine the possibility of nuclear power as a long-term development.

Another important factor in the transition to oil power was the determination of postwar economies to make this switch during phases of economic fast growth. In the latter part of the 1960s, Japan's economic development grew at 11 per cent annually and oil needs expanded at 18 per cent. Consequently, by the end of the decade, oil comprised 70 per cent of Japan's energy consumption, up from a mere 7 per cent during the preceding decade.[50]

But the relevance of coal and its utility often seems counterbalanced by the availability of other fuels, especially in periods of oil shortage. Prior to 1973, the world seems to have transitioned smoothly from coal to oil, largely because of oil's tremendous abundance. To some extent the affordability of oil facilitated, for much of the world, the costs of the postwar reconstruction, the costs of recovery and of industrialization. Speaking clearly to this point, Daniel Yergin notes that coal made up two-thirds of global energy supply in 1949, but that oil and natural gas fulfilled that spot and that quantity by 1971.[51] It took a dramatic political impact of the 1973 oil embargo to raise global awareness of the importance of oil supply stability. This also caused the world to reflect on the obvious visible and hidden costs of non-oil alternative fuels.

In other words, coal's fate seems almost inversely related to and directly opposite that of oil. A revival of coal use occurred in the 1973 oil crisis sparked off by the Middle East conflict. Because of rising oil prices, new coal power stations were built, based on affordable coal importations. Another coal revival was sparked off by a Middle Eastern oil crisis in 1979.[52] The use of coal in this instance appears to be correlated with the availability of other types of imported fuels. In such a narrative, market forces determine coal's continued use and relevance is not self-contained, but dependent on the availability of other fuels.

Ironically, Dannreuther argues that China's efforts to engage fuels other than coal caused it to lose the self-sufficiency that coal-sourced energy permitted.[53] There is no doubt that the mission to engage cleaner fuels also caused the North-East Asian economies to become more dependent on Middle Eastern crude.

The practicalities of economic growth and transportation systems have moved China along the path to greater oil consumption, and displacement of coal. From 1995, until 2004, the percentage of oil in Chinese energy consumption increased from 19 per cent to 22 per cent, respectively. For the same time period, China's use of coal declined from 77 per cent to 69 per cent.[54]

China's shift from coal to oil should be considered neither exceptional nor unique. Still, within North-East Asia, when Japan's domestic factories manufactured 4.1 million vehicles, with 85 per cent of this quantity for domestic use, these decisions sparked off an increase in petroleum use as regards transportation.[55] Under these lenses, it becomes apparent that oil, petrol and petroleum are symbolic, not only of fast economic growth, but also the middle-class desire to use automobiles to enjoy the freedom of travel and to experience automobile ownership as a lifestyle choice.

The discourses and narratives about coal and oil appear to be associated with themes, ideas and fantasies as to independence, ownership, security, modernity, and overconsumption and feelings of sufficiency. Narratives that mention coal, and its large reserves in China, India and Russia, arguably invoke themes of sufficiency, independence and, perhaps, strength. On the other hand, narratives that deal with fuels based in other regions, including such ideas or words as foreign, (over)dependence, Middle Eastern oil and maritime routes, convey feelings of dependency and, by implication, vulnerability.

On a pragmatic level, it may be that, even though self-sufficiency is not attainable, the theme itself acts as a counter-narrative that conveys political, economic and social desires to impose limits on foreign oil use during times of high oil prices or oil shortage. Even perceived examples of domestic self-sufficiency appear to have their weaknesses. Wishnick argues, for example, that there are other limitations on China's coal deposits. She contends that, although China has 114 billion tons of coal reserves, these reserves are generally of comparatively lower quality,[56] if energy yield is the criterion. She also contends that access to these massive reserves may be impeded by logistical challenges that work against shipping them affordably for use in the south.

Questions as to the acceptability of foreign oil use appear to emerge and rear their heads with every oil crisis, with price hikes and with fear of socio-economic instabilities. Some of these fears encourage aggressive responses, and others simply encourage irrational responses, for instance taxi drivers rioting or housewives stocking up on toilet paper. Given its importance to social order, issues as to energy security may represent either a desire to return to normalcy and to a stable energy supply, or alternatively, anxiety as to whether such a return is possible. These themes would persist, whether in the demographically sizeable North-East Asian units or on resource-scarce island nations.

Discourse about demography related to coal energy may prove to be extremely interesting. Two examples may include the size of population growth, middle class emergence and economic growth in emerging economies like India and China and their eventual consumption of coal energy.

Even though China has large coal reserves, narratives, studies and discourses point to increasing coal imports as signs of demographic challenge. With regard to Japan, the prevailing narrative focuses on the maintenance of living standards and how persistently high levels of coal-energy use result from the great longevity of its aging population. The argument seems to say that, by virtue of the fact that people are living longer, Japan may require long-term supplies of coal for its socio-economic development, sustenance and maintenance.

The Return of Coal?

Even now, in spite of the fuel transition away from coal, North-East Asian economies continue to be dependent on it. Among the four economies, Katayama highlights China and Russia as the two economies that are especially coal-intensive.[57] Harris predicts that China will remain dependent on coal relatively longer than other North-East Asian economies, even as it considers cleaner sources like natural gas and nuclear energy.[58] In fact, relative to North-East Asia as a region, David von Hippel, Timothy Savage and Peter Hayes predicted that coal usage may increase by 65 per cent between 2005 and 2030.[59]

It may be interesting to point out that even greater development of renewable energy resources cannot totally and completely remove other fuels from the national energy mix and/or avoid the intimate relationship between different fuels. According to Morse and He, public transportation infrastructure and other systems that are subjected to natural climatic factors, such as storms, can affect the costs of coal commodities, as can less than ideal conditions for renewable energies such as hydropower and solar.[60] Therefore, while the ratio and percentages of different energy resources within the overall national usage may change proportionately, they remain important and influential with regard to pricing, and with regard to one another.

The thoughts reflected in this chapter probably belong to the school of pragmatist observers, who continue to see a mix of fuels as necessary for continuing economic growth, and consumption. These pragmatist place little faith in the false hopes that alternatives, domestic sources or other sources, will replace the mainstays of oil, gas, coal, among a very few others.

The pragmatic view seems to comport with Kaplan's argument that, even as China focuses on coal, biomass, nuclear and renewables and alternatives, it will continue to consume large quantities of fossil fuels, including crude oil and natural gas.[61] Coal, even if out-trended by oil and gas, may continue to be crucial for a number of industries that form the backbone of the manufacturing sector. The pragmatic approach is crucial for East Asia's reputation as the world's manufacturing platform.

In consultations for this chapter, Nagy agrees with the pragmatic approach. He argues that it appears that current economic development is based on a coal/oil intense infrastructure that demands more and more of these products. He believes that, to change the technology and use different energy sources may be problematic, because these new technologies may not be compatible with the current manufacturing infrastructure.

Nagy argues that the shift to non-fossil fuel sources requires reinvestment, reinvestment means less profit and less growth, less growth can lead to decreased economic security and subsequently social and political instability. With this domino affect, he believes that the end result will be the continued dependence on the current coal and oil-centred economy.

Even with the shift to cleaner sources of energy, some crucial industries cannot do without coal energy. According to Ekawan, Duchêne and Goetz, while coal demand has declined in the West, Japan, South Korea, Taiwan and China continue to demonstrate growth in demand. Among these North-East Asian nations, coal may be most crucial for China, which is rapidly developing its steel industry.[62]

By contrast, Ekawan, Duchêne and Goetz argue that, in terms of Japanese coal use for the steel industry from the early 1960s to 1974, the peak was reached in 1973 at 90.9 million tons from 12 million tons in 1960.[63] Knights and Hood provide a glimpse into the historical intimacy between Japan's steel industry and coal energy, brokered by the Mitsui family group and other partners, resulting in Australia's Bowen Basin as the nucleus of coal output in the subcontinent.[64] Such developments coincided with the decade of the 1960s which was a period of fast-growth and income-doubling for Japanese economic development. Other industries that use coal include paper pulp and cement.[65]

Although, of Japan's overall types of fuel at the beginning of the 1950s, coal made up more than 50 per cent and oil 7 per cent, oil was increasingly taking over as the fuel of choice.[66] While Japan's coal use to fuel fast growth and its rapid switch to oil during the same period may be comparatively more historical, similar analogies are made with emerging economies in the contemporary setting. Even by the 1990s, Wishnick argues that China relied on coal for up to 70 per cent of its energy needs and though there was a slight decrease from the middle part of the 1990s (75 per cent), it was compensated by a small rise to 66–9 per cent from 1999 to 2001. In other words, coal energy remained an important component of China's energy needs.[67] According to the important MIT Study on the Future of Coal in 2007, China continues to build two 500-megawatt coal-based power facilities per week.[68]

Even for Japan, according to Wyciszkiewciz's paper, Japanese coal occupies 8.9 per cent of its total energy makeup, fourth after oil, nuclear and gas.[69] Based on such developments, it may be unlikely that coal as part of the energy mix will be linearly and deterministically replaced. In fact, according to von Hippel, Savage and Hayes, coal accounted for much of the increase in fuel use between 1990 and 2007 in North-East Asia with coal average growth of slightly below 5 per cent between 1990 and 2007 (but 9 per cent yearly from 2000 to 2007).[70] Highly technical technological arguments based on clean coal technologies may be likely to address this. They are not covered in detail in this chapter and deserve a separate analysis of their own.

In his consultation for this chapter, Nagy argues that developmental levels and the broad sophistication of the Japanese and Korean economies in both a historical and contemporary sense provided them with the capacity to diversify their energy consumables. He notes that these nations changed from producing low-value products to high-valued products for consumption abroad. The focus on consumables, which can vary widely within short time periods, contributed in part to the evolution of an infrastructure that can not only diversify energy consumption, but diversify the kinds of energy resources that are used.

Therefore, Nagy concludes that, no longer are the economic engines of these two economies genuinely dependent on coal. Development, diversification and design enabled these nations to accept new energy consumption patterns, which – at the same time – encourage the creative space that investigates and designs new innovative ways to consume tradition energy forms, such as carbon.

The transition from coal to oil may not have been fully completed for the large emerging JUICE economies. There continues to be some JUICE constituents that continue to use traditional fuels. Pranab Bardhan explains that individuals in both India and China continue to cause 'indoor air pollution' by the use of firewood when cooking.[71] If the transition away from traditional, wood-based fuel to oil power continues, the demand for oil may only grow. This pattern could, perhaps, be mitigated by energy conservation measures, alternative renewable energy, green education and more energy-efficient technologies. Newly emerging economies try energy consumption patterns that reduce the undesirable effects of technology in the already developed economies and perhaps that even enable the more populous JUICE country to leapfrog them in renewable energy use. For example, China's official media revealed that the country which is globally the biggest manufacturer of solar heaters and photovoltaic cells has put in place a schedule to motivate its private sector to develop renewable energies, including solar power.[72] This transition requires time to displace conventional applications of fossil fuels for economic purposes.

Since most JUICE entities are consumers, decisions made in the Gulf region impact their energy supplies. During the 1990s, explains Smil, the Gulf region had twelve of the globe's fifteenth largest oilfields and 66.3 per cent of the world's oil reserves.[73] The region will probably remain the world's major oil and gas supplier, for some time to come, barring the impact of rising suppliers, such as Russia.

In reviewing this chapter with a focus on 'energy hedging' in international energy relations, Nagy argues that each JUICE member will be influenced differently, based in part on the resources in its own site. The US, for example, not only invested massively in the Canadian oil sands, but is engaged in constructing a pipeline to pump oil from Canada to the US. Nagy explains that the US's pipe construction project is not to use Canada's oil sands to supplant the need for oil and gas, but to provide options. Nagy argues that Japan seems to balance oil supplies from Iran and the Persian Gulf with its security needs, even while it continues to invest in energy efficiency and to implement other forms of technology. For their parts, both India and China actively look at renewable energy supplies.

All JUICE energy consumers appear to yearn to see supply stability in the Gulf region, given its importance to their energy needs, economic growth and socio-political stability. Such desires to see stability in energy supply from the region underlines the importance of the US in providing that stability because it may be possible that none of the other JUICE constituents are prepared or inclined to play that role at the moment. It could be argued that, while the JUICE energy entities are highly important energy consumers, that fact alone may not necessarily translate to better, more efficient and rational energy use by some of their economies and households. In other words, some JUICE economies may need more help than others in learning and utilizing energy-efficient techniques, technologies and management.

As regards social perception, some Chinese and Indians along with other JUICE constituents may be increasingly aware of the importance of a clean environment. According to Bardhan, the environmental performance indicator for China in 2008 is pegged at 65.1 (105th in the world out of 149 states covered in the survey while India is ranked at 120th with 60.3 score).[74] Both aspire to improve their environmental cleanliness, taking into account the progress that they have made and are making thus far. Their efforts are complementary with the green technologies that Japan and the US can offer. These technologies may address important resources needed for livelihoods, including the air that humans breathe, the land that food is extracted from, the waters where seafood originates and aqua resources needed for life. In other words, energy and its use may impact the environment and the survivability of its inhabitants.

With these green technologies, there may be a functional method to apportion energy between industrial, household and transportation sectors. Of these three arenas, the industrial sector consumed more than 50 per cent of the total oil supply.[75] Again, these sectors were of critical importance to Japan's fast growth economic period between 1960 and 1973. These may be the same three sectors that form the bulk of energy use in other fast-growing economies. While stories of large emerging, energy-driven JUICE economies may be well-known in the past, Japan's role in expanding its green technologies in the region may occupy popular media coverage in the future. Pollution-mitigation devices, and the tough automobile emissions regulations instituted in Japan in the 1970s helped to put it on the path towards a green economy.[76]

In China, some natural resources became part of the local common pool of resources, which restricted collective use to ensure the sustainability of those resources. Bardhan, however, highlights the difficulties involved in effectively gauging local use of resources in India and China – as local authorities found it challenging to effectively allocate costs to small-scale rural agriculturalists, based on their energy usage.[77] Bardhan also points out the realistic difficulties that vast, highly populated economies, such as India and China, experience in preventing environmental damage at the local level. Problems sometimes result from the close and complex relationships between local business interests and authorities.[78] Contradictions of this type may be challenging and require patience and time to resolve.

Some observers may consider political solutions to resolve the contradictions of development. All JUICE entities have governments that play important and significant roles in planning their energy systems. There are some historical exceptions to the strong state role in energy industries in East Asia. In Hong Kong, for example, public utilities in gas and electricity fall within the purview of the private sector but are regulated by the state.[79] Another example could be where Standard Oil was supplying kerosene to Chinese consumers in the late nineteenth century. These examples may reflect historically exceptional circumstances when states were weaker or in laissez-faire market economic systems.

Generally, however, because they received state scrutiny, energy industries were among the first to receive the state help required to recover during the immediate, post-1945 period. With the exception of the coal industry, Japanese energy industries recovered rapidly. State economic bureaucracy may also control foreign technological transfers, including those in the energy sector, through regulations that govern financing – as energy industries are capital-intensive – licensing, entry restrictions and requirements for technological transfers in technical design, operational and maintenance standards, and mechanical/technical specifications that bestow minimal expertise on the recipient of any technology transfer.[80] These devices apparently helped Japan and other Asian JUICE members obtain their energy technologies from the West and built up their indigenous production and operational capabilities.

Among North-East Asian economies, Japan likely had the earliest engagement with the Middle Eastern account of the oil crisis in 1973. Just as the 1970s oil crises emphasized the status of the Gulf region in the global economy, it had other unintended effects in North-East Asia.

Japan, which then was the most industrialized and developed economy in North-East Asia, suddenly found its economic growth trajectory, which enjoyed economic growth due to a favorable global economic climate, interrupted by the oil embargo and desperate to find new sources of oil. Panic and fear of oil shortage spurred Japanese housewives to stock up on daily necessities including toilet paper and tissue paper.

The oil crisis coincided with the Sino-US rapprochement that President Nixon's visit to China facilitated. With the normalization of relations between these two countries (known as the so-called 'Nixon shocks' in Japan), Japan reached out to China as a possible source for oil, particularly the discovery of the Chinese oilfield known as the Daqing.

China responded eagerly because it needed foreign capital and required foreign technological input. These exchanges would later be characterized as an exchange of Japanese steel for Chinese oil deals. The new Japan–China nexus was a tool for luring Japan away from making provisions to acquire Russian oil. Information exchanges occurred through mechanisms, with American and Chinese journalists engaging in dialogues and exchanging information with one another other.

Not only did Japan seek alternative sources of oil, including from its immediate neighbours, it quickly made efforts to mend fences with Arab oil producers. Acting through energy diplomacy, Japan persuaded the Arab nations to reclassify it as a friendly nation. In this method, greatly enhanced Gulf-North-East Asian economic interactions occurred through a flurry of exchanges. The challenge was to depict Japan as having a relatively friendly, balanced diplomatic stance towards the Middle East.

Japan had been one of the world's most generous donors to the ODA between 1980 and 1995. Regions, such as South-East Asia, and economies like Indonesia and China benefited from this aid. Sezai Özçelik explains that, with the exception the of Gulf War period, Japan's ODA to the Middle East region made up 10 per cent of the ODA's total funding.[81] This may also have been a legacy of the 1973 oil crisis, when Japan realized that it needed to build bridges with the Middle Eastern region to ensure a stable energy supply.

Japan and other Asian economies joined in experiencing increases in oil imports. Swanström explains that, as early as the eve of the first postwar oil crisis in 1971, the Asia Pacific region consumed only 14.8 per cent of the global energy supply. However, this consumption comprised 28.1 per cent by 2000 and may increase to a projected 34.9 per cent in 2030, if one takes into account the economic expansion of developing economies, the dependence on Middle Eastern crude oil and the lack of alternatives.[82]

Imports of Middle Eastern crude oil into North-East Asia increased with the newly emerging economies of China and India, and with their rising demands, experiencing a dwindling domestic energy supply. Tsutomu Toichi explains that the industrialization and vehicle usage within these two economies could account for the higher utilization. With increasing environmental awareness, natural gas could also increase with the perception that this energy commodity offers greater environmental friendliness.[83]

Hyun Ahn Se and Michael T. Jones explain that South Korea is currently the second biggest LNG importer and that its company Korean Gas Corporation (KOGAS) is globally the largest importing firm. Since 1999, KOGAS has imported substantial amounts of LNG imports from the Middle East region, particularly from Oman and Qatar.[84]

China shifted from a pure economic focus on energy supplies and sought to negotiate in other arenas, such as free trade. To some commentators, these negotiations resulted in a form of interdependence, layered upon each other, to ensure that energy supplies are not the only point of contact with the Arab region.

For example, Angelica Austin, Danila Bochkarev and Willem van der Geest point out that China Power Investment Corp invested US$1.8 billion in 3-GW, gas-fired power generation capacity, and by 2001, China inked and signed almost 3,000 contracts in the Gulf worth US$2.7 billion, inclusive of infrastructure construction agreements.[85]

China itself may also be trying to upgrade its capabilities to accept Middle Eastern supplies that do not necessarily consist of light, low grade sulphur crude oil. China also upgraded or constructed new refineries to handle heavy high sulphur content crude oil. Zha Daojiong argues that the emphasis on heavy-oil-processing facilities may be beneficial globally, since this may help to relieve supply pressures in the international market for light oil.[86]

Zha also notes that China began building relations with the Middle East in the 1980s, and by 1985, China's crude oil exports reached a peak at 30 million tonnes, before declining with lower production. China, then, imported crude oil from Oman in 1983 as a transitional solution to energy delivery problems at the Yangtze River.[87] In 1988, Zha notes that, with augmented demand, Chinese importation of both crude and processed energy fuels increased quickly. He believes that, in 1993, China's self-sufficiency may have ended as it became a net importer of oil products.[88]

Traditionally, East Asia's own limited sources of energy had supplied a part of the regional energy needs. For example, Indonesian crude oil supplied Japanese energy needs. But, with the growth of North-East Asian economies, the region's own energy resources were no longer sufficient or faced depletion for this purpose. According to the International Energy Agency, by 1997 Oman replaced Indonesia as the main energy supplier because Chinese refineries were constructed with specifications to process sweet Chinese crude oil and were therefore suitable for refining Omani crude oil.[89]

Daniel Rosen and Trevor Houser explain that China's own largest oilfields, for example Daqing and Shengli, have relatively low sulfur (sweet) crude oil – unlike the usual Arabian Gulf crude oil that may be higher comparatively in sulphur content and that perhaps Japanese and South Korean refineries may be equipped to process.[90] Consequently, Rosen and Houser conclude that Chinese oil companies may prefer comparatively sweeter, lower sulphur crude oil from Asian and West African sources for processing in Chinese refineries.[91] The IEA pointed out that modifying refinery specifications to process sulphur content, particularly heavier crude oil, and the upgrading of existing refineries may facilitate China's ability to use more varieties of crude oil from the Middle East.[92]

Despite sulphur content being a factor in oil-refining processes, Zha points out that the Middle East may continue to be China's biggest source of energy and that its refineries may have to adjust to large imports, including Middle East high-sulphur crude oil (sulphur content of 1 per cent or more).[93]

In terms of pricing, Swanström argues that Middle Eastern oil is imported into North-East Asia with a premium amounting possibly to US$1-2 a barrel because of overreliance on this single source, the lack of competitive alternatives, and expensive transportation/freight charges.[94] According to Craig Parsons and Jeffrey Brown, North-East Asian economies, for example, Japan, South Korea, and increasingly China, may be worried about the Asian premium because it translates to lower profits for petroleum refiners.[95]

Some explanations of the Asian premium have been advanced. One school of thought, according to Parsons and Brown, argues that North-East Asian state energy companies and private entities that are either closely related to or regulated by the state had been responsible for purchasing oil, and these, they contend, may not be concerned with market forces to the same extent as wholly private firms and, therefore, willing to pay more for energy resources such as oil. At the same time, these public-private partnerships may have less motivation to upgrade technology to lower costs of oil.[96]

According to Parsons and Brown, another reason for the Asian premium is that, because Middle East oil producers occupy a large percentage of global oil exports, they possess a degree of control over regional markets in the US, Europe and Asia. This market control also facilitates their influence over energy pricing.[97]

Parsons and Brown argue that the premium may come about because the Middle East dominates a large portion of Asia's energy market. Asia seems to have limited reserves of its own, and may, unlike the US or Europe, lack plausible alternatives.[98] Parsons and Brown argue that Europe may have a number of alternative sources of energy, inclusive of the North Sea, Russia, the Caspian Sea region and Africa, compared to Asia which is comparatively more isolated from these areas except for the Russian alternative.[99]

Consequently, North-East Asian economies turned to non-Middle Eastern sources of oil. Ronald Soligo and Amy Jaffe highlight China's global drive for oil to make up for supply pressures from domestic energy sectors, for example, state-owned CNPC has invested in energy resources in locations like Kazakhstan, Angola, Russia and Peru.[100] Chinese or Indian firms may also try to acquire energy resources and facilities, whose ownership by others have expired or been relinquished.

According to Bernard Cole's article, China appears to be interested in a Pan-Asian Continental Oil Bridge that links the Middle East, South-West and Central Asia, Russia, and South-East Asia to China, as a means of channelling energy resources.[101] However, such an initiative is likely to encounter enormous challenges and require monumental efforts to actualize its objectives. In other words, it is far from becoming reality.

In terms of natural gas, South-East Asia, Australia and Russia may also increase gas availability, given the perception that natural gas may be environmentally friendlier than crude oil. South Korea appears to be active in utilizing natural gas resources. Anh and Jones project that by 2020 approximately 80 per cent of South Korea's LNG imports may come from the Middle East region, restricted only by the shortage and limitations of liquefaction capacity in the Middle East.[102]

Some of these new sources may be located nearer than others. For example, Russia may be considered more proximate than Kazakhstan or Peru, which could affect the pricing of oil coming from these sources. For now, however, these alternatives may not be as competitive in pricing as Middle Eastern crude oil. In this regard, Soligo and Jaffe analyse the competitiveness of the pricing of Kazakh oil vis-a-vis Middle East crude oil. They point out that Kazakh oil pricing must bear transport costs, currently pegged approximately at US$1.00 a barrel.

Soligo and Jaffe add that Kazakh oil may be higher in quality than Gulf-originated oil so this may counterbalance its higher pricing in terms of attractiveness. Yet, transport costs must still be added to transit tariffs, as the pipeline, which goes through Russia to Novorossyisk, and negotiates the Bosporus, leads to delays. But nearer or farther, there may be unavoidable competition among other economies that are reliant on foreign imports of energy resources. Adam Blinick's important work on the Kazakh-China oil pipeline highlights other rationale for the pipeline that may be as important if not more important than pricing considerations: diversification exercises, avoidance of contact with other major powers, preventing overreliance on pariah states and sensitive issues associated with them and the emerging potential of Kazakh gas.[103]

Jiang Wenran argues that the oil sands of Canada may represent other energy sources, given that Alberta outputs more oil from oil sands than from conventional reserves. Although the cost of extraction for sands may be higher at approximately US$12 a barrel (as opposed to US$4 a barrel for Middle East conventional extraction), profitability may still be possible in times of high oil prices above US$40–50 range.[104] According to Jiang, current Alberta production at 3 million barrels daily may still have surplus even after 50 per cent has been exported to the US. Therefore, infrastructural investments in this energy resource may be considered.[105]

According to Michael Thorpe and Sumit Mitra, despite spending over US$15 billion between 2003 and 2008 to purchase more than 100 oilfields and firms globally in more than thirty countries, China may still have to depend on Middle Eastern oil.[106] All North-East Asian and other large economies in the world appear to focus on the common goal of avoiding overreliance on Middle Eastern oil. Large emerging Asian economies seemingly made joint efforts to reduce friction and to mitigate excessive competition between themselves through focusing on common challenges but, even if these initiatives bear fruits, it will be a long-term venture. It may not mean the end of competitive instincts but rather a mitigation of its excesses. Both China and India are large economies, in which development may rely on affordable crude oil from the Middle East and in which interests may converge in keeping prices low.

Projections of increases in Middle Eastern oil to North-East Asia are no longer something new. According to Kang Wu, economies in Asia Pacific utilize three times more oil than they produce domestically and consumption is growing twice as fast in the region compared to the world, and so with less than 4 per cent of global proven oil reserves, the region may have to increase domestic production, diversify to energy such as natural gas or rely on renewable energy that seems to require long-term effort.[107] Japan's technology may also help make oilfield extraction of crude oil more efficient and sustainable.

As for the future, according to Thorpe and Mitra, the IEA (2007) forecasts an average early growth in global oil consumption of 1.1 per cent over the next twenty years, starting from 2008, and Asia may make up two-thirds of this increase due to economic and transportation needs.[108]

According to John Calabrese, who also studied the IIF report, China is the internationally second largest oil consumer and the fastest growing market for GCC petrochemical and metals exports.[109] India and Japan are also major consumers of such products. Overall, according to Swanström Asia's dependence on imported oil hovered a little above 70 per cent in 2000, but may be projected to be significantly higher than 90 per cent in 2030, in spite of possible future shortages.[110]

Wu suggests that one way to cope with the Asian premium may be to coordinate emergency energy stockpiles among economies in the region. Better endowed economies in the region may provide assistance to less developed regional economies, to maintain such stockpiles.[111] Another possibility, according to Wu, may be collective bargaining to lower prices and negotiate on better terms for Middle Eastern oil, something in which economies in East Asia appear to be interested. No concrete strategies have been implemented, because of uncertainties that oil producers have about such schemes, among other reasons.[112]

In the non-energy sector, Asian exports of goods and products may also not be surprising. Many see Asia as a global platform for production and manufacturing. Middle Eastern importation of Asian-made goods may not be an exception. There is also the matter of infrastructure construction projects that involve the engineering skills of North-Eastern Asia's advanced economies, and investments from both North-East Asia and the Arabian Gulf region. With advanced engineering skills and capabilities, Japan and South Korea may be active in building tankers, pipelines, offshore maritime projects, refineries and other energy-related facilities for the Middle East.

According to the IEA, Saudi Arabia and Kuwait detect profit-making opportunities in China, for crude oil exports and monetary investment in the petrochemical sector.[113] Calabrese notes that the Saudis appear to be cognizant of China's market size. Calabrese points out that the SABIC has a strong presence in East Asia with sales and marketing facilities in Indonesia, Philippines, Vietnam, Hong Kong, Taiwan, China, South Korea and Japan (in excess of 2,500 employees across Asia), and 50 per cent of them are based in China with its new petrochemicals projects.[114]

Thorpe and Mitra explain that Saudi Arabia and Kuwait may be keen on long-term investments in downstream infrastructure (such as refining and pet-rochemical plants) in China, augmenting the value-chain of oil production. Aramco (Saudi Arabia) has invested in a US$5 billion refinery/petrochemical facility (inclusive of Chinese retail distribution of petrol) in partnership with Chinese state-owned Sinopec and ExxonMobil in the southern Chinese province of Fujian.[115]

In another example that Thorpe and Mitra provide, Chinese Sinopec con-tracted with Saudi Aramco for a thirty-year supply contract that included constructing China's largest oil refinery in the northern port city Qingdao. Their agreements also included an award of licenses to distribute fuels in China whole-sale.[116] Thorpe and Mitra also note that Saudi Basic Industries (globally largest petrochemical company) concluded a joint venture with Chinese-owned Sin-opec, to invest over US$1billion in a petrochemical plant in China.[117]

Mehmet Ögütçü points out that many Middle East oil exporters seem-ingly demonstrate interest in investing in the downstream facilities of their oil-importing clientele before granting long-term import contracts; for exam-ple Saudi Aramco's US$1.5 billion joint investment and oil supply agreement for Chinese refineries domestically and as re-exports; and in 2002, Aramco negotiated for expansion and improvement upgrades at the Thalin refinery at Qingdao in Shandong Province and at the Saudi involvement in Guangdong's Maoming refinery.[118] According to the International Energy Agency, reports indicate that Thalin may receive 10 million tons of Saudi oil annually for half a century.[119]

Calabrese contends that the crude oil trade may remain the basis of Gulf–Asia energy relations especially since Gulf oil producers export more oil to Asia than to Europe and North America combined. Approximately two-thirds of Gulf oil exports are sold to the Asia Pacific market, where GCC countries may fulfill the majority of future energy needs, particularly for oil rather than for gas.[120] Toichi argues that, because the Middle East apparently sees the importance of the Asian market, the Middle Eastern nations may have stakes in the formation of a stable global energy market and forum. Such a forum would increase the communication and cooperation between Asia-Pacific Economic Cooperation (APEC) member nations (Japan, Korea, China and South-East Asia) and the GCC.[121]

At the same time, however, the Middle Eastern economies may also detect opportunities in the refinery business in China. Cole argues that China's refinery sector may be overconstructed and overconstituted by smaller refineries that cannot make profits, which is analogous to the Chinese coal-mining industry. These smaller Chinese refineries may also be less able to process the heavier crude variety that is characteristic of Middle Eastern-originated oil.[122]

Cole also points out that, even though Beijing plans to close many small refineries, it feels compelled to moderate the process. By moderating the process, Beijing hopes to absorb the unemployment resulting from the shutdowns. These shutdowns may, in part, be motivated by Beijing's desire to streamline costs for producing oil and gas (Chinese firms pay, on the average US$1.50 a barrel, compared to the US$1.20 a barrel costs that Western companies pay).[123] In such restructuring efforts for its refineries, it may be possible that China will seek joint ventures with foreign partners, including those from the Middle East and this may present some energy infrastructure construction opportunities for these partners.

As large emerging JUICE economies move away from energy-intensive economic development to environmentally conscious development, the state may also play a functional role in this transition. Bardhan argues that the state-led developmental model in China seems to motivate local governing and political units away from a focus on pure economic growth to environmental concerns; this may be an ongoing process that needs time to peter out and the consequences/impacts are relatively unknown at this stage.[124]

India, which may lack the same level of centralized mobilization, could consider long-term policy solutions, including educational initiatives, to teach the benefits of environmentalism. The balancing of local and central governmental interests may be more challenging in large economies like India and China, compared to comparatively smaller economic units like Japan.

Regardless of centralized or decentralized systems, governing units may not be able to directly, and successfully, tackle the issue of subsidized or underpriced fuels, given its politically explosive nature. Political and policy solutions in this sense have their limits. In the early 1950s for example, Japan tried to revive the coal industry through policy and economic incentives but failed.[125] Along a similar vein in the 1960s, Japan found that oil use in industrial and refinery processes generated substantial amounts of air pollution. To resolve this problem, the state discovered that – given the developmental priorities at that time – it had to gradually and patiently direct these energy industries towards other uses.[126] Japan's dynamics reflect many of the developmental issues that India and China currently face.

The delicate balancing of developmental objectives and environmental sustainability may present another inherent contradiction that older JUICE economies faced in the past and that currently confront newly developing JUICE economies. One difference is that newly developing economies may study historical precedents that older JUICE members established and perhaps avoid these developmental excesses. Nations adapting the experiences of others must be mindful that their own idiosyncratic, demographic make-up may necessitate innovative measures suited for local conditions. Emerging economies face challenges in developing the necessary social, cultural, educational, political, legal and economic infrastructure necessary for environmentally positive living standards compatible with economic development and employment-growth opportunities.

Jared Diamond illustrates, in a dramatic manner, the dilemma of being caught between economic development/industrialization and environmental protection.

From Diamond's view, China may be on a tightrope between conservation and development, given its sizeable demography and economy. China's bureaucracy and leadership may understand that its environmental challenges could sprout into bigger issues than perhaps previous problems – whether real, projected or merely perceived – that were cast into Malthusian problems.

China may, in fact, feel compelled to take bold steps in this area to resolve environmental contradictions.[127] Given such predictions, North-East Asia may consider cleaner fuels, for which there are numerous options.

Some Gulf states appear to be strategizing and positioning early for a predicted post-oil age and a diversification initiative. A move to natural gas coincides with the needs of the Middle East. According to Gawdat Bahgat, Saudi Arabia's Natural Gas Initiative is a scheme to augment employment opportunities for new entrants into the workforce, and to establish a self-contained, integrated gas platform for powering economic development at affordable prices.[128]

At the same time, North-East Asian economies are apparently discussing possibilities of alternatives to oil, such as natural gas, which is perceived as a cleaner resource, especially when compared to coal. Airborne particles of coal pollution may remain suspended in the sky as transnational acid rain that can harm the North-East Asian region. This may be remedied in part by protective technology and by converting to natural gas, which is generally a cleaner alternative.

According to Fereidun Fesharaki, Kang Wu and Sara Banaszak, coal made up 42 per cent of Asia's fossil fuel use but accounted for 54 per cent of carbon dioxide emissions. By comparison, natural gas made up 11 per cent of the fossil fuel use for calendar year 1998, but only 8 per cent of the regional carbon-dioxide emissions.[129] Relative to North-East Asia, Doh Hyun-jae argued that, while coal use is declining in North-East Asia, it continues to make up 64 per cent of China's energy use. Even though South Korea and Japan use coal less than China, they still are heavily coal dependent. As a consequence, all three nations are exposed to environmental challenges.[130]

Flynt Leverett and Jeffrey Bader call for the US to share and export its clean coal technologies to China. This will enable China to utilize its domestic coal supply, which is one of the largest globally,[131] to mitigate reliance on fossil fuels and to contribute to environmental quality upgrade.[132] But such initiatives may not be utilizable immediately, even though they may be promising, advantageous and possibly inject no detriments into nature.

Beyond the realm of long-term, advanced technologies and any solutions they permit, there could exist a region-wide incentive for North-East Asian economies to study the implementation of possibly cleaner fuels like natural gas. This transition may fit into regional lifestyle trends and into North-East Asia's environmental consciousness.

Despite rising interest in the environmentally friendly natural gas resource and the substantial quantities of gas found in the Middle East, Bahgat argued at the turn of the twenty-first century that relatively fewer efforts were directed into such resources for either local consumption or exports.[133]

In 2003, Doh noted that gas in North-East Asia was less than 10 per cent of the region's overall energy consumption.[134] On a more individual basis, the regional economies reflected the following consumption figures: gas comprised 3 per cent of China's energy use total in 2001;[135] from 2001 to 2025, projected Japanese oil consumption would increase at an average annual rate between 4 percent and 1 per cent; Korean annual growth for gas consumption averaged 18 per cent from 1988 to 2003 (11.3 per cent in 2002) is expected to slow down to 4.8 per cent in the period from 2003 to 2023.[136]

Relatively lower use of gas resources may have changed since then, as Fesharaki, Wu and Banaszak argue in their important article 'Natural Gas: The Fuel of the Future in Asia'. The title of their article embodies their main argument. If natural gas is, indeed, Asia's 'fuel of the future', it will likely play a critical role in the growth and enlargement of Asia-Gulf energy exchanges.

Fesharaki, Wu and Banaszak argue that gas allows consumers and suppliers to forge deeper relationships compared to other fuels because both parties require 15–20-year-old contracts that determine the distribution, pricing and other important details, such as the loans from large multinational banks willing to fund such expensive projects.[137] At the same time, other factors that influence the prospect of Asia–Gulf exchanges may involve non-oil sectors. Not only that, but energy trade between Asia and the Gulf region may move into related areas, including infrastructure construction.

The gas sector seems to be making inroads made into the infrastructure development necessary for gas delivery and processing, rather than merely focusing on sales and delivery. Such infrastructure upgrading and construction may be important because, according to Doh, the quality of energy infrastructure and facilities, their proximity and integration into the region's overall energy system may impact the effectiveness, deployability and reliability of energy supply.[138]

Cole notes that the Gulf is involved in a LNG project in Guangdong, China to supply the industrialized and densely populated coastal areas with an eventual capacity of 5 trillion cubic metres annually, construction that involves building six 320-MW gas-fired power plants, and converting existing oil-fired plants with a capacity of 1.8 GW to LNG.[139] Another refinery investment that Saudi Arabia made in China involves upgrading a refinery in southern Fujian province, with collaboration from Sinopec of China and ExxonMobil of the US.[140]

Cole indicates that the Guangdong construction project initially received indications of interest from firms in Australia, Indonesia, Iran, Malaysia, Qatar, Russia and Yemen. Investments in these gas-fields flowed in from Dutch Shell, French TotalFina, ExxonMobil and Australia LNG. However, in April 2002, China's planners limited the selection process to companies from Australia, Indonesia and Qatar.[141]

Perhaps as a sign of diversification from reliance on the Middle East, Cole noted that China gave Australia a US$13.5 billion contract to provide Guangdong with 3 million tons of LNG yearly for 25 years. The purpose of the contractual bid was to facilitate CNOOC's relationships, so that it might 'develop natural gas in Australia', in collaboration with Australia Natural Gas.[142]

China may not be the only North-East Asian recipient of refinery infrastructure investments from the Gulf. Saudi Aramco also owns S-Oil, which is part of the Aramco group owned partly (35 per cent) by the Kingdom. S-Oil obtained a deal to construct a new refinery in Seosan in western South Korea to possibly facilitate exports to China.[143] Investments also move the other way, from North-East Asia to the Middle East. According to Leverett and Bader, Sinopec obtained one of the three gas resource concessions (non-associated) that Saudi Arabia offered for foreign bidding.[144]

Even while North-East Asian economies like China are strengthening economic engagements with the Middle East, others like Japan have a history of long economic and energy contact with the same region. These arrangements, however, may not be comparable to the long-time US engagement in the region and its strong and established partnerships with economies like Saudi Arabia.

Diversification of gas energy resources may also extend to one's own resources. North-East Asian economies, like China, may simultaneously focus on developing domestic resources. Doh 's article on North-East Asia argues that domestically, North-East Asia may be equipped with usable energy resources like gas, coal and hydropower. In fact, one-third of the globe's gas and coal reserves and a quarter of the earth's hydropower are located here, generally in Russia and China, but – to a lesser extent – Korea and Japan.[145]

According to Kaoru Yamaguchi and Keii Cho, China emphasized the importance of developing its own domestic reserves to achieve energy supply stability.[146] These writers also explained that most Chinese gas reserves are located in Tarim, Junggar Qaidam, Ordos and Sichuan, which as the largest among these reserves makes up 30 per cent of the overall national output.[147]

Pricing may be a crucial factor in developing domestic reserves. Soligo and Jaffe calculated that China's Tarim oil may incur costs of roughly US$10 a barrel in production at the site itself.[148] They found that Tarim oil's retail price in the industrialized southern China market may be US$13 a barrel and additional right of way costs may increase that amount to US$15 a barrel.[149] With tanker costs of about US$1 a barrel from the Middle East (not including any right of way costs or transit tariffs), Soligo and Jaffe argued that Tarim Basin oil may be price-competitive with lighter Middle Eastern crudes at prices of US$12 and, from their calculations, assuming a US$1 a barrel premium for quality differ- ences between Tarim and the sour crudes from Iran, Iraq and Saudi Arabia, Tarim oil may also be competitive at US$10–11 for Middle East-originated sour crudes.[150]

But in terms of consumption, domestic demand appears to continue to out- strip supply. According to Leverett and Bader, electricity generation may be increasingly provided by power stations that run on natural gas energy. Trans- portation energy needs may continue to grow, since China had 23 million cars in 2005 and Sinopec projections pegged the number of cars at 130 million by the year 2030.[151] Given such growth, it may be possible that domestic resources alone cannot meet heightened needs. Soligo and Jaffe raised the caveat that, even if Tarim were developed, output may not be enough to cover growing import demand.[152]

In terms of dependence, Asia may, in fact, need Middle Eastern supplies more than the US. Some comparisons here may be helpful. According to Calder, the Middle East provides 70.8 per cent of Asia's oil needs, but only provided 23 per cent of US overseas oil imports for 2004.[153] Doh argues that Russia is in the vicinity of North-East Asia and has surplus energy resources that can be exported. These facts may be increasingly important for, perhaps, the first thirty years of the twenty-first century.[154] For now, however, it is unlikely for any domestic Asian source to fully wean itself off Middle Eastern energy engagements. That may not mean, however, that other forms of economic interactions cannot take place.

However, North-East Asian economies are also examining other possibilities like nuclear energy. The LDP, which governed Japan for most of the postwar period eagerly examined nuclear energy development as a priority non-oil energy source.[155] A 1987 White Paper identified nuclear power as an option, during an era when it made up 28 per cent of Japan's energy industry.[156] Even though South Korea and Japan are considered prolific users of nuclear energy, Calder predicts that China will become the largest global user by 2050.[157] Leverett and Bader contend that China intends to build as many as forty nuclear plants by the year 2020.[158]

Other East Asian efforts involve seeking alternative, non-Middle Eastern foreign energy sources. Turkmenistan and Uzbekistan may be other sources of natural gas for North-East Asia, with their proximity to China and South Asia.[159] One IEA report argues that Caspian oil may compete with Middle Eastern oil for market share in Asia, since incremental output from Central Asia may reasonably reach 2 million barrels a day.

Moreover, pipelines are being considered that will export oil through Central Asia[160] in spite of the enormous challenges involved. Not only Central Asia, but Africa is another possible source of gas. At the turn of the twenty-first century, Alaska appeared as a further source.[161]

East Asian diversification from reliance on Middle East crude oil may be accompanied by other interactions between economies within the two regions beyond mutual interests based on energy. Trade in non-oil-related export goods and cross-investments in each other's economies may increase, and lead to other economic and trade exchanges between the two regions.

One example of multidimensional engagement is Japan's involvement in the Middle East, which Naitoh, among others, discusses. As the first North-East Asian economy to engage the Middle Eastern region, Japan's relationships may be multifaceted and possibly complicated with engagements in economics and individually based support. Japan is highly aware of the need to be on harmonious relations with the region that provides 90 per cent of Japan's oil energy needs.[162]

Japan remains comparatively less engaged in the Middle East than the US. There have been extensive interactions between the Middle East and the US in the past, some initiatives more far-ranging and broader than others. Christopher Candland, formerly a Principal Advisor, to the Federal Advisory Committee on Labor Diplomacy, U.S. Department of State, during the George W. Bush administration, gives an excellent example of an initiative that promotes extensive engagement.

Specifically, Candland explained that the Bush administration may have had plans to engage with the Middle East in the form of a Greater Middle East Initiative that geographically covers Morocco's Atlantic coastal areas, the northern region of Pakistan, the northern coastal areas of Turkey and southern Yemen.[163] Within this initiative, some objectives include political economic programs, FTAs to promote trade, civil-society development, funding from endowments and human development activities.[164]

Given the importance of governments in shaping their policies towards the Middle East, the various states continue to play a role in working with North-East Asian gas firms. For example, Fesharaki, Wu and Banaszak note that Korea's Kogas played a dominant role in the investment of a national gas transmission system. Japan's firms were sensitive to Japan's economic ministries that coexisted alongside privatization. State-corporate relationships were also impacted by deregulation trends at the turn of the twenty-first century.[165] In regard to China, Fesharaki, Wu and Banaszak note that the state influences gas prices in China through subsidies in favour of industries and households.[166]

Steven Lewis argues, however, that, despite the fact that both non-Chinese and China-based scholars have singled out the central government as the primary entity in tackling China's energy and environmental challenges, foreign investors going into these industries have to interact with both the state and with local/regional authorities, given their early involvement in China's market economy and China's economic opening since 1978.[167]

Large state companies face peculiar issues in the international gas industry, as they fight to compete more effectively in soliciting investments and contracts with Saudi-based state firms in the energy sector. Yoshikazu Kobayashi suggested a 'Hinomaru alliance' between Japanese firms for economy of scale to compete with Western entities. He observes that the projects that Saudi Aramco appear to be interested in are multifaceted, high in value and big in scale.[168]

For example, Fesharaki, Wu and Banaszak, made estimates that pipeline costs in Saudi deals may range from US\$10 a barrel to US\$30 a barrel, typically with lengths reaching from 2,000 to 7,000 km.[169] Massive size and scale also appear to be characteristic of the growing trade between Asia and the Gulf.

According to Lewis, many Chinese, American and Japanese academics and researchers concur that collaboration in the gas industry may develop into more extensive work in energy and environmental industries.[170] Doh, explained how proposed schemes for regional cooperation may take place.

Relative to Japan, Doh explained in 2003 that most such gas cooperation initiatives clustered around Irkutsk, Yakutsk, Ohka (Sakhalin) and that an aspect of these agreements pertained to pipeline delivery to end users.[171] Even if these initiatives succeed, they will probably require time, patience and the reaching of a very delicate political consensus, which could be in consideration of the contentious issues, such as transit fees, profitability, sovereignty, security, etc.

Using Japan's experience as a gauge, NGOs and the private sector played significant roles in its energy system, as advocates of awareness, information exchange, local community interfacing, consumption watchdogs, etc. Networking these organizations may contribute to an awareness of energy and environmental issues. One example is the networked, anti-golf movement in Japan with regard to environmentalism.[172] Given the different political systems and societal make-ups in the newly developing economies of India and China, they may have to innovate their own mechanisms for interfacing with local communities.

The consensus appears to be that both China and India made commitments to put in considerable efforts and resources that implement alternative sources of energy. As Bardhan points out, India has globally the fourth largest installed wind power capacity. China has done well in wind turbines and is ranked the third biggest producer of solar cells (Suntech Company).[173] There appears to be consensus that such achievements are impressive, laudable, even though they must be accelerated or deepened. Renewable energy resources and technologies are important in the long-term to mitigate dependence on fossil fuels but they cannot immediately replace the need for oil.

India and China are not the only ones that seek to shift to environmentally safe mechanisms. JUICE conservation efforts may also be decisive in determining whether conservation can make a dent in energy consumption. Some JUICE members are more experienced than others in managing the environment. Japan, which was able to recover quickly from the 1970s oil crisis and environmental challenges, became a model for others to follow. Japan continues to innovate with energy-efficiency technologies and to incorporate rational production techniques in the interest of cost-cutting through energy use reduction.

Perhaps Japan is no longer under the sort of international media spotlight on its environment compared to when its pollution incidents were highlighted as a case study of development excesses. Japan may be able to help its Asian JUICE partners, India and China, undo some of the excesses of fast growth and benefit from reduced transnational pollution on its own shores. In fact, environmentally friendly renewable energy use is not entirely new in Japan. There were historical uses of renewable energy in Japan. For example, the Japanese electric power industry relied on hydropower as a source of energy in the 1920s.[174] Its use of hydropower may date back to at least the Tokugawa period (1603–1867) when it was used for agricultural processes.

As China and India go through the same fast-growth phase, they may shorten the learning curve by examining the Japanese developmental example and perhaps even work with Japan and the US to develop new, environmentally friendly technology. This will likely be a continuous process of improvement rather than a one-off procedure. For example, there have been calls in the US, the most developed and advanced JUICE constituent, to rebuild older infrastructure according to contemporary needs and specifications that should include energy efficiency and environmental friendly measures.

Some schools of geopolitical thought contend that, when growth reaches a natural limit, there may be more similarities among the JUICE entities. There may be a long-term convergence, after which certain aspects of the Indian and Chinese economic development begin to resemble the more mature economies of US and Japan. When that happens, JUICE challenges may be more similar than dissimilar.

In other words, very little is cast in stone as the dynamics among the JUICE constituents shift fluidly from one context to the next and from one historical scenario to the other. The net result may remain the same as large, influential JUICE economies get concerned with internal development and attempt to gain mileage, with resources from global interests. Smaller JUICE economies, which are already highly organized and mobilized, continue their search for prosperity and resources, even while the largest JUICE economies maintain comfortable positions – adjusting to changing dynamics and adapting to new geopolitical situations. Ultimately, the net result of the movement may be stability and accommodations of positions.

In the geopolitical sense, the US is probably the strongest and most significant JUICE entity, because it has vast resources that underline the phrases used to describe its geopolitical reach, including 'hyperpower' or 'deep power' in addition to the traditional 'superpower'. Perhaps, another possible description may be that it is a unique power, able to influence the global energy industry more than the other JUICE constituents. Regardless of the description, the US may likely be the hub around which the other JUICE constituents revolve, because of the embeddedness of US role, and its position in the global energy sector and the world economy. The US role, to many, may also reflect an element of stability, of dependence and reliability.

Some JUICE constituents may need to be closer to the US than others, for example, Japan. Basically, however, all JUICE entities are dependent on the US in one way or another. Japan relied on American petroleum products shortly after Meiji Restoration of 1868 when it embarked on modernization.[175] During the period of recovery after the war, Japan was also able to absorb American technologies to recover quickly, helped by favorable global oil prices. Bilaterally, the US and Japan are in a unique and close relationship that may have shared interests in the global economy, geopolitics and energy systems.

Within certain subregions too, there are important subregional relationships. For example, the triangle of US–Japan–China has determined the shape and outcome of geopolitical, socio-economic, political-economic and energy allocation for a long time, before and after the Pacific War. It is unlikely that this will change subregionally. The US and Japan may also be working with India, given India's emerging role as an interconnector between North-East Asia and the Arabian Gulf area. India's unique location places her in the Indian Ocean and in Central Asia.

Other subregional initiatives that relate to energy in the past among North-East Asian-based JUICE economies include the 2005 Shenyang Declaration of the North-East Asian Economic Forum and the North-East Asian gas and electricity pipelines.[176] These subregional initiatives may require tremendous political will, determination and effort to implement plans that may not be immediately realizable. Sub-regional initiatives may be more important and crucial to information exchange – and as regular forums for familiarity of personalities – rather than as vehicles that resolve energy needs completely. Better communication and exchanges tend to mitigate uncertainties and shocks.

It could be that only the US, among JUICE constituents, guarantees the stability of the Gulf, of its oil supply, and of its energy commodities that feed the needs of other JUICE constituents. The US has close ties with that region's ruling elite, as shown by the fact that the US has historically established economic engagements with the region. While there may have been differing views on the desire of each JUICE constituent to influence the oceanic energy transportation routes, no JUICE entity will be able to achieve this without reactions from the others. It may really be a scenario where some entities will work closely with the US to keep the energy flow going, even as others may free-ride upon this arrangement. The US remains core to the process.

Finally, all JUICE members may face the common challenge, as energy supplies may be vested into less accessible areas, including underwater arenas and oil shale that, as George Friedman noted, may require considerable financial resources for extraction and to compensate technical and maintenance personnel.[177] These may be common issues for JUICE entities to work on since they may all face the net impact of such resource inaccessibility that raises the costs of energy.[178] Combined JUICE resources and economies of scale may make such extraction economically more practicable if political consensus may be reached.

It is well known that historically Japan was adversely affected by the 1973 oil crisis, but that it, thereafter, coped effectively through energy measures. Mito Takamichi noted a less well-known fact – Japanese policymakers, its bureaucratic leaders and its private sector elite did not worry about the initial oil crisis, but only became aware of its magnitude when crude oil supplies dwindled by 10 to 30 per cent.[179] Therefore, another issue that JUICE economies may work on would involve information-sharing systems and networks: surprises and the lack of preparedness of pending energy price instabilities may create developmental and social challenges internally for each JUICE economy. Information may be exchanged on the basis of need or be sent simultaneously to subregional consultations. It may be sent, inclusively, to all stakeholders, rather than exclusive arrangements, given the interconnectedness and global nature of energy needs.

Other common challenges may also be tackled through the collective use of resources. For example, collective JUICE resources may reduce piracy, by implementing a more effective energy delivery. Piracy may be challenging for energy delivery systems, particularly at chokepoints on maritime routes that enable ambushes. Piracy may raise costs, based on the impact on maritime insurance premiums and it may disrupt supplies. This may be a common issue that may drive some or all JUICE constituents to collaboration.

Some JUICE members may be more advanced than others in developing non-petroleum-based technologies. As an example, Japan achieved leadership in environmental technologies and knowhow. Yet, because all JUICE economies are likely to continue their reliance on fossil fuels, this reliance may encourage all JUICE constituents to engage in future collaboration with regard to green technologies and non-fossil-fuel based applications. Collaboration may be market-driven, based on comparative advantages, or in the form of technological transfers from more advanced to less developed economies.

These are long-term measures, with which benefits may only be realized in its full potential in the future, but which may be initiated currently due to JUICE developmental needs. As problematic challenges emerge (including Japan's demography, the US's and China's mature infrastructure, Japan's fast-growth environmental impact) and converge on JUICE constituents, these economies may find more in common and more reasons for collaboration. Living with energy giants may also involve an issue of these giants living and accommodating one another.

8 CHINA AND ITS ENERGY NEEDS

There is a close relationship between economic growth in China and energy demand, exacerbated by the absence of local resources in China to match the amount needed for its own economic growth, while energy efficiency remains a challenging issue as total Chinese energy usage is 40 quadrillion BTU per annum or approximately 6,500 BTU per dollar of GDP, below the rate and efficiency of developed economies.[1] Due to these factors, among others, China has to turn outwards for its energy needs.

To meet its energy needs, the Middle East/Gulf region is its primary supplier of petroleum and natural gas for the foreseeable future. There are many schools of thought about China's energy links and connections with the Gulf region and the Middle East. Historically, during the ideological divide of the Cold War, Mohamed Bin Huwaidin argued that there had been perceptions of China as a power sufficiently distant from the USSR, despite being in the socialist bloc, and a possible source of support for the developing world, especially with Chinese provision of monetary and other forms of help for the developing world along with the promotion of the Chinese developmental model to developing economies.[2]

The 1955 Bandung Conference was perceived by some as an event of Sino-Arab mutualism as some Arab states founded official relationships with China as the latter provided finances and other forms of non-monetary support for various Arab causes.[3] The ideological relationship and perceptions of fraternity that began in the Cold War eventually became predicated on economic and trade exchanges with the market economic transformation and opening up of China.

An early Chinese energy exchange with the Gulf was its crude oil importation from Oman in 1983 as a transitional policy for managing supply routes from northern to Yangtze upper-end regions of China.[4] Seven years later, China and Saudi Arabia established an official bilateral relationship,[5] which would eventually place the Saudis as the number one oil supplier to China. By the 1990s, China was supplied with crude oil from the Middle East, mainly from countries such as Oman which was eventually joined by other suppliers like Saudi Arabia and Yemen by 1997, and at the same time, China was also reliant on Asia Pacific economies for refinement of these oil supplies.[6]

In 1997, oil was the majority item in bilateral trade between China and Oman (100% per cent of bilateral trade) and Yemen (83 per cent of bilateral trade) while Saudi Arabia and the UAE had become China's main trading entities in the Middle Eastern region.[7] By the turn of the twenty-first century, some of these Gulf states had move up the ranks to become China's major energy suppliers. According to Bernard Cole's report *'Oil for the Lamps of China' – Beijing's 21st-Century Search for Energy*, in 2001, Saudi Arabia and Oman were ranked the second most prolific supplier to China, supplying 44.1 million barrels each to China.[8]

In 2004, China overtook Japan to emerge globally as the world's second largest consumer of petroleum, utilizing up to 7.4 million barrels daily in 2006, almost a half a million barrels more on a daily basis in comparison with the previous year of 2005.[9] In 2007–8, Chinese oil importation from the Middle East stabilized at approximately 60 per cent.[10] Besides availability, the attraction of Middle Eastern crude could be found in the highly affordable cost of production in the Gulf within the prices of US$2–4 a barrel.[11]

Cautious of increasing (over)dependence, China began to explore alternatives. More contemporarily, some observers see China's search for alternative energy sources, alternative energy and diversification policies as indicative of lessening dependence on Middle Eastern crude. However, an IEA report *China's Worldwide Quest for Energy* indicated that China may try to limit dependence on the Middle East to a certain extent but cannot wean itself off completely from their oil supply.[12]

Moreover, even future sources of oil appear to be found mainly in the same locations. According to Maurizio Cociancich and Fabio Massimo Parenti, major oil reserves are still contained in the Middle East (66 per cent) compared to other regions like Latin America (10 per cent), Africa (9 per cent), Eastern Europe (5.4 per cent), developing states in Asia Pacific (3.1 per cent), North America (3 per cent), Central Asia (1.5 per cent) and Western Europe (1.3 per cent).[13]

There appears to be some occasions when alternative non-Middle Eastern sources seem to have an upper hand in terms of crude supply. For example, according to some estimates, non-Middle Eastern sources of oil have at times momentarily displaced Gulf states as China's main crude source. For example, in 2006, Angola was China's largest crude provider pushing Saudi Arabia to second place followed by Oman and Yemen (not in particular order) and, other than Yemen, most of these suppliers increased their output to China between 2005 and 2006.[14] Even so, in 2006, the Middle East provided 45 per cent of China's energy importation while Russia supplied 8 per cent.[15]

Nevertheless, in most other years, such as 2003 for example, much of China's oil inflow originated from the Middle East (51.8 million tons or 380 million barrels) and a South-East Asian source.[16] According to Niklas Swanström, China may place equal premium on acquisition of energy resources and pipelines in Central Asia as it will do on Middle Eastern pipelines, and the significance of these facilities and resources is set to grow in importance as the Middle East may be expected to produce output to the extent of 45 per cent of global crude supply by as early as 2010 along with Venezuela.[17] As for future projections in terms of consumption, according to the East-West Center, 70 per cent of China's crude supply will be from the Middle East by 2015 while the remainder will originate from Russia, central Asia and shipped from Africa.[18]

Given that most North-East Asian economies are looking for alternatives to Middle Eastern sources of energy, in particular crude oil, it is reasonable that they examine the resource-rich African continent. According to the Asia Pacific Energy Research Centre, almost 25 per cent of China's crude oil presently comes from Africa compared to nearly 50 per cent in the year 2002.[19] From such statistics, Africa does not replace the Middle East as a source of crude oil but rather presents an alternative source of diversification. Africa itself may also be considered a growth region. According to Raghav Bahl, Africa has an annual economic growth rate of 6–7 per cent, with 150 million 'elite' consumers and a 500 million-strong middle class seeking similar lifestyle choices.[20]

There have been many views of China's role in Africa. The first school of thought focuses on China's no-conditions-attached arrival in the continent. The scale of views of China's role in Africa ranges from realist views that see China as intruding with little emphasis on help for the region. In this perspective, the 'no-strings' activities apply to China's offer of aids, loans and capacity-building opportunities (or debt cancellation – 150 debt items owed to China by thirty-two African nations, according to Raghav Bahl[21]) to other world regions, including Africa. Brahma Chellaney points out another example of Angola which obtained a US$3 billion loan from China along with technicians to open up offshore oilfields.[22]

The second school of thought has a stronger view of Chinese economic presence. China is presented as a neo-colonial presence, with long-term resource interests that may eventually lure armed intervention to protect those interests. The strongest interpretation of this view perceives China's needs to have a foothold in the continent as part of a zero-sum game to oust other players. Ben Simpfendorfer argues that Chinese help for Africa amounted to US$19 billion and that China created a US$5 billion investment vehicle, which, he argues, is mainly comprised of Chinese firms and manpower that benefit from Africa's infrastructure projects.[23] According to Joseph Stiglitz, China's demand for African raw materials increased the continent's growth trate by 7 per cent per annum.[24]

On the other end of the spectrum, the scale moves into more benign depictions. This involves the historical school of thought engulfing the Ming dynasty model, where China's Ming-dynasty Admiral Zheng sailed to the African continent and set up vassal relationships with no intentions of colonization. Another school of thought follows the now-familiar 'Peaceful Rise of China', in which China seeks peaceful contact and coexistence for its continued economic growth to continue. According to Indian strategist Chellaney, Sino-African bilateral trade increased from US$10 billion in 2000 to US$107 billion in 2008.[25]

Besides these two doctrinal schools, an institutional viewpoint is that of the functionalist school, whereby China is in Africa for cooperation, hoping that increased interlinkages can lead to future interdependence and mutualism. According to Bahl, Sino-African bilateral trade reached US$73 billion in 2007; in fact, Africa is expected to become China's second largest project (infrastructure) destination and China's third biggest investment recipient.[26] According to Christopher Davidson, Sino-African trade attained US$107 billion in 2009, largely because of trade with economies located in the northern portion of Africa.[27] Related to this school of thought is the inter-regional worldview that focuses on the continent's exchanges with a major economy. Usually, inter-regional links are between two world regions but some conceptions of inter-regionalism also include a region's relations with a major economy in the world.

The two contrasting images of Chinese presence in Africa are probably eclectic snapshots of Chinese diplomacy and interests in Africa. There are other subgenres in the range of worldviews on Chinese presence in Africa. For example, Sino-Japanese paradigms that present Chinese presence in Africa as an offshoot of grand Asian rivalries. This is related to the realist school of thought, except that it is narrowed down to the East Asian context. The realist school, however, is aware that Africa is far away from North-East Asia – meaning that mere geographic distance works against both Japan and China. Some analyses of Sino-Japanese presence in Africa thus focus on the speed and extent of their influence in the continent.

Somewhere in between these polemic interpretations are the pragmatic schools of thought. The pragmatic schools of thought see China considering Africa as a diversification exercise, one of the larger numbers of regions in the world that is a possible repository for the procurement of resources that facilitate economic growth. Bahl argues that China is in Africa to procure resources, including platinum and iron ore from Zimbabwe, not to find a customer base for its consumer products.[28]

Yet, others within the realism school take a more global perspective of China's resource hunt. Africa is only one of many sources of resources that China can turn to for its industrialization and economic growth needs. China's renewable energy technologies may develop so that China is either self-sufficient or that it has credible alternatives to crude oil. In these events, China's renewable energy technologies will take precedence over its African engagements.

The realistic school of thought may argue that, in fact, China, which sends confusing signals, lacks a coherent African strategy at all. Chinese top leaders visit Africa, on grounds of the centrality of the continent to Chinese interests. Yet, the Chinese appear to be happy to evacuate its workers from the continent and opt for non-intervention, with the first sign of trouble. China sometimes appears ready to confront the West, with regard to certain issues. On other occasions, it is prepared for international cooperation with peacekeeping troops. The confusing signals may denote the lack of coherent African strategy.

The economic school of thought may see China as a customer of African resources. Transactions are at arm's length and no real emotional stakes are involved. China is a net importer of energy, with few domestic resources (besides coal), to hedge against resource providers. Therefore, it has no cards to play against the energy suppliers. Views of Chinese presence may be important because these views sometimes may underlie the efforts of resource regions to hedge and balance major economies, powers and states against each other.

Aside from looking beyond the Middle East, a limiting factor on more Chinese importation of Gulf and Middle Eastern crude appears to be the availability of the refinery facilities. In the mid-2000s, with slightly above 1.35 million barrels per day capacity to refine lesser grade Gulf oil in 2005, Ronald Soligo and Amy Jaffe argue that China did not have the capabilities to process large volumes of less than optimal grades of oil produced in the Gulf by producers such as Saudi Arabia and Kuwait and thus relied more on oil suppliers with minimal sulphur content from Abu Dhabi, Oman and Yemen.[29] In the early to mid-2000s, China mainly has relied on processing sweet crude from Oman and Yemen but was less equipped to deal with sour crudes.[30]

Zha Daojiong points out that China must learn to expand its capacity for churning out greater output from Middle Eastern high-sulphur crude defined as having sulphur content of 1 per cent or more through upgrading the quality of the oil products.[31] In a 2006 article, Zha argues that this is a bit of myopia on the part of China not to have studied the post-oil crisis (1970s) Japanese example to upgrade their facilities to refine heavy Middle Eastern crude and perpetuate dependence on low-sulphur that only comes from certain sources in the Middle East, creating a market squeeze on such products.[32] This issue may likely be a priority for corrective measures in the coming years in terms of energy development in China, thereafter, it is predicted that Chinese consumption for both heavy and light crudes may expand in tandem.[33]

Consequently, according to Soligo and Jaffe, southern China witnessed a mid-2000s flurry of refinery construction, catering to economic growth in that region of coastal China.[34] Refining business therefore presents opportunities for Middle East and Gulf investors. In the early 2000s, Saudi investors recognized the potential in the Chinese market for crude sales and energy investments.[35] Other investors interested in infrastructure businesses such as building more refineries to handle heavy high-sulphur crude and also upgrading older obsolete refineries in China included the Kuwaits.[36]

According to Mehmet Ögütçü, Saudi energy firm Aramco increased the scale and also improved the Thalin refinery located in Qingdao in northern China while establishing a foothold in the Maoming refinery in southern China in 2002.[37] Aramco and Exxon also inked a memo of understanding (MOU) to place funds into improving a refinery facility at Fujian province in the mid-2000s.[38]

According to the IEA, the negotiations in the early 2000s involved Saudi funding for petrochemical investments, including refineries in exchange for Chinese purchase of Saudi crude.[39] In accordance with such arrangements, for example, Thalin would process about 10 million tons of crude oil annually at the start of its operations.[40]

China has tried various strategies to diversify, regulate dependence and lessen overdependence on Middle Eastern and Gulf sources of oil. One reason behind China's diversification exercise is to avoid paying the so-called premium for Middle Eastern crude,[41] a reference to Asian economies paying higher prices due to lack of coordination and other factors that would help to bring down regional competition and/or increase price competitiveness for consumers within a particular region.

Some strategies were less successful than others. In some ways, there has been less than successful attempts to lessen dependence on Middle Eastern energy resources by controlling prices, for example, according to C. Fred Bergsten, Charles Freeman, Nicholas R. Lardy and Derek J. Mitchell, the Chinese authorities attempted to regulate natural gas prices to make them competitive against Middle Eastern prices for supporting industries that consume significant amounts of gas as the petrochemicals industry but the strategy did not succeed in increasing gas production to meet domestic needs and so the authorities liberalized price controls.[42] Therefore, Angie Austin suggests that instead of focusing on net volumes of Middle Eastern crude imports by China, it may be possible to look instead at the formulation and development of regulations to align Chinese energy prices and processes with market prices to bring about productive and efficient use of energy.[43]

In some industries, China had to yield to market pressure and draw down production with a positive spinoff of lesser energy consumption. According to Bergsten, Freeman, Lardy and Mitchell, in 2007, because of increasing output and competition in the Middle Eastern chemicals industry (and corresponding lower production from China), and lower output for Chinese steel, cement and basic chemicals production since 2006, energy consumption intensity was expected to be lowered by 20 per cent by 2010, which was a goal that the Chinese industries intended to achieve.[44]

One strategy that China has adopted is to embed oil within a more complex and comprehensive set of bilateral trade connections with Middle Eastern economies focusing on longer range views, mutually beneficial economic exchanges and diversified trade that does not only include crude.[45] According to John Calabrese, Chinese products needed for daily use like electronics and other goods began to enter the Middle East in 1993 when China became a net crude importer.[46]

Eight years later, according to Angelica Austin, Danila Bochkarev and Willem van der Geest, China negotiated approximately three thousand agreements related to oil services in the Gulf by 2001 that were valued at US$2.7 billion.[47] In 2007, an advisor to the Saudi Minister of Commerce and Industry, Fawaz al-Alami indicated that in 2002, Saudi trade with China was worth US$200 million and it became US$14 billion in 2007 and projected to increase by US$45 billion in 2012.[48]

In 2006, the Chinese Premier (second after former French President Jacques Chirac to talk to the Saudi Consultative Council) travelled to Saudi Arabia and, three months after this visit, Saudi King Abdallah visited China officially, it was his first trip outside the Middle East since August 2005 when he became the head of state and these visits resulted in deals on energy, health and trade.[49] An Arab–China Business Conference with over 200 Arab private sector participants was held in the capital of China with the follow-up conference in the Gulf as bilateral trade expanded from US$300 million from the start of Sino-Arab relationship to US$10 billion in 2006.[50]

More recently, in accordance with this comprehensive bilateral economic relations strategy, China initiated negotiations with the GCC economies to construct a free trade area and shift emphasis away from purely energy trade to diversify into other forms of economic interactions with the Middle East with the goal of increased interdependence.[51] Along with this goal of interdependence, China also has about 20 million Muslims with Chinese citizenship inside its borders,[52] it remains unclear what role they will play in future Sino-Arab relations.

While alternative energy resources technologies still had a long way to go in the late 1990s in terms of pricing and other factors, Chinese development and advancements in such technologies has improved substantially in the twenty-first century and may eventually contribute to alleviating dependence on Middle Eastern fossil fuels to a certain extent. Even for fossil fuels, improvements in technologies appear to have increased the possibilities of greater output.

According to Dan Child in 2004, the proven reserves of most Middle Eastern states, including entities such as Saudi Arabia have upped their estimates over the period of 1994–2004 while, in 2004, China's oil output is estimated approximately at 3.4 million barrels daily, accounting for the sixth ranking output volume globally.[53] If an even longer time span is used, between 1965 and 2004, according to Child, China's petroleum output expanded from 11.3 to 169.3 million tons (up by 1,400 per cent) while Saudi output expanded by 327 per cent.[54]

Given the importance of the Middle Eastern and Gulf region to China, the two regions may likely witness an expansion in ties, including energy relations. According to Mikkal Herberg, China's interactions with the Arabian Gulf and the Middle East is likely to expand as the Gulf states themselves increase relations with Asia (including China) where oil exports will increase, up from the two-thirds of the Gulf's current flow.[55]

According to Herberg, even for non-oil fossil fuels like LNG, China may derive some of its stock from Oceania and South-East Asia but will continue to depend on the expansion of its Gulf supply, including suppliers like Qatar, Oman and probably Yemen.[56] In terms of gas reserves, the Middle East remains the main supplier with 40.5 per cent of the estimates and Russia accounts for 26.3 per cent.[57]

There may be some possible non-Middle Eastern, non-Gulf fossil fuel alternative sources under consideration by Chinese consumers and likely others in the region. One example is the oil sands (such as those found in Alberta, Canada, which produced about 3 million barrels daily in 2005) where the cost of extraction (of oil from sand) is approximately US$12 per barrel (2005 price) compared to around US$4 per barrel (2005 price) for crude extraction in the Middle East and thus, oil sands may be considered viable and/or profitable if global oil prices are above US$12 per barrel.[58] Canada also appears to be a possible alternative source of crude oil for global consumption. According to Jiang Wenran's estimation, Canada's oil reserves ranks second at 176 billion barrels after Saudi Arabia and may be more quantitatively than some Gulf/Arab states.[59]

Despite alternative sources, Middle Eastern/Gulf crude oil and energy supply continues to be important. In 2007, Cociancich and Parenti point out that the energy relationship between the Gulf suppliers and East Asian states (with China at the top of the ranking) has expanded above the extent projected by International Energy Agency's 2002 study until the year 2030. Cociancich and Parenti argue that one strategy for China may be to look at Saudi Arabia as a major source of oil given its comparatively prolific output while, in the long run, building up strategic reserves and refineries and seeking treaties with other energy suppliers.[60]

Therefore, for the foreseeable future at least, collective insurance of peace and stability may be an important policy for secured energy supplies. Even the state pronouncement from the Information Office of the State Council of the People's Republic of China appears to officially indicate this as it says that 'the international community should work collaboratively to maintain stability in oil producing and exporting countries, especially those in the Middle East, to ensure the security of international energy transport routes and avoid geopolitical conflicts that affect the world's energy supply.'[61]

According to Zha's interpretation, China shares a vested interested in maintaining the political and economic stability of the Arabian Gulf with the US and other major powers for stable energy supply (a main Chinese priority), even if it means a pre-eminent US security position in the region.[62] China appears to rely on the US and its alliances for stability and flow of energy resources from the Middle East. According to Zha's interpretation, China itself maintains what Zha perceives as a policy that tries to strike a balance between different factional interests in Middle Eastern conflict to minimize political tensions disruptive to energy supply from that region.[63]

Not all agree with this view as they see a potential clash of interests. Some private sector competition may be inevitable. According to John Keefer Douglas, Matthew B. Nelson, and Kevin L. Schwartz, China's state energy firms (CNPC (Petrochina), China Petrochemical Corp (Sinopec), and China National Offshore Oil Corp (CNOOC)) have sunk their finances into the Middle East while in 2004, Sinopec competed with many US energy companies to access an oilfield development project in Saudi Arabia while partnering in 2007 with another rising power India to purchase a sizeable portion of Syria's oilfields.[64]

Regardless of the various interpretations of the situation, it appears to serve the collective interests if there is more cooperation and collaboration than conflicts. One possible interpretation of Gulf relations with other major powers may be detected in a 2007 example. In 2007, Prince Turki Al-Faisal, Saudi Ambassador to the US in 2007, was interviewed by the American media and clarified that the Kingdom did not prioritize friendships with US and China over one another and did not see one as a buffer against the other (China over the US, for example).[65]

Given the vintage and proven record of US participation and involvement in the Middle Eastern/Gulf region, the US remains the principal entity in the region where it enjoys long-entrenched alliances, partnerships and other forms of arrangements. In addition, there is no existing coherent, coordinated Arab policy towards relations with China or any other Asian countries.[66]

Indeed one Arab perception notes that China consciously considers itself a regional entity/player rather than a global one like the US and these perceptions also note that Chinese interests tended to be predominantly economic rather than political,[67] unlike American wide-ranging interests, which along with other Western economies, are able to provide advanced technological offerings as well as education, health and training[68] capacity-building items. The US consequently remains the most globalized and institutionalized source of relationship in that respect and has shared interests with all major powers.

This appears to be the point advocated by Richard Hu. He argues that, given the reliance that both China and the US have on oil flow from the Gulf, there are shared incentives to maintain Middle Eastern oil production and export.[69] Ever since China started importation of Gulf oil from Oman in 1983, according to Hu there has been no major US effort to thwart this crude oil supply and, consequently, China has indirectly benefited from what was made possible by the US and its allies, and therefore it is not in the interests of any of the two (US or China) or other major powers to upset this balance.[70]

Hu highlights the economic interdependence among non-state actors like major energy multinationals in extracting and transporting Gulf crude oil globally, due to the close coordination needs for various components of the supply chain through which energy resources are able to reach their consumer markets, and such mutual reliance applies to state-owned enterprises (SOEs) as well.[71]

9 ADDRESSING THE UAE NATURAL GAS CRISIS: STRATEGIES FOR A RATIONAL ENERGY POLICY[1]

Introduction

Although it seems inconceivable, the UAE is facing an enormous energy shortage. Much of the world views the UAE – and the rest of the Gulf countries by extension – as an inexhaustible reserve of hydrocarbons. However, as with many of the other Gulf countries, the UAE confronts a potentially far-reaching energy crisis. Despite increased energy production and imported Qatari gas through the Dolphin natural gas pipeline, UAE domestic gas demand substantially exceeds available supply.[2] This disparity created a shortfall met by an increasing use of fuel oil, natural gas liquids, and in certain circumstances, coal. But it is natural gas that continues to be the UAE's most important domestic energy source.

This chapter explains the origins of the UAE energy crisis, forecasts developments for 2010–20, and posits recommendations for overall sector rationalization. If Emirati authorities take a proactive stance and address the structural elements of the natural gas shortage, the more extreme elements of the crisis would be mitigated without lasting damage to Emirati economic growth. As the UAE has prodigious natural gas reserves, slight modification of the natural gas pricing and the power sector tariff structures would be able to resolve the most serious issues facing the UAE in its drive towards industrialization and diversification.

Overview of the Emirati Gas and Power Shortage

The UAE has massive natural gas reserves. After the Russian Federation, Iran, Qatar, and Saudi Arabia, the UAE holds the fifth largest proven gas reserves in the world, namely 3.5 per cent of the total global reserves. Estimated at 6.43 trillion cubic meters (tcm) at the end of 2009, Emirati reserves should last another eighty-five years at 2009 rates of production.[3] The bulk of Emirati gas is located in the capital of the UAE, the Emirate of Abu Dhabi, which holds approximately 5.62 tcm of the UAE's total reserves, or more than 90 per cent of Emirati gas (see Table 9.1).

Table 9.1 UAE gas reserves (2009)

	tcm	Share of total (per cent)
Abu Dhabi	5.98	92.58
Dubai	0.11 (113 bcm)	1.87
Sharjah	0.303 (303 bcm)	4.99
Ras Al Khaimah	0.03 (34 bcm)	0.56
Ajman	---	0
Umm Al Quwain	0.01 (14.16 bcm)	0
Fujairah	---	0
Total	6.43	100

The Emirate of Dubai holds 2 per cent respectively (113.3 Billion cubic meters (bcm)), while the emirates of Sharjah[4] and Ras al-Khaima contain the remaining amounts of 303 bcm and 34 bcm, respectively.[5] Because the gas fields in those two emirates have matured, their respective production rates have fallen in recent years. The UAE produced 48.8 bcm of natural gas in 2009, or 1.6 per cent of global natural gas production for that year.[6] However, it consumed 59.1 bcm that same year, resulting in a shortfall of 10.3 bcm.[7] Because the UAE is almost totally reliant on natural gas for power generation, its total gas consumption is expected to reach 107.5 bcm per year by 2020 (see Table 2). Its gas demand has steadily outstripped incremental production increases since late 2006 (see Figure 9.1).

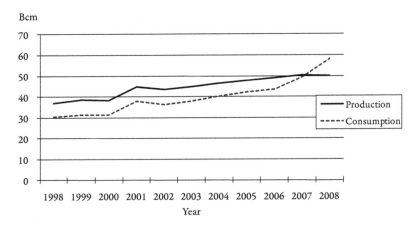

Figure 9.1 UAE natural gas production and consumption
Source: BP, 'Natural Gas: Production/Consumption', BP Statistical Review of World Energy (June 2009), pp. 24, 27.

One reason Emirati natural gas demand is so high is because of the dispropor-
tionate role it plays in power generation: it accounts for 98 per cent, with fuel oil
comprising the rest.[8] Additionally, the UAE's rapid economic and demographic
growth caused it to have the second highest consumption rate in absolute terms,
after Saudi Arabia, among members of the Organization of Arab Petroleum
Exporting Countries (OAPEC).[9] In 2010, the UAE National Human Resources
Development and Employment Authority (Tanmia) announced that the UAE
population doubles approximately every 8.7 years – largely due to expatriate
labour – as opposed to every fifty-five years for the world's population.[10] In 2010,
the population reached 8.19 million and was continuing to grow at a robust
rate; despite the global economic crisis. This population growth will increase the
demand pressures on scarce natural gas reserves.[11]

During 2009, the UAE imported, through the Dolphin natural gas pipeline, 17.25 bcm (approximately 47.3 million cubic meters per day) of natural gas
from Qatar.[12] It exported 7.01 bcm of natural gas in the form of LNG that same
year.[13] Because much of the UAE's gas is either associated with oil reservoirs or
is sour (i.e. sulphurous) gas in non-associated fields, it has focused on increasing
production capacity primarily by advancing its technical expertise on sour gas
treatment technology, as well as developing oil and gas separation technology.
The production limits attached to OPEC's quota system make future UAE gas
production difficult to predict, since associated gas production is determined by
oil output and thereby dependent on the global economy's health.[14]

The UAE's energy situation has interrupted the government's industrialization, modernization, and environmental conservation plans. Before the
Dolphin gas imports came online in 2007, it appeared that the UAE was head-
ing for an economic implosion, as it was not able to meet its basic energy and
power requirements. Rolling blackouts had spread through the various Emirates,
and gas shortages, having a decisive impact on power production, had precipi-
tated major project delays and cancellations.[15] To mitigate the economic fallout
of this crisis, the UAE undertook several innovative approaches, ranging from
the promotion of nuclear energy to organizing energy conservation campaigns.
However, in the absence of a thorough review of the domestic gas and electricity tariff structures, many energy policy adjustments will only have a cosmetic
impact and ultimately leave the major structural problems unresolved.

However, officials at the Dubai Electricity and Water Authority (Dewa)
disputed the use of the term 'energy crisis', and instead contended that Dubai
did not experience any type of electricity shortage. They argued that Dewa fully
satisfied peak demand while still holding approximately 1,200 MW in reserve in
2009, a year of tremendous demand pressure. Other analysts conclude that the
main issue may not be a gas shortage by itself, but rather a distribution bottleneck
largely located in the Northern Emirates (Ajman, Fujairah, Ras al-Khaimah and

Umm al-Quwain).[16] These contentions are justifiably disputed, since they focus merely on meeting peak demand; however, they neglect the fact that fuel oil and coal – which in an Emirati context are much less economical fuels for electricity generation – were used to meet the significant repressed demand.[17]

Dubai and Abu-Dhabi were spared the brunt of the gas shortage because Dolphin imports enabled them to avoid consuming significant amounts of expensive fuel liquids. Yet, while these two emirates were able to escape crippling blackouts, the gas shortage was most glaring in the Northern Emirates. These Emirates were in the worst position, and had to burn fuel liquids even during off-peak demand.[18]

Dubai and Abu Dhabi will likely not have to grapple with blackouts prior to 2015. Despite the threat of runaway gas demand, Dolphin gas imports will spare the two emirates that fate. However, the less wealthy Northern Emirates will likely face continued blackouts. Dubai and Abu Dhabi have the financial resources to burn expensive fuel liquids and import LNG, while the Northern Emirates do not.

The situation in the Northern Emirates may be symptomatic of the fate that awaits the rest of the UAE if a rational gas development strategy is not pursued. Chronic and unrelenting energy shortages in Sharjah and the Northern Emirates have posed grave economic and ecological threats that heighten the urgency of the crisis. Substantial adverse economic consequences resulted from the twin challenges of persistent electricity shortages and the global recession. Furthermore, the Emirati real-estate market dried up as investors and banks stopped funding new development projects due to the lack of liquidity and the collapse of the housing market.[19]

Balancing Competing Needs: Solving the Emirati Gas Supply Crunch

Given the massive gas reserves in the UAE, it appears that the major gas deficit predicted by some to take place as early as 2017 is almost entirely self-inflicted.[20] Gas is supplied to the domestic market at close to the wellhead price of US$1 per million British thermal units (MMBTU). Artificially low domestic prices make gas import through the Dolphin pipeline a more attractive proposition for the UAE than developing the relatively expensive-to-produce domestic non-associated natural gas reserves. Selling North Field gas at US$1.30/MMBTU while international LNG prices range from US$6–10/MMBTU, Qatar incurs a significant opportunity cost that indirectly subsidizes the UAE's industrialization. Qatar initially agreed to such a low natural gas price to the UAE in a bid to buttress its political influence with its neighbour. However, as of late, Qatar has been much more concerned about its own budget, and securing the best price possible for its natural resources.

The Emirati government is extremely concerned that its prodigious natural gas reserves will be unable to provide for its future power needs. Even though the UAE has increased its electricity generating capacity by 24 per cent per annum over the last thirty years, this frenetic pace has not been sufficient.[21] On 20 April 2008, the Emirati government explicitly recognized the problem with the release of a white paper, entitled *Policy of the United Arab Emirates on the Evaluation and Potential Development of Peaceful Nuclear Energy*, outlining the national energy challenges. The white paper concluded that national annual peak demand for electricity is likely to rise to more than 40,000 MW by 2020, from the level of around 15,000 MW in 2010. This predicted increase portends a major threat to Emirati economic growth. To meet the expected power demand increase, the UAE has developed a plan to construct several nuclear power plants

The four 1,400 MW nuclear plants are planned to provide 25 per cent of the country's electricity demand by 2020. These four plants, to be built by a consortium led by Korea Electric Power Co (Kepco), have an estimated construction cost of US$20.4 billion.[22] As with the Abu Dhabi solar project, Shams 1, there are enormous subsidies involved with plant construction and nuclear power generation.[23] Nuclear power plants are notoriously expensive compared with gas-fired power plants (including the full production chain, from construction, enrichment and generation, to decommissioning, etc.).[24] However, while the financial burden will still be quite large, Emirati officials have allowed for financial risk allocation with the development of a Public–Private Partnership where Kepco is in charge of designing, building and operating the nuclear power plant.[25]

The primary impetus behind the UAE's plan to establish a civilian nuclear programme is the expected natural gas shortfall. Although the first nuclear plant is expected to come online by 2017, there will be an interregnum when the UAE will still be highly vulnerable to supply disruptions. Mohamed al-Hammadi, chief executive of the Emirates Nuclear Energy Corporation (ENEC), promised that more nuclear plants could be forthcoming if Emirati electricity demand continues to rise.[26]

A secondary consideration for the UAE in its nuclear drive is the conservation of its oil for export, as opposed to its inefficient use in power plants. By approximately 2018, if the nuclear plants come online as planned, the UAE could substantially increase its oil export volumes. By reliance on nuclear and other alternative energy sources for power generation, natural gas would also be conserved and made available to the petrochemical sector.

In an effort to diversify its energy imports, the UAE also seeks to develop linkages with energy-rich Central Asian countries. For example, it has shown interest in Turkmenistan's gas fields to supply its own needs.[27] Mubadala Development Company (Mubadala) joined ConocoPhillips Inc in a bid to develop Turkmen gas fields. The two companies are also planning to jointly drill in the Kazakh portion of the Caspian Sea in the third quarter of 2010. However, without a comprehensive gas swap agreement with Iran, going as far afield as Turkmenistan for natural gas would make little economic sense. Deliveries from Turkmenistan would be just as expensive as domestic UAE non-associated gas production, if not more.

Production and Demand Estimates 2015-20

Even though the global economic crisis weakened natural gas demand growth in the UAE, as the global economy seems poised to return to growth by 2012, it is likely that robust Emirati natural gas demand growth would return soon thereafter. The global economic recovery would also increase global oil demand, which in turn would cause OPEC to increase its production quotas to allow the UAE to drastically boost oil and associated gas production to somewhat meet any Emirati demand growth.[28] Even without global economic recovery, the broad infrastructure development projects planned in the UAE would still drive natural gas demand.[29] The global economic crisis was both an obstacle and a catalyst for sectoral evolution.

While there were significant liquidity challenges for natural gas companies because the international credit market dried up, one benefit was that the many energy project cancellations caused commodity (steel, aluminum, concrete, etc.) and construction costs to decline precipitously.[30] In the event that the global economic crisis deepens and spreads due to economic difficulties in the Eurozone, it is possible that the decline in UAE gas consumption from 2008 to 2009 of 0.4 bcm could drop further if European and global oil, steel and petrochemical demand weakens.[31]

While the massive governmental stimulus measures and infrastructure plans could be a major consumer of already scarce natural gas supplies, governmental funds could also be directed to natural gas development. In 2009, the UAE developed a comprehensive plan to pump nearly US$1 trillion into the Emirati economy, building roads, power plants, and the metro system.[32] However, it is extremely likely that Emirati gas demand only temporarily diminished during the peak of the global economic crisis of 2008–9. Natural gas demand growth may have the same unrestrained increase that typified the hydrocarbon 'boom' years of 2002–8, when natural gas demand grew by 20.2 bcm. It is estimated that Emirati natural gas demand will continue to grow at approximately 7 per cent per annum due to the expanding power and industrial sectors the increase in global oil demand, government investment in strategic industrial sectors, and the Emirati stimulus plans.[33]

Emirati associated gas production will likely remain constrained, at least until the predicted return to economic growth by 2012 or until OPEC loosens its strict oil production quotas for the UAE.[34] The Abu Dhabi National Oil Company's (ADNOC) stated strategy is to increase oil production by 14 per cent by 2014. Although it is uncertain what the OPEC quotas will be at that time, such an increase would boost associated gas production significantly.[35] However, non-associated natural gas production projects are expected to gradually come online from 2012 to 2016, especially from the smaller natural gas reserves in the Northern Emirates, as well as the Hail Gas and Integrated Gas Development projects. The exit of ConocoPhillips from the Shah field in May 2010 is likely to result in a two-year delay, with production starting up around 2016–17, under the most optimistic scenario. The UAE may have to contend with a precarious gas supply until 2014–15, with blackouts plaguing the Northern Emirates during peak summer months (May–August).

In the event that the UAE continues its robust industrialization drive over the next decade with a 7 per cent annual demand growth, the UAE is likely to face a severe gas shortfall in 2015 (see Table 9.2) despite additional non-associated gas production, Dolphin natural gas imports, and Shell/QatarGas LNG.[36] Even under the most optimistic scenario that the various domestic non-associated gas fields will come online as planned, there would still be a 29.4 bcm per year shortfall by 2020. If the UAE is able to utilize nitrogen or carbon for its enhanced oil recovery operations, that would liberate an approximate 18 bcm per year for domestic consumption. Furthermore, since 2007, the UAE has been developing a nascent carbon-trading platform, with the expectation of an eventual cap-and-trade system. However, the onset of the global financial crisis in 2008, combined with the lack of a binding global compact at the Copenhagen climate negotiations in 2009, decisively constrained its realization. Nevertheless, the development of a comprehensive Gulf carbon trading platform would have significant benefits for the UAE.

If a Gulf carbon-trading platform instituted a credible cap-and-trade system, the carbon caps would forge a type of Darwinian environment, forcing the energy-intensive industries to become more efficient.[37] The energy gains from binding carbon limitations would translate into enormous gains in the natural gas sector, as gas would be utilized more effectively in the industrial and retail sectors.

The above measures, in addition to demand-side energy efficiency and peak demand imports from regional suppliers, should be sufficient to allow the UAE a razor-thin margin to escape from crippling blackouts. If the nuclear plants do come online by 2018 (an extremely optimistic scenario), and the various energy efficiency and renewable energy projects are able to exert significant downward pressure on natural gas demand, the prognosis will not be as dire. Incorporating a robust gas sector rationalization plan would mitigate the future gas shortage. Nonetheless, the foregoing would have a significant impact in only the most optimistic scenarios.

Conclusions: The Way Forward

Between 2015 and 2020, the UAE will continue to import 18.61 bcm per year of Dolphin gas under the Phase One contract. Since this exceeds exports of LNG from the Abu Dhabi Gas Liquefaction Limited plant (ADGAS is a part of the ADNOC group of companies), the country is already a net gas importer. As discussed above, no additional long-term pipeline supply contracts are to be expected from Qatar (Phase Two Dolphin) without a significant reformulation of the pricing schedule. Even then, Qatar is unlikely to want to remain locked into an additional long-term pipeline gas export relationship. Much of Qatar's reluctance depends on whether there is a sustained downturn in the global economy and whether an abundance of global gas continues to depress international gas prices. Nonetheless, a scenario of a protracted downturn in natural gas prices could be the very development to push the UAE and Qatar into a mutually agreeable contract for additional long-term gas sales.

By 2015–16, natural gas production in the UAE is predicated to increase significantly, by an estimated 14.4 bcm per year when several non-associated fields start producing. But this increase will be accompanied by a significant increase in gas demand over the same period (see Table 9.2). In spite of the gas allocation issues, the UAE's state-owned companies are pressing ahead with diversification into petrochemicals, building additional plants that demand large quantities of gas. At the time of writing, Abu Dhabi has selected its state-owned petrochemical company National Chemicals (Chemaweyaat), to spearhead construction of a $20 billion industrial city christened, 'Madeenat Chemaweyaat Al Gharbia' or Western Chemical City. The focus of Western Chemical City is to diversify the Emirati economy away from its overwhelming reliance on oil production. However, the diversification into petrochemicals comes at a price, being increased natural gas feedstock allocated to the Emirati natural gas sector at a time of significant shortfalls.[38]

With such a large projected increase on its natural gas from the petrochemical sector, the UAE is researching the viability of using other types of feedstocks in the production process.[39]

It is likely during the forecast period that the UAE will still be in dire need of 'interruptible' gas supplies from Dolphin or additional LNG imports during the peak demand summer months, and perhaps significant imports during the off-peak season. If the UAE is successful in its quest to replace the massive amounts of natural gas for oilfield reinjection (18 bcm per year) with nitrogen or carbon, additional gas supplies should be liberated for domestic consumption in the industrial and retail sectors.

Table 9.2 UAE natural gas production and demand 2000–20 (bcm)

	Production	Demand
2000	38.4	31.4
2008	50.2	58.1
2015 (est.)	64.6	88.5
2020 (est.)	78.1	107.5

Gas import from Dolphin is likely to remain at its Phase One commitments of 18.61 bcm per year until the contract expires in 2032. The UAE's currently net import position is therefore expected to not only continue but increase over the next decade.

The Emirati strategy to increase its natural gas supply and reduce demand will likely be superficial unless power and natural gas prices are increased substantially. The ConocoPhillips withdrawal from the Shah sour gas project in 2010 is a harbinger of events to come unless structural pricing reform is undertaken. It is beyond the scope of this brief to consider the implications of the World Trade Organization's Agreement on Subsidies and Countervailing Measures (ASCM) on Emirati natural gas pricing reconfiguration, but Emirati authorities should explore the feasibility of adopting a dual pricing formula for the industrial and retail sectors. The retail sector contributes less to economic growth and modernization than the industrial sector does. Therefore, in terms of gas allocation, the industrial sector should be given preferential pricing, perhaps cost-plus, to encourage the development of the horizontal and vertical value-added industries such as petrochemicals, fertilizers, and steel and aluminium smelting. The retail sector should be brought as close as possible to market-based pricing to discourage overconsumption of the UAE's natural gas patrimony.

However, judging by the lack of political commitment for a comprehensive restructuring of the natural gas and power sector, it does not seem that the UAE will be able to effectively rationalize natural gas supply and allocation within the next decade. A fragmented natural gas and power policy focusing on the promotion of nuclear and renewable energy, gas imports, coal plant construction and energy efficiency measures, rather than full natural gas price liberalization, is the more likely scenario, at least until 2020.[40]

If the UAE desires to truly liberate itself from its natural gas impasse, it will need to proactively create a viable strategy for increasing natural gas production, while moderating demand for electricity. If the UAE does not undertake a comprehensive restructuring of its disjointed energy policy, it will face enormous challenges in the coming decades to its hitherto successful economic growth model. Furthermore, its role as an LNG exporter to North-East Asia and other markets could be severely undermined placing the viability of North-East Asia dependence on Emirati LNG exports in doubt.

10 CONCLUSION

Justin Dargin, Stephen Nagy and Lim Tai Wei

This volume remains a work in progress, given the complexity of the topic and evolving interrelationships between the two regions. Some of the major trends and developments discussed in the volume include: the importance of openness to trade and the ability for developing economies to benefit from it including poverty reduction; the importance of India's strategic position in trade and energy transmission between North-East Asia and the Middle East; GCC harmonization of energy production and minimization of redundancies in the power sector; Middle Eastern economies' interest in investing in future growth prospects in Asia; and increasing people-to-people contact between North-East Asia and the Middle East in various fields, such as in the field of education (tertiary education), cultural exchanges, art shows and exhibitions.

Overall, it appears that East Asian diversification away from reliance on Middle East crude oil may be accompanied by other interactions between economies within the two regions beyond mutual interests in energy. Trade in non-oil-related export goods and cross-investments in each other's economies may increase, leading perhaps to other economic and trade exchanges between the two regions.

This trend towards increased investments show that Gulf financial and investment interests in Asia are not restricted to large emerging economies like India and China, but that they also seek mature and established economies in North-East Asia, such as South Korea and Japan. These exchanges increase contact at the individual level. They take place according to market forces and happen in the normal course, with other non-East Asian partners such as persons within the US, EU and other regional economies within the Middle East. If open to all, these exchanges will benefit participants in the global economies and will benefit MNCs that have a global presence. Collaborative project sharing capital and technologies resources may benefit stakeholders, in accordance with market forces and economic complementarity. While the US does not have a physical presence in both regions, its presence and interests are interdependent with those of both areas. The US also plays an important balancing and tilting function. It balances between different interests in the regions within the inter-regional trade and also intermediates the inter-regional trade itself. Its tilting function is either sought or expected (directly or indirectly) by other entities in the region and the direction towards which the US tilts is crucial for any important initiatives and decision-making process to attain success. The US is also a generator of ideas, concepts and innovative thinking which is emulated or referenced by other entities in the inter-regional trade and Middle East/North-East Asian region. These ideas are then particularized, adapted to fit local conditions with modifications.

The other model of study in North-East Asia has been Japan. Ideas of ongoing infrastructural change for a mature economy, models of emulation for developing states, options and discussions of energy diversification, and instances of events requiring the energy cooperation and collaboration of regional stakeholders can all be detected in Japan in the wake of the 11 March 2011 earthquake, tsunami and nuclear incident in the Tohoku region of Japan. Nuclear technologies remain a possible priority for oil-dependent nations in North-East Asia, although in the short and medium term, this aspect may be slowed down or mitigated by the nuclear accident at the Fukushima nuclear plant in Japan as countries reassess their dependence on nuclear energy. The main challenge may be on to minimize the risk factor.

Neighbouring Asian countries and the world witnessed a plethora of graphic images of the death and destruction that took place in the areas that were immediately affected by the earthquake. Media outlets from around the world showed images of homes, cars and buildings being swept through seaside villages. They showed the post-tsunami devastation of whole villages being swept out to sea with no bodies to recover and no one to claim their missing family members. The bare, grey landscape was reminiscent of the black and white images which depicted the aftermath of the atomic bombing of Hiroshima and Nagasaki in 1945. In contrast to the images and video feeds of the destruction and death, the media also showed images of stoic Japanese citizens lining up in queues to get food and water; they also noticed that there was an absence of crime and looting.

Although not a perfect response to the unprecedented disaster, the Japanese government successfully evacuated Japanese residents from the affected region within days of the disaster. Furthermore, they provided shelter, blankets, and food and water for the victims. They also opened their doors to international aid from neighbouring countries such as China, South Korea, Russia as well as their traditional ally, the United States. The response was a stark contrast when comparing the 1995 Kobe disaster response when rescue dogs from overseas where quarantined instead of being used for searching for survivors. Collectively, the images conveyed to us through television and on the internet have demonstrated to viewers both the tremendous destruction brought to Japan but also the deep reservoir of resources that Japan has. In order for interdependency to work, continued engagement by all major participants in Asia may be essential, including the US as well as Asian economies such as the Gulf states, Japan, China and India. Interdependency requires proactive and intricate coordination by all these parties and a cooperative climate that elicits collaboration and exchange.

With this in context, what the concluding chapter of the book argues is that Japan's post-disaster response, although not without problems demonstrated a different kind of soft power and rallying point for the region and the world, in the sense of *behavioural power*. In particular, the post-disaster response enhanced Japan's attraction in the region as a nation that was efficient, well organized and orderly (disciplined) and that could maintain a semblance of social cohesion and civility despite being significantly burdened by the natural disaster that occurred. It is this soft power that may represent the next phase of emulation and source of study by other emerging and developing economies, including those in North-East Asia and the Middle East. The values are not absorbed and taken wholesale by stakeholder entities in both regions. Instead, they are localized, adapted, adjusted and assimilated selectively to fit local and regional conditions according to their national interests and domestic priorities.

Japan's post-disaster management demonstrated to nations in the region and around the world that the Japanese and their government displayed behaviour that saved lives and prevented a large-scale humanitarian crisis through behavioural power which comprises of behavioural norms, organizational skills and planning. For observing nations such as China, another Asian country plagued by frequent natural disasters, watching how the ordinary Japanese citizen and local governments have responded to this unprecedented disaster has been not only an exceptional demonstration of Japan's disaster preparation but also a salient demonstration of Japan's exceptional ability to remain an orderly society even in the most desperate of situations. There has been no reported crime or looting, no mass panic and none of the chaos that we have seen in recent disasters in other parts of the world.

Japan's post-disaster responses demonstrated how good, detailed planning can limit damage, how a transparent-legal system can create the circumstance in which building codes are met, how societies can be organized through training to prevent the worst. The images displayed on television screens and newspapers following the disaster displayed powerful and meaningful images. Onlookers saw the Japanese government and Japanese people response to the earthquake in an orderly, cohesive manner. General Secretary Edano gave hourly updates on the progress of the recovery; Prime Minister Kan similarly was engaging with the media and reaching out to political friend and foe alike. It is this aspect that lends support to the possibility of regionalism in North-East Asia as long as external stakeholders are involved and given access to initiatives and cooperation.

In exploring the issue of the possibility of regionalism in North-East Asia, the Japanese ruling party also accepted the international aid of other countries and regions. We saw China immediately offer 20,000 tons of fuel and supplies as well as expertise and advice. Importantly, this generosity has not been limited to the state but also local and provincial municipalities, individual citizens and China's Red Cross. This reciprocates Japanese generosity and past aid following devastating earthquakes in China. It is illustrative of the will, capacity and crucial ability to cooperate despite tensions in other aspects of their relationship. The United States sent two aircraft carriers, groups to the region to help transport supplies and offered technical assistance. South Korea offered aid in the form of fuel, supplies and expertise as well.

At the citizen level, we saw no looting or chaos. Ordinary citizens reacted in orderly ways that are in part related to culture, preparedness and level of development, including technology. Japan is a nation that is plagued by natural disasters. Understanding its precarious position vis-a-vis nature, Japan has systematically inculcated educational awareness and training into many aspects of Japanese life. Companies, universities, schools and the public sector are all required to conduct earthquake training drills, ensure that a minimal amount of survival equipment is available for employees and students. Preparedness requires close cooperation with the community, police and local leaders to design and implement appropriate responses to disasters. Judging by the number of individuals directly killed because of the 9.0 magnitude earthquake on 11 March, and its subsequent aftershocks, one could conclude that Japan was successful in dealing with the immediate aftermath of the earthquake. They were also able to provide supplies to effected individuals and evacuate over 200,000 people to evacuation zones. In this case, preparedness limited the loss of life and permitted a relatively quick response to the unfolding events.

In the post-earthquake/tsunami (3 March 2011, Japan) energy world of North-East Asia, the following future trends are worth watching: Middle Eastern economies themselves are now increasingly reliant on energy for their growing population and manufacturing capabilities; attempts by North-East Asia and India to mitigate the use of oil and increase reliance on natural gas from the Middle East; Asian partnership with Western and Japanese firms for environmentally friendly and green technologies; outcomes of investments in energy-saving technologies and automobiles which may in turn signal lower demand for OPEC oil; the development of alternative energy sources as a means for lessening reliance on the Middle East in terms of North-East Asian energy consumers; the utilization of Russian energy resources; contradictions of development centring upon the ability to feed populations of developing areas, keeping them employed, locating enough resources for them to utilize; Gulf economies as an important model for others in the Middle East.

There may be new emerging areas for collaboration and cooperation in sectors of mutual interests to both East Asian and Middle Eastern economies. For example, the future may hold possible collaboration, trade or exchanges in green technologies that may be of interest to both East Asia and the Middle East in the near future, if not now. Because East Asia industrialized and manufactured products for the world, rapid economic development impacted the environment and raised questions of sustainability, and natural resource use. Middle Eastern economies, including those in the Gulf that have been developing rapidly, may see the middle classes clamor for higher standards of living and quality of life. Energy-efficient and environmentally friendly technologies developed in resource-scarce North-East Asia may be useful for technological transfers to the Middle East.[1]

NOTES

1 Introduction

1. G. Kemp, *The East Moves West: India, China and Asia's Growing Presence in the Middle East* (Washington, DC: Brookings Institution, 2010), pp. 3–4, note the quote on p. 6 by Kemp: 'The scale of the Asian powers' involvement in the Middle East can be measured in multiple ways, including by the amount of energy flowing east to Asian markets, the value of Asian exports to the middle East, financial investment by Asian firms in the Middle East and by Middle Eastern firms in Asia, the number of tourists travelling in both directions, and the number of Middle Easterners enrolling for higher education in key Asian countries.'; B. Simpfendorfer, *The New Silk Road: How a Rising Arab World Is Turning Away from the West and Rediscovering China* (Basingstoke: Palgrave MacMillan, 2009), pp. 28–75 (pp. 1–6 also frames the observation for the publication in a multidimensional view of inter-regional trade between the Middle East and Northeast Asian entities); C. M. Davidson, *The Persian Gulf and Pacific Asia: From Indifference to Interdependence* (New York: Columbia University Press, 2010), note the quote by Davidson on p. 1: 'As this book will demonstrate, the powerful and multidimensional connections that are being forged by the very eastern and western extremities of the continent are posed to become a central pillar of this process'.

2. R. C. Mohan, 'India and the Asian Security Architecture', in M. J. Green and B. Gills (eds), *Asia's New Multilateralism: Cooperation, Competition and the Search for Community* (New York: Columbia University Press, 2009), pp. 128–53, on p. 141.

3. G. Rozman, *Northeast Asia's Stunted Regionalism: Bilateral Distrust in the Shadow of Globalization* (New York and Cambridge: Cambridge University Press, 2004), p. 3.

4. C. M. Dent, 'The International Political Economy of Northeast Asian Economic Integration', in C. M. Dent and D. W. F. Huang (eds), *Northeast Asian Regionalism: Learning from the European Experience* (London: RoutledgeCurzon, 2002), pp. 65–95, on p. 79.

5. S. V. R. Nasr, *Meccanomics: The March of the New Muslim Middle Class* (Oxford: Oneworld, 2010), p. 15.

6. D. Rothkopf, *Superclass: The Global Power Elite and the World They are Making* (New York: Farrar, Straus and Giroux, 2008), p. 136.

7. Pioneered by Peregrine Worsthorne and then adopted by contemporary commentators like Amy Chua to described dominant powers with overwhelming strength in multiple sectors.

8. H. J. Wiarda (ed.), *Non-Western Theories of Development: Regional Norms versus Global Trends* (Fort Worth, TX: Harcourt Brace College Publishers, 1999).

9. V. Smil, *Energy in Nature and Society: General Energetics of Complex Systems* (London and Cambridge, MA: The MIT Press, 2008), p. 376.

10. L. Margonelli, *Oil on the Brain: Petroleum's Long, Strange Trip to Your Tank* (New York: Broadway Books, 2008), pp. 62–3.

11. Ibid., p. 265.

12. Ibid., p. 136.

13. J. Hofmeister, *Why We Hate the Oil Companies: Straight Talk from an Energy Insider* (New York: Palgrave Macmillan, 2010), p. 71.

14. Margonelli, *Oil on the Brain*, p. 265.

15. P. Roberts, *The End of Oil: On the Edge of a Perilous New World* (Boston, MA and New York: Houghton Mifflin, 2005), p. 257.

16. D. L. Goodstein, *Out of Gas: The End of the Age of Oil* (New York and London: WW Norton and Company, 2004), p. 35.

17. G. Heal, 'Are Oil Producers Rich?', in M. Humphreys, J. D. Sachs and J. E. Stiglitz (eds), *Escaping the Resource Curse* (New York: Columbia University Press, 2007), pp. 155–72, on p. 156.

18. Roberts, *The End of Oil*, p. 103.

19. Ibid., p. 8.

20. A. Morita, *Made in Japan: Akio Morita and Sony* (London: HarperCollins Business, 1994), p. 54.

21. S. D. King, *Losing Control: The Emerging Threats to Western Prosperity* (New Haven, CT: Yale University Press, 2010), p. 164.

22. V. I. Ivanov, 'Russian Crisis: Will Northeast Asia Links Help?', in T. Akaha (ed.), *Politics and Economics in Northeast Asia: Nationalism and Regionalism in Contention* (New York: St Martin's Press, 1999), pp. 227–46, on p. 241.

23. King, *Losing Control*, p. 163.

24. H. Nakanishi, 'Overcoming the Crises: Japanese Diplomacy in the 1970s', in M. Iokibe (ed.), *The Diplomatic History of Postwar Japan, Winner of the 1999 Yoshida Shigeru Prize*, trans. R. D. Eldrige (Abingdon: Routledge, 2009), pp. 108–43, on pp. 123–24.

25. Roberts, *The End of Oil*, p. 117.

26. Margonelli, *Oil on the Brain*, p. 265.

27. According to the International Monetary Fund (IMF), 'SWFs are defined as special purpose investment funds or arrangements, owned by the general government', see S. Willson, 'Wealth Funds Group Publishes 24-Point Voluntary Principles', *IMF Survey Online*, 15 October 2008, at http://www.imf.org/external/pubs/ft/survey/so/2008/new101508b.htm [accessed 24 June 2011].

28. J. Dargin, 'Trouble in Paradise – The Widening Gulf Gas Deficit', *Middle East Economic Survey*, 29 September 2008.

29. Ibid.

30. J. Dargin, 'Lights Out in the Gulf', *Alexander's Gas and Oil Connections*, 13:21 (2008), at http://www.gasandoil.com/goc/news/ntm84847.htm [accessed 1 January 2010].

31. Dargin, 'Trouble in Paradise'.

32. J. Dargin, *The Dolphin Project: The Development of a Gulf Gas Initiative* (Oxford: Oxford Institute for Energy Studies Press, January 2008).

33. Dargin, 'Lights Out in the Gulf'.

34. Dargin, 'Trouble in Paradise'.

35. Ibid.

36. J. Dargin, 'The Islamization of Project Finance in the Gulf', *Oil and Gas Financial Journal*, 6:2 (2009), at http://belfercenter.ksg.harvard.edu/files/xstandard/Islamic%20 Finance%20Dargin.pdf [accessed 24 June 2011].

37. H. Caldicott, *If You Love This Planet: A Plan to Heal the Earth*, rev. and updated edn (New York and London: WW Norton, 2009), p. 104.

38. B. Cumings, *Korea's Place in the Sun: A Modern History* (New York: WW Norton, 1997).

39. K. Armstrong, G. Rozman, S. S. Kim and S. Kotkin (eds), *Korea at the Center: Dynamics of Regionalism in Northeast Asia* (Armonk, NY: ME Sharpe, 2006).

2 Progress and Development

1. B. Meng and S. Inomata, 'Production Networks and Spatial Economic Interdependence: An International Input-Output Analysis of the Asia Pacific Region', *Institute of Developing Economies Discussion Paper*, 185 (March 2009), at https://ir.ide.go.jp/dspace/bitstream/2344/818/1/ARRIDE_Discussion_no.185_BoMENG.pdf [accessed 3 January 2011], p. 1.

2. A. Vespignani, 'The Fragility of Interdependency', *Nature: News & Views*, 464 (15 April 2010), at http://polymer.bu.edu/hes/articles/nv-vespignani10.pdf [accessed 3 January 2011], p. 984.

3. A. Aydin, 'Choosing Sides: Economic Interdependence and Interstate Disputes', *Journal of Politics*, 70:4 (October 2008), pp. 1098–108, on p. 1098.

4. J. Smith, N. Clark and K. Yusoff, 'Interdependence', *Geography Compass*, 1:3 (May 2007), pp. 340–59, on p. 340.

5. Ibid.

6. Readers may wish to refer to: S. P. Huntington, *Political Order in Changing Societies* (New Haven, CT: Yale University Press, 1968) and/or W. W. Rostow, *The Stages of Economic Growth: A Non-Communist Manifesto* (Cambridge: Cambridge University Press, 1960) among other references.

7. W. Zapf, 'Modernization Theory – and the Non-Western World', Paper presented to the conference 'Comparing Processes of Modernization', University of Potsdam, 15–21 December 2003, Wissenschaftszentrum Berlin für Sozialforschung (WZB), Beim Präsidenten, Emeriti Projekte, Best.-Nr. P 2004-003, June 2004, at http://bibliothek.wz-berlin.de/pdf/2004/p04-003.pdf [accessed 13 January 2011], p. 8.

8. P. Johannessen, 'Beyond Modernization Theory: Democracy and Development in Latin America', (Outstanding Senior Honors Thesis, Pi Sigma Alpha, the National Political Science Honor Society in the US, the University of Vermont, 2009), at http://www.uvm.edu/~polisci/Johannessen_Thesis-2009.pdf [accessed 13 January 2011], p. 7.

9. A. Gould, 'Resisting Postmodernity: Swedish Social Policy in the 1990s', *Social Work & Society: Series on European Services in Transition (I)*, 3:1 (2005), pp. 72–84, at http://www.socwork.net/2005/1/articles/473/Gould2005.pdf [accessed 13 January 2011], on p. 73

10. B. Nicol, 'Introduction: Postmodernism and Postmodernity' in *The Cambridge Introduction to Postmodern Fiction* (Cambridge: Cambridge University Press, 2009), p. 2.

11. Ibid., p. 3.

12. P. Verdoux, 'Transhumanism, Progress and the Future', *Journal of Evolution and Technology*, 20:2 (December 2009), pp. 49–69, on p. 49.

13. For further reading, see J. A. Schumpeter, *Business Cycles: A Theoretical, Historical, and Statistical Analysis of the Capitalist Process* (New York, London: McGraw-Hill, 1964); I. Wallerstein, *The Modern World-System: Capitalist Agriculture and the Origins of the European World-economy in the Sixteenth Century* (New York: Academic Press, 1974); T. K. Hopkins, I. Wallerstein, R. L. Bach, C. Chase-Dunn and R. Mukherjee, *World-Systems Analysis: Theory and Methodology* (Beverly Hills, CA: Sage, 1982).

14. T. P. Soubbotina, 'What is Development?', *Beyond Economic Growth: An Introduction to Sustainable Development, Second Edition* (Washington, DC: the World Bank, 2004), at http://www.worldbank.org/depweb/english/beyond/beyondco/beg_all.pdf [accessed 3 June 2011], pp. 7–11, on pp. 7–8.

15. International Institute for Sustainable Development (IISD), 'Business Strategies for Sustainable Development', at http://www.iisd.org/business/pdf/business_strategy.pdf [accessed 24 January 2011]. This article is based on the book *Business Strategy for Sustainable Development: Leadership and Accountability for the '90s* (Winnipeg: IISD, jointly with Deloitte and Touche and the World Business Council for Sustainable Development, 1992).

16. UN Millennium Project, *Innovation: Applying Knowledge in Development* (UN: Task Force on Science, Technology, and Innovation, 2005), p. iii.

17. United Nations Environment Programme (UNEP)'s developmental initiatives in former areas of conflict can be found in the publication: UNEP, *From Conflict to Sustainable Development: Assessment and Clean-up in Serbia and Montenegro* (Switzerland: UNEP, 2004).

18. R. W. Kates, T. M. Parris and A. A. Leiserowitz, 'What is Sustainable Development', *Environment: Science and Policy for Sustainable Development*, 47:3 (April 2005), pp. 8–21, on pp. 14–15.

19. Ibid., pp. 10–11.

20. Y. Eghbalnia, 'Natural Resource Curse: Special Experience of the Persian Gulf States', Munich Personal RePEc Archive Paper No. 22325, 30 July 2006, at http://mpra.ub.uni-muenchen.de/22325/1/MPRA_paper_22325.pdf [accessed 24 January 2011].

21. Ibid., pp. 13, 14, 18.

22. For more on this aspect, a possible reference: G. D. Aharonovitz, 'Development and the Increasing Prices of Natural Resources: Have You Missed the Last Boat to Sustained Growth?', Washington State University, School of Economic Sciences, April 2008, at http://www.ses.wsu.edu/people/Aharonovitz/nr_prices_dev_2.pdf [accessed 24 January 2011].

23. M. Suzuki, 'Realization of a Sustainable Society – Zero-Emission Approaches', Introductory Articles, Zero Emissions Forum, United Nations University, at http://archive.unu.edu/zef/publications_e/suzuki_intro_ZE.pdf [accessed 10 June 2011].

24. National Science Foundation (NSF), Division of Science Resources Statistics, *Asia's Rising Science and Technology Strength: Comparative Indicators for Asia, the European Union, and the United States*, NSF 07-319 (Arlington, VA: NSF, 2007).

25. R. C. Levin, 'Speeches & Statements: The Rise of Asia's Universities', Yale Office of Public Affairs & Communications, 1 February 2010, at http://opa.yale.edu/president/message.aspx?id=91 [accessed 22 December 2010].

26. Ibid.

27. B. D. Romulo, 'Asia's Rising Middle Class', *Manila Bulletin*, 29 September 2010, at http://www.mb.com.ph/node/279682/a [accessed 22 December 2010].

28. P. McCulley and R. Toloui, 'Asia Rising', *Time*, 13 September 2007, at http://www.time.com/time/magazine/article/0,9171,1661477,00.html [accessed 22 December 2010].

29. World Economic Forum (WEF), 'EU Commissioner Mandelson Urges Europe to Look at a Rising Asia as an Opportunity, Not a Threat', 29 April 2005, at http://www2.weforum.org/en/media/Latest%20Press%20Releases/PRESSRELEASES139.html [accessed 22 December 2010].

30. Finfacts Team, 'Asia's Rising "Clean Technology Tigers" – China, Japan, and South Korea – to Overtake United States', *Finfacts Ireland Business & Personal Finance Portal*, 20 November 2009, at http://www.finfacts.ie/irishfinancenews/article_1018490.shtml [accessed 22 December 2010].

31. S. Silverthorne, 'The Rise of Innovation in Asia', Harvard Business School Working Knowledge, 7 March 2005, at http://hbswk.hbs.edu/item/4676.html [accessed 22 December 2010].

32. R. S. Anderson, 'Asia: Important to All of Us', *Phi Delta Kappan – Problems and Promises of Education in Asia*, 39:3 (December 1957), pp. 81–3.

33. Shorenstein APARC, 'No One Can Now Ignore or Overlook the Importance of Asia, Says APARC Director Dr. Gi-Wook Shin', Korean Studies Program (KSP) News, Freeman Spogli Institute for International Studies at Stanford University, 19 July 2010, at http://fsi.stanford.edu/news/no_one_can_now_ignore_or_overlook_the_importance_of_asia_says_aparc_director_dr_giwook_shin_20100719/ [accessed 22 December 2010].

34. M. Majid, 'The Big Idea: US Diplomacy in Rising Asia: Through the Glass Darkly', *IDEAS Today – Deals, Denials and Declassification: Israeli-South African Nuclear Collaboration*, 5 (The London School of Economics and Political Science (LSE), September 2010), at http://www2.lse.ac.uk/IDEAS/publications/ideasToday/05/majid.pdf [accessed 22 December 2010], pp. 4–6.

35. C. Martin, 'Crafting a US Response to the Emerging East Asia Free Trade Area', *Whitehead Journal of Diplomacy and International Relations*, 8:2 (Summer/Fall 2007), pp. 73–84.

36. F. S. T. Hsiao, M. W. Hsiao and A. Yamashita, 'The Impact of the US Economy on the Asia-Pacific Region: Does It Matter?', *Journal of Asian Economics*, 14:2 (April 2003), pp. 219–41.

37. S. Kaufman, 'Obama's Trip Underscores Asia's Importance', US Department of State's Bureau of International Information Programs, 29 October 2010, at http://www.america.gov/st/peacesec-english/2010/October/20101029142757nehpets5.151629e-04.html?CP.rss=true [accessed 22 December 2010].

38. The National Bureau of Asian Research, 'Emerging Leaders in East Asia', *National Bureau of Asian Research Project Notes* (May 2008), at http://www.nbr.org/downloads/pdfs/PSA/EL_PN_May08.pdf [accessed 22 December 2010].

39. M. Noland, 'United States Economic Policy toward Asia', *East-West Center Working Papers*, 103 (June 2009), at http://www.eastwestcenter.org/fileadmin/stored/pdfs/econwp103.pdf [accessed 22 December 2010], p. 1.

40. M. Schuman, 'What Asia Can Really Teach America', *Time*, 4 February 2010, at http://www.time.com/time/business/article/0,8599,1959065,00.html [accessed 22 December 2010].

41. L. H. Summers, 'The U.S.-India Economic Relationship in the 21st Century: Remarks to the U.S.-India Business Council', US Government National Economic Council, 2

June 2010, at http://www.whitehouse.gov/administration/eop/nec/speeches/us-india-economic-relationship [accessed 22 December 2010].

42. Ibid.

43. W. H. Cooper, 'US-Japan Economic Relations: Significance, Prospects, and Policy Options', *Congressional Research Service Report for Congress* (2007), at http://www.fas.org/sgp/crs/row/RL32649.pdf [accessed 22 December 2010], unpaginated Summary.

44. A. E. Kornblut and B. Harden, 'In Japan, Obama Stresses Asia's Role in U.S. Economy', *Washington Post*, 14 November 2009, at http://www.washingtonpost.com/wp-dyn/content/article/2009/11/13/AR2009111304272.html [accessed 22 December 2010].

45. M. Brahmbhatt and L. Christiaensen, 'Rising Food Prices in East Asia: Challenges and Policy Options', Faculty of Economics, Thammasat University, May 2008, at http://econ.tu.ac.th/archan/rangsun/ec%20460/ec%20460%20readings/global%20issues/Food%20Crisis/Policy%20Issues/Rising%20Food%20Price%20in%20East%20Asia-%20Challenges%20and%20Policy.pdf [accessed 22 December 2010].

46. International Monetary Fund (IMF), 'Asia in the World Economy Asia's Importance Growing in Global Economy', *IMF Survey Online*, 12 May 2010, at http://www.imf.org/external/pubs/ft/survey/so/2010/car051210a.htm [accessed 22 December 2010].

47. A. Bull and S. Desai, 'U.S. Britain Press G8 to Help Poor Nations', *Reuters*, 26 June 2010, at http://in.reuters.com/article/2010/06/25/idINIndia-49637420100625 [accessed 15 August 2010].

48. M. Nissanke and E. Thorbecke, 'Linking Globalization to Poverty in Asia, Latin America and Africa', *United Nations University WIDER Policy Brief*, 3 (2010), at http://www.wider.unu.edu/publications/policy-briefs/en_GB/unupb3-2010/_files/83351175411204184/default/Policy%20Brief%20no%203%202010-Web-.pdf [accessed 22 December 2010], p. 10.

49. European Commission, *The World in 2025: Rising Asia and Socio-Ecological Transition* (Luxembourg: Office for Official Publications of the European Communities, 2009).

50. D. F. Von Hippel and P. Hayes, 'Growth in Energy Needs in Northeast Asia: Projections, Consequences, and Opportunities', paper prepared for the 2008 Northeast Asia Energy Outlook Seminar, Korea Economic Institute Policy Forum, Washington, DC, 6 May 2008, at http://www.keia.org/Publications/Other/vonHippelFINAL.pdf [accessed 22 December 2010], p. 1.

51. D. L. Alles (ed.), 'Asian Air Pollution', Western Washington University, 18 December 2009, at http://fire.biol.wwu.edu/trent/alles/AirPollution.pdf [accessed 22 December 2010].

52. UNEP, 'Alternative Policy Study: Reducing Air Pollution in Asia and the Pacific', *Global Environment Outlook (GEO)-2000*, at http://www.unep.org/geo2000/aps-asiapacific/index.htm [accessed 22 December 2010].

53. T. Yamamoto and S. Itoh (eds), *Fighting a Rising Tide: The Response to AIDS in East Asia* (Tokyo: Japan Center for International Exchange, 2006), pp. 1–18.

54. United States General Accounting Office (GAO), 'Emerging Infectious Diseases: Asian SARS Outbreak Challenged International and National Responses', Report to the Chairman, Subcommittee on Asia and the Pacific, Committee on International Relations, House of Representatives, April 2004, at http://www.gao.gov/new.items/d04564.pdf [accessed 22 December 2010], p. 3.

55. World Health Organization (WHO), 'TB a Threat to Economic Progress in Asia: TB Control Must be Effectively Supported to Reverse Losses', 29 November 2006, at

http://www.searo.who.int/LinkFiles/Events_JakPressRelease.pdf [accessed 22 December 2010], p. 2.

56. Asia Business Council, 'Containing Pandemic and Epidemic Diseases in Asia' (2010), at http://www.asiabusinesscouncil.org/docs/DiseaseBriefing.pdf [accessed 22 December 2010].

57. C. W. Freeman and M. Goodman, 'Crafting US Economic Strategy toward Asia: Lessons Learned from 30 Years of Experience', *A Report of the CSIS Asia Economic Task Force* (Washington, DC: Center for Strategic and International Studies (CSIS), October 2008), at http://csis.org/files/media/csis/events/081016_freeman_craftusecon_web.pdf [accessed 22 December 2010], p. 2.

58. M. Kelton, 'US Economic Statecraft in East Asia', *International Relations of the Asia-Pacific*, 8:2 (April 2008), pp. 149–74, on p. 152.

59. The Task Force on the Future of American Innovation, 'The Knowledge Economy: Is the United States Losing its Competitive Edge?', *Benchmarks of Our Innovation Future*, 16 February 2005, at http://www.futureofinnovation.org/PDF/Benchmarks.pdf [accessed 22 December 2010], p. 1.

60. Most East Asian ones covered in this study.

61. L. J. Lau and J. Park, 'The Sources of East Asian Economic Growth Revisited' (Stanford University and the State University of New York at Buffalo, September 2003), at http://www.stanford.edu/~ljlau/RecentWork/RecentWork/030921.pdf [accessed 22 December 2010], p. 1.

62. L. Ryan, 'The "Asian Economic Miracle" Unmasked', *International Journal of Social Economics*, 27:7–10 (2000), pp. 802–15.

63. K. de Boer and J. M. Turner, 'Beyond Oil: Reappraising the Gulf States', *McKinsey Quarterly* (January 2007), at http://mkqpreview1.qdweb.net/Middle_East/Beyond_oil_Reappraising_the_Gulf_States_1902 [accessed 22 December 2010].

64. B. Abdullah, 'The Growing Economic Presence of Gulf Countries in the Mediterranean Region', *Mediterranean Yearbook: Med.2009* (2009), pp. 203–209, at http://www.iemed.org/anuari/2009/aarticles/a203.pdf [accessed 22 December 2010], p. 203.

3 Challenges – Contradictions of Development?

1. E. Ostrom, *Governing the Commons: The Evolution of Institutions for Collective Action* (Cambridge: Cambridge University Press, 1990), p. 1

2. Ibid., p. 6.

3. T. Toichi, 'Energy Security in Asia and Japanese Policy', *Asia-Pacific Review,* 10:1 (May 2003), pp. 44–51, on p. 51.

4. Ostrom, *Governing the Commons*, p. 22.

5. Ibid., p. 186.

6. G. H. Sahlgren, 'The United States-South Korea Free Trade Agreement: An Economic and Political Analysis', *Competitive Enterprise Institute Issue Analysis*, 10 (October 2007), at http://cei.org/pdf/6189.pdf [accessed 24 January 2011], p. 11.

7. K. Calder, 'Sino-Japanese Energy Relations: Prospects for Deepening Strategic Competition', Paper presented at the conference on Japan's Contemporary Challenges in Honor of the Memory of Asakawa Kanichi, Yale University, New Haven, CT, 9–10 March 2007, at http://eastasianstudies.research.yale.edu/japanworld/calder.pdf [accessed 24 January 2011], p. 2.

8. Ibid., p. 3.

9. Toichi, 'Energy Security in Asia', p. 45.
10. J. Diamond, *Collapse: How Societies Choose to Fail or Succeed* (London: Penguin, 2006), pp. 9–10.
11. M. Cociancich and F. M. Parenti, 'Will Iran Meet China's Energy Demand? The Effects of Globalisation on the Energy Demand Allocation and on the Strengthening of Iran's Market Power', Paper for the Sixth Pan-European Conference on International Relations, Session 6-10: Greater Asia, The Middle East, and Energy Security, IPE, Developing Countries and Development, 14 September 2007, University of Turin, Italy, 12–15 September 2007, at http://www.turin.sgir.eu/uploads/Cociancich-Cociancich%20 Iran%20China.pdf [accessed 24 January 2011].
12. Toichi, 'Energy Security in Asia', pp. 46–7.
13. Calder, 'Sino-Japanese Energy Relations', p. 7.
14. G. Friedman, *The Next Decade: Where We've Been – and Where We're Going* (New York: Doubleday, 2011), p. 183.
15. Ibid., p. 185.
16. Ibid., p. 192.
17. P. Wickramasekera, 'Asian Labour Migration: Issues and Challenges in an Era of Globalization', *International Migration Papers*, 57 (International Labour Organization, August 2002), at http://www.ilo.org/public/english/protection/migrant/download/imp/ imp57e.pdf [accessed 24 January 2011], pp. 4–6.
18. S. V. Lall, H. Selod and Z. Shalizi, 'Rural-Urban Migration in Developing Countries: A Survey of Theoretical Predictions and Empirical Findings', *World Bank Policy Research Working Paper*, 3915 (May 2006), at http://www-wds.worldbank.org/servlet/ WDSContentServer/WDSP/IB/2006/05/05/000016406_20060505110833/Rendered/PDF/wps3915.pdf [accessed 24 January 2011], p. 48.
19. K. Saeed, 'Sustainable Trade Relations in a Global Economy' (Worcester Polytechnic Institute, January 1998), at http://www.wpi.edu/Images/CMS/SSPS/08.pdf [accessed 24 January 2011], p. 26.
20. S. A. Mason and A. Muller, 'Transforming Environmental and Natural Resource Use Conflicts', in M. Cogoy and K. W. Steininger (eds), *The Economics of Global Environmental Change: International Cooperation for Sustainability* (Cheltenham, UK and Northampton, MA: Edward Elgar, 2007), pp. 225–72, on p. 225.
21. International Fund for Agricultural Development (IFAD), *Environment and Natural Resource Management IFAD's Growing Commitment* (Rome: IFAD, February 2002), at http://www.ifad.org/pub/enviorn/EnvironENG.pdf [accessed 24 January 2011], p. 1.
22. Ibid.
23. T. Johns and P. B. Eyzaguirre, 'Nutrition and The Environment', in *Nutrition: A Foundation for Development: Why Practitioners in Development Should Integrate Nutrition*, Environment Brief 5 of 12 (Geneva: Administrative Committee on Coordination/Sub-Committee on Nutrition, January 2002), at http://www.unscn.org/files/Publications/ Briefs_on_Nutrition/Brief5_EN.pdf [accessed 24 January 2011], p. 1.
24. Aydin, 'Choosing Sides', p. 1099.
25. Ibid.
26. Ibid.
27. Lau and Park, 'The Sources of East Asian Economic Growth Revisited', p. 68. For more, refer to C. A. Johnson, *MITI and the Japanese Miracle: The Growth of Industrial Policy, 1925-1975* (Palo Alto, CA: Stanford University Press, 1982).
28. Lau and Park, 'The Sources of East Asian Economic Growth Revisited', p. 68.

29. Z. X. Zhang, 'Asian Energy and Environmental Policy: Promoting Growth While Preserving the Environment', Munich Personal RePEc Archive Paper No. 12224, January 2008, at http://mpra.ub.uni-muenchen.de/12224/ [accessed 24 June 2011], p. 54.

30. D. F. Simon and C. Cao, *China's Emerging Technological Edge: Assessing the Role of High-End Talent* (Cambridge: Cambridge University Press, 2009), p. xix.

31. J. R. Kennedy and R. J. Orr, 'The "New Market" for Emerging Markets Infrastructure: China, Other New Players and Revised Game Rules', *Collaboratory for Research on Global Projects Working Paper*, 32 (Palo Alto, CA: Stanford University, April 2007), at http://crgp.stanford.edu/publications/working_papers/GCR3_April07_Proceedings_3_v2.pdf [accessed 24 June 2011], unpaginated.

32. UN Millennium Project, *Innovation*, p. 7.

33. S. Gray and M. I. Blejer, 'The Gulf Cooperation Council Region: Financial Market Development, Competitiveness, and Economic Growth', in M. D. Hanouz, S. El Diwany and T. Yousef (eds), *The Arab World Competitiveness Report 2007 – Sustaining the Growth Momentum* (Geneva: World Economic Forum, 2007), pp. 41–51, on p. 44.

34. Ibid.

35. A. B. Bernard, J. B. Jensen, S. J. Redding and P. K. Schott, 'Firms in International Trade', *Journal of Economic Perspectives*, 21:3 (Summer 2007), pp. 105–30, on p. 127.

36. Nissanke and Thorbecke, 'Linking Globalization to Poverty in Asia, Latin America and Africa', p. 23.

37. W. Keller and S. R. Yeaple, 'Multinational Enterprises, International Trade, and Productivity Growth: Firm-Level Evidence from the United States', *Review of Economics and Statistics*, 91:4 (November 2009), pp. 821–31, on p. 821.

38. Ibid.

39. UN Millennium Project, *Innovation*, p. 37.

40. Ibid., p. 5.

41. K. R. Al-Rodhan, *The Saudi and Gulf Stock Markets: Irrational Exuberance or Markets Efficiency?* (Washington, DC: Center for Strategic and International Studies, 2005), at http://csis.org/files/media/csis/pubs/051025_saudi_gulf_mrkts.pdf [accessed 24 June 2011], p. 4.

42. European Commission, *The World in 2025*, p. 10.

43. Ibid., p. 20. For more on this important topic, please refer to: H. Ku and A. Zussman, 'Lingua Franca: The Role of English in International Trade', *Journal of Economic Behavior and Organization*, 75:2 (August 2010), pp. 250–60.

44. Nissanke and Thorbecke, 'Linking Globalization to Poverty in Asia, Latin America and Africa', p. 26.

45. Ibid.

4 Important Advanced Economies: US and Japan as Development Models

1. N. Roubini, 'Japan's Economic Crisis: Comments for the Panel Discussion on "Business Practices and Entrepreneurial Spirit in Japan and the United States"', 12 November 1996, at http://library.thinkquest.org/28837/japan.pdf [accessed 27 June 2011], unpaginated.

2. S. R. Schwenninger, 'US/Europe: Shaping a New Model of Economic Development', in C. Degryse (ed.), *Social Developments in the European Union 2009: Eleventh Annual Report* (Brussels: European Trade Union Institute, 2010), pp. 23–36, on p. 23.

3. Ibid., p. 26.

4. A. Alesina, E. Glaeser and B. Sacerdote, 'Why Doesn't the US Have a European-Style Welfare State?', *Brookings Papers on Economic Activity*, 2001:2 (2001), pp. 187–254, on p. 202.

5. Ibid., p. 222.

6. J. Heintz, R. Pollin and H. Garrett-Peltier, *How Infrastructure Investments Support the U.S. Economy: Employment, Productivity and Growth* (US: Political Economy Research Institute and Alliance for American Manufacturing, January 2009), at http://www.americanmanufacturing.org/wordpress/wp-content/uploads/2009/01/peri_aam_finaljan16_new.pdf [accessed 30 June 2011], p. 1.

7. Ibid., p. 2 .

8. Ibid., p. 6.

9. I. D. Wyatt and K. J. Byun, 'Employment Outlook: 2008-18 – The US Economy to 2018: From Recession to Recovery', *Monthly Labor Review*, 132:11(November 2009), pp. 11–29, on p. 14.

10. E. G. M. Parker and T. C. Shaffer, 'India and China: The Road Ahead', *South Asia Monitor*, 120 (1 July 2008), at http://csis.org/files/media/csis/pubs/sam120.pdf [accessed 5 July 2011], p. 3.

11. The MEPI aims to expand opportunities for women and youth, empowering their economic, social and political opportunities among other goals. (For more details: The Middle East Partnership Initiative (MEPI), 'About MEPI', U.S. Department of State, MEPI, at http://mepi.state.gov/about-us.html [accessed 5 July 2011].)

12. C. Candland, 'The U.S. Greater Middle East Initiative: Implications for Persian Gulf Economies and Polities', *Iranian Journal of International Affairs* (Spring 2007), at http://www.wellesley.edu/Polisci/Candland/USGMEI.pdf [accessed 5 July 2011], unpaginated.

13. Ibid.

14. A. Insel and M. Tekce, 'Econometric Analysis of the Bilateral Trade Flows in the Gulf Cooperation Council Countries', Munich Personal RePEc Archive Paper No. 22130, 15 April 2010, at http://mpra.ub.uni-muenchen.de/22130/1/MPRA_paper_22130.pdf [accessed 5 July 2011], p. 4.

15. A. M. Jaffe, 'Energy Security: Oil-Geopolitical and Strategic Implications for China and the United States' (Houston, TX: The James A. Baker III Institute for Public Policy of Rice University, 2004), at http://www.rice.edu/energy/publications/docs/SIIS_AJAFFE_worldenergy071805.pdf [accessed 5 July 2011], p. 2.

16. Ibid.

17. N. Hayashi, *The Japanese Economy Today – 50 Years after World War II*, Series of the Research Institute for Economics, No. 2 (Japan: Osaka University of Economics and Law, 1996), p. 13.

18. Parker and Shaffer, 'India and China', p. 1.

19. C. J. Rusko and K. Sasikumar, 'India and China: From Trade to Peace?', *Asian Perspective*, 31:4 (October 2007), pp. 99–123, on p. 111.

20. Ibid., p. 107.

21. Calder, 'Sino-Japanese Energy Relations', p. 27

22. J. Calabrese, 'The Consolidation of Gulf-Asia Relations: Washington Tuned in or out of Touch?', *Middle East Institute Policy Brief,* 25 (June 2009), at http://www.mei.edu/Portals/0/Publications/Consolidation-of-Gulf-Asia.pdf [accessed 5 July 2011], p. 2.
23. Ibid., p. 4.
24. Ibid., p. 2.
25. Insel and Tekce, 'Econometric Analysis of the Bilateral Trade Flows in the Gulf Cooperation Council Countries', p. 9.
26. Calabrese, 'The Consolidation of Gulf-Asia Relations', p. 4.
27. Ibid., p. 7.
28. Parker and Shaffer, 'India and China', p. 1.
29. Ibid., p. 3.
30. Rusko and Sasikumar, 'India and China', p. 114.
31. T. N. Srinivasan, 'China and India: Economic Performance, Competition and Cooperation: An Update', Economic Growth Center, Yale University, February 2004, at http://www.econ.yale.edu/~srinivas/C&I%20Economic%20Performance%20Update.pdf [accessed 6 July 2011], p. 16. (This paper draws on 'China and India: Economic Performance, Competition and Cooperation', which was originally presented at a seminar on WTO Accession, Policy Reform and Poverty sponsored by the World Trade Organization in Beijing, China in June 2002 and on T. N. Srinivasan, 'Economic Reforms and Global Integration', in F. R. Frankel and H. Harding (eds), *The India-China Relationship: What the United States Needs to Know* (Washington, DC: Woodrow Wilson Center Press, 2004), pp. 219–66.)
32. A. Panagariya, 'India and China: Trade and Foreign Investment', *Stanford Center for International Development Working Paper,* 302 (Palo Alto, CA: Stanford University, November 2006), at http://www.stanford.edu/group/siepr/cgi-bin/siepr/?q=system/files/shared/pubs/papers/pdf/SCID302.pdf [accessed 6 July 2011], p. 2.
33. H. J. Wiarda, 'Introduction: The Western Tradition and its Export to the Non-West', in H. J. Wiarda (ed.), *Non-Western Theories of Development: Regional Norms versus Global Trends* (Fort Worth, TX: Harcourt Brace College Publishers, 1999), pp. 1–19, on p. 2.
34. A. H. Somjee, 'India: A Challenge to Western Theories of Development', in H. J. Wiarda (ed.), *Non-Western Theories of Development: Regional Norms versus Global Trends* (Fort Worth, TX: Harcourt Brace College Publishers, 1999), pp. 44–63, on p. 46.
35. Wiarda, 'Introduction', pp. 2, 10.
36. H. J. Wiarda, 'Conclusion: Development in its Regional and Global Dimensions', in H. J. Wiarda (ed.), *Non-Western Theories of Development: Regional Norms versus Global Trends* (Fort Worth, TX: Harcourt Brace College Publishers, 1999), pp. 149–63, on p. 160.
37. H. J. Wiarda, 'Preface', in H. J. Wiarda (ed.), *Non-Western Theories of Development: Regional Norms versus Global Trends* (Fort Worth, TX: Harcourt Brace College Publishers, 1999), pp. vii-ix, on pp. vii-viii.
38. M. S. Qureshi and G. Wan, 'Trade Expansion of China and India Threat or Opportunity', *United Nations University World Institute for Development Economics Research (UNU-WIDER) Research Paper,* 2008/08 (February 2008), at http://www.environmentportal.in/files/rp2008-08.pdf [accessed 6 July 2011], p. 1.
39. US Congress Office of Technology Assessment, *Technology Transfer to the Middle East OTA-1 SC-173* (Washington, DC: US Congress Office of Technology Assessment, September 1984), at http://govinfo.library.unt.edu/ota/Ota_4/DATA/1984/8428.PDF [accessed 7 July 2011], p. 4.

40. N. Armitage, 'From Crisis to Kyoto and Beyond: The Evolution of Environmental Concerns in Japanese Official Development Assistance', *Graduate School of International Development Nagoya University Discussion Papers*, 176, November 2009, at http://www.gsid.nagoya-u.ac.jp/bpub/research/public/paper/article/176.pdf [accessed 7 July 2011], p. 9.

41. S. Özçelik, 'The Japanese Foreign Policy of the Middle East between 1904-1998: Resource, Trade and Aid Diplomacy', *Humanity & Social Sciences Journal*, 3:2 (2008), pp. 129–42, on p. 130.

42. Ibid.

43. C. M. Davidson, 'Persian Gulf – Pacific Asia Linkages in the 21st Century: A Marriage of Convenience?', *Kuwait Programme on Development, Governance and Globalisation in the Gulf States*, 7 (London: London School of Economics and Political Science, The Centre for the Study of Global Governance, January 2010), at http://www.lse.ac.uk/collections/LSEKP/documents/Davidson%20paper.pdf [accessed 7 July 2011], p. 3.

44. Armitage, 'From Crisis to Kyoto and Beyond', p. 11.

45. Özçelik, 'The Japanese Foreign Policy of the Middle East between 1904-1998', p. 137.

46. J. T. Jensen, *The Development of a Global LNG Market: Is It Likely? If So When?* (Oxford: Oxford Institute for Energy Studies, 2004), at http://www.jai-energy.com/pubs/Oxfordbook.pdf [accessed 7 July 2011], p. 10.

47. D. Stewart, 'Japan: The Power of Efficiency', in G. Luft and A. Korin (ed.), *Energy Security Challenges for the 21st Century: A Reference Handbook* (Santa Barbara, CA: Praeger Security International, 2009), pp. 176–90, on p. 179.

48. Calabrese, 'The Consolidation of Gulf-Asia Relations', pp. 3–4.

49. M. Thorpe and S. Mitra, 'Growing Economic Interdependence of China and the Gulf Cooperation Council', *China & World Economy*, 16:2 (March–April 2008), pp. 109–24, on p. 117.

50. Davidson, 'Persian Gulf – Pacific Asia Linkages in the 21st Century', p. 3.

51. M. Abo-Kazleh, 'Transformations in Japanese Foreign Policy toward the Middle East: From Low to More Active Political Engagement', *Uluslararasi Hukuk ve Politika (Review of International Law & Politics)*, 5:17 (2009), pp. 165–93, on p. 195.

52. Davidson, 'Persian Gulf – Pacific Asia Linkages in the 21st Century', p. 11.

53. US Congress Office of Technology Assessment, *Technology Transfer to the Middle East*, p. 7.

54. Calabrese, 'The Consolidation of Gulf-Asia Relations', p. 5.

55. Ibid., p. 3.

56. H. Yoshimatsu, 'Japan's Quest for Free Trade Agreements Constraints from Bureaucratic and Interest Group Politics', in M. Pangestu and L. Song (eds), *Japan's Future in East Asia and the Pacific: In Honour of Professor Peter Drysdale* (Canberra: Asia Pacific Press, Australian National University, 2007), pp. 80–102, on p. 95.

57. Jensen, *The Development of a Global LNG Market*, p. 6.

58. Abo-Kazleh, 'Transformations in Japanese Foreign Policy toward the Middle East', p. 195.

59. S. Itoh, 'Can Russia Become a "Regional Power" in Northeast Asia? Implications from Contemporary Energy Relations with China and Japan' (Center for East Asian Studies Monterey Institute of International Studies, May 2006), at http://gsti.miis.edu/CEAS-PUB/2007_Itoh.pdf [accessed 7 July 2011], p. 17.

60. Ibid.

61. Ibid., pp. 17–18.

62. R. P. Suttmeier, 'The Japanese Nuclear Power Option: Technological Promise and Social Limitations', in R. A. Morse (ed.), *The Politics of Japan's Energy Strategy: Resources-Diplomacy-Security* (Berkeley: Institute of East Asian Studies Research Papers and Policy Studies, 1981), pp. 106–33, on pp. 132–3.
63. L. Newby, *Sino-Japanese Relations: China's Perspective* (London: Routledge, 1988), p. 26.
64. Stewart, 'Japan: The Power of Efficiency', p. 180.
65. Armitage, 'From Crisis to Kyoto and Beyond', p. 10.

5 Emerging Economies: Asia and the Gulf

1. Davidson, 'Persian Gulf – Pacific Asia Linkages in the 21st Century', p. 2.
2. Ibid., pp. 28–9.
3. A. Sager and G. Kemp, 'Introduction', in Gulf Research Center, *India's Growing Role in the Gulf: Implications for the Region and the United States* (Dubai: Gulf Research Center and the Nixon Center, 2009), at http://www.cftni.org/Monograph-Indias-Growing-Role-in-the-Gulf.pdf [accessed 11 July 2011], pp. 11–13, on p. 12.
4. X. Liu, *The Silk Road: Overland Trade and Cultural Interactions in Eurasia* (Washington, DC: American Historical Association, 1998), p. 4.
5. Ibid.
6. Ibid.
7. There was specific interest from the Chinese in a breed of horses whose sweat takes on the idiosyncratic color of blood. (For more: 'China Enthusiastic about "Blood-Sweating" Horse', *People's Daily*, 5 August 2002, at http://english.peopledaily.com.cn/200208/05/eng20020805_100885.shtml [accessed 12 July 2011].)
8. Liu, *The Silk Road*, p. 4.
9. Ibid., p 5.
10. Ibid.
11. Calder, 'Sino-Japanese Energy Relations', p. 5.
12. Liu, *The Silk Road*, p. 15.
13. Ibid., p. 26.
14. C. J. Halperin, *Russia and the Golden Horde: The Mongol Impact on Medieval Russian History* (Bloomington, IN and Indianapolis, IN: Indiana University Press, 1987), p. 25.
15. Ibid., p. 75.
16. Ibid., p. 82.
17. Ibid.
18. S. Pradhan, 'India's Economic and Political Presence in the Gulf: A Gulf Perspective', in Gulf Research Center, *India's Growing Role in the Gulf: Implications for the Region and the United States* (Dubai: Gulf Research Center and the Nixon Center, 2009), at http://www.cftni.org/Monograph-Indias-Growing-Role-in-the-Gulf.pdf [accessed 12 July 2011], pp. 15–39, on p. 16.
19. J. Weerahewa and K. Meilke, 'Indo-China Trade Relationships: Implications for the South Asian Economies', The Ohio State University, Department of Agricultural, Environmental, and Development Economics, 22 June 2007, at http://aede.osu.edu/programs/anderson/trade/34Weerahewa.pdf [accessed 11 June 2011], p. 3.
20. Rusko and Sasikumar, 'India and China', p. 114.
21. Liu, *The Silk Road*, p. 1.
22. C. Werner, 'The New Silk Road: Mediators and Tourism Development in Central Asia', *Ethnology*, 42:2 (Spring 2003), pp. 141–59, on p. 145.

23. International Energy Agency (IEA), *China's Worldwide Quest for Energy Security* (Paris: OECD/IEA, 2000), p. 69.

24. Özçelik, 'The Japanese Foreign Policy of the Middle East between 1904-1998', p. 130.

25. J. Townsend and A. King, 'Sino-Japanese Competition for Central Asian Energy: China's Game to Win', *China and Eurasia Forum Quarterly*, 5:4 (November 2007), pp. 23–45, on p. 41.

26. N. Norling, *First Kabul Conference on Partnership, Trade, and Development in Greater Central Asia* (Washington, DC and Sweden: Central Asia-Caucasus Institute & Silk Road Studies Program and the First Kazakhstan President Foundation, 2006), at http://www.silkroadstudies.org/new/docs/0604Kabul.pdf [accessed 12 July 2011], p. 6.

27. This point was argued in: S. Nagy and T. W. Lim, 'The Future Trend of Inter-Regionalism in East Asia', paper presented at the conference 'Major Trends in the Contemporary World', College of International Studies of Tamkang University, March 2011, p. 9. (unpublished at the time of this writing).

28. Ibid.

29. Ibid., p. 16.

30. Ibid.

31. Ibid.

32. Source of the three different forms of inter-regional arrangements: H. Hänggi, 'Inter-regionalism: Empirical and Theoretical Perspectives', paper prepared for the workshop 'Dollars, Democracy and Trade: External Influence on Economic Integration in the Americas', The Pacific Council on International Policy, Los Angeles, CA; The Center for Applied Policy Research, Munich, 18 May 2000, at http://www.ipw.unisg.ch/org/ipw/web.nsf/SysWebRessources/h%C3%A4nggi/$FILE/Haenggi.pdf [accessed 1 September 2010], p. 3. This point was argued in Nagy and Lim, 'The Future Trend of Inter-Regionalism in East Asia', p. 18.

33. See Hänggi, 'Interregionalism', p. 3 for the four different groups of inter-regionalism. This point was argued in Nagy and Lim, 'The Future Trend of Inter-Regionalism in East Asia', p. 18.

34. This point was argued in Nagy and Lim, 'The Future Trend of Inter-Regionalism in East Asia', p. 19.

35. Ibid., p. 21.

36. Ibid., p. 29.

37. For more on this issue, please refer to Calabrese, 'The Consolidation of Gulf-Asia Relations'.

38. Calabrese, 'The Consolidation of Gulf-Asia Relations', p. 5.

39. Y. Kobayashi, 'Corporate Strategies of Saudi Aramco' (The James A. Baker III Institute for Public Policy of Rice University, March 2007), at http://www.rice.edu/energy/publications/docs/NOCs/Papers/NOC_Kobayashi%20SAramco.pdf [accessed 12 July 2011], pp. 26–7.

40. Calabrese, 'The Consolidation of Gulf-Asia Relations', p. 5.

41. Kemp, *The East Moves West*, p. 3.

42. Thorpe and Mitra, 'Growing Economic Interdependence of China and the Gulf Cooperation Council', p. 116.

43. Kemp, *The East Moves West*, p. 12.

44. Calabrese, 'The Consolidation of Gulf-Asia Relations', p. 7.

45. Thorpe and Mitra, 'Growing Economic Interdependence of China and the Gulf Cooperation Council', p. 117.

46. Calabrese, 'The Consolidation of Gulf-Asia Relations', p. 3.
47. Ibid., p. 5.
48. Ibid.
49. Ibid., pp. 3–4.
50. Kemp, *The East Moves West*, p. 12.
51. R. D. Kaplan, *Monsoon: The Indian Ocean and the Future of American Power* (New York: Random House, 2010), p. 8.
52. Kemp, *The East Moves West*, p. 12.
53. Ibid., p. 15.
54. Kaplan, *Monsoon*, p. 9.
55. Kemp, *The East Moves West,* pp. 15–16.
56. K. Calder, 'East Asia and the Middle East: A Fateful Energy Embrace', *The China and Eurasia Forum Quarterly*, 3:3 (November 2005), pp. 5–9, on p. 7.
57. Calabrese, 'The Consolidation of Gulf-Asia Relations', pp. 5–6.
58. Ibid., p. 3.
59. Kemp, *The East Moves West*, p. 15.
60. Thorpe and Mitra, 'Growing Economic Interdependence of China and the Gulf Cooperation Council', p. 116.
61. Calabrese, 'The Consolidation of Gulf-Asia Relations', pp. 4–5.
62. Calder, 'East Asia and the Middle East', p. 7.
63. Kemp, *The East Moves West*, p. 3.
64. Calabrese, 'The Consolidation of Gulf-Asia Relations', pp. 4–5.
65. Ibid.
66. Kemp, *The East Moves West*, p. 15.
67. M. B. Oren, *Power, Faith, and Fantasy: America in the Middle East, 1776 to the Present* (New York and London: WW Norton, 2007), p. 501.
68. Calabrese, 'The Consolidation of Gulf-Asia Relations', p. 2.
69. Thorpe and Mitra, 'Growing Economic Interdependence of China and the Gulf Cooperation Council', p. 116.
70. Calabrese, 'The Consolidation of Gulf-Asia Relations', p. 6.
71. Ibid.
72. Thorpe and Mitra, 'Growing Economic Interdependence of China and the Gulf Cooperation Council', p. 116.
73. Calabrese, 'The Consolidation of Gulf-Asia Relations', p. 5.
74. Kemp, *The East Moves West*, pp. 12, 15.
75. Ibid.
76. Calabrese, 'The Consolidation of Gulf-Asia Relations', p. 5.
77. Ibid.
78. Ibid.
79. Kemp, *The East Moves West*, p. 12.
80. Calabrese, 'The Consolidation of Gulf-Asia Relations', p. 3.
81. Kobayashi, 'Corporate Strategies of Saudi Aramco', p. 15.
82. Ibid.
83. Kemp, *The East Moves West*, p. 15.
84. Kobayashi, 'Corporate Strategies of Saudi Aramco', p. 1.
85. Ibid., p. 20.
86. Gulf Research Center, *India's Growing Role in the Gulf: Implications for the Region and the United States* (Dubai: Gulf Research Center and the Nixon Center, 2009), at http://

www.cftni.org/Monograph-Indias-Growing-Role-in-the-Gulf.pdf [accessed 12 July 2011], on pp. 11–12.

87. Kemp, *The East Moves West*, p. 16.
88. Ibid.
89. Oren, *Power, Faith, and Fantasy*, p. 572. At the point of Oren's writing, the membership number was 2,600 but as of 20 June 2011, MESA's website states the membership has grown to more than 3,000 individuals (source: Middle East Studies Association (MESA), 'Description', at http://www.mesa.arizona.edu/about/description.htm [accessed 20 June 2011]).
90. Kemp, *The East Moves West*, pp. 11–12.
91. Ibid.
92. Ibid.
93. S. Zhang, 'The Environmental Impact of the Financial Crisis: Challenges and Opportunities', The Carnegie Endowment for International Peace, 11 April 2009, at www.carnegieendowment.org/events/?fa=eventDetail&id=1328http://www.carnegieendowment.org/events/?fa=eventDetail&id=1328 [accessed 1 April 2010].
94. This point was argued in Nagy and Lim, 'The Future Trend of Inter-Regionalism in East Asia', p. 6.
95. Ibid., pp. 22–3.
96. Ibid.
97. Ibid., p. 23.
98. Ibid.
99. Ibid.
100. Kobayashi, 'Corporate Strategies of Saudi Aramco', p. 27.
101. Yoshimatsu, 'Japan's Quest for Free Trade Agreements Constraints from Bureaucratic and Interest Group Politics', p. 95.
102. Ibid.
103. Kemp, *The East Moves West*, pp. 16–17.
104. Ibid.
105. K. Nagasu and Y. Sakamoto, *Jichitai no Kokusai Kōryū: Hirakareta Chihō o Mezashite* (*International Cooperation of Local Governments: Toward Open Local Regions*) (Tokyo: Gakuyō Shobō, 1983); K. Hirano, 'Sengo Nihon no Kokusai Bunka Kōryū' ('International Cultural Relations of Postwar Japan'), in K. Hirano (ed.), *Sengo Nihon no Kokusai Bunka Kōryū* (*International Cultural Relations of Postwar Japan*) (Tokyo: Keisō Shobō, 2005), pp. 81–129. This point was argued in Nagy and Lim, 'The Future Trend of Inter-Regionalism in East Asia', p. 22.
106. Calabrese, 'The Consolidation of Gulf-Asia Relations', p. 4.
107. Ibid.
108. J. Ghosh, 'Poverty Reduction in China and India: Policy Implications of Recent Trends', *Department of Economic and Social Affairs Working Paper*, 92:ST/ESA/2010/DWP/92 (January 2010), at http://www.un.org/esa/desa/papers/2010/wp92_2010.pdf [accessed 8 July 2011], p. 2.
109. S. Muller-Kraenner, 'China's and India's Emerging Energy Foreign Policy', *German Development Institute Discussion Paper*, 15/2008 (Bonn: German Development Institute, 2008), at http://www.die-gdi.de/CMS-Homepage/openwebcms3.nsf/(ynDK_contentByKey)/ANES-7HJAZ8/$FILE/DP%2015.2008.pdf [accessed 8 July 2011], foreword.

110. M. G. Plummer, 'The Global Economic Crisis and Its Implications for Asian Economic Cooperation', *East-West Center Policy Studies*, 55 (2009), at http://www.eastwestcenter.org/fileadmin/stored/pdfs/ps055.pdf [accessed 14 July 2011], p. viii.

111. E. Lincoln, 'Japan: Using Power Narrowly', *Washington Quarterly*, 27:1 (Winter 2003–4), pp. 111–27, on p. 111.

112. For more details on the connection between the element of technology in Japanese development which has served as a model for other East Asian economies, please refer to: D. L. Doane, *Cooperation, Technology, and Japanese Development: Indigenous Knowledge, the Power of Networks, and the State* (Boulder, CO: Westview Press, 1998).

113. Toichi, 'Energy Security in Asia and Japanese Policy', p. 6.

114. J.-Y. Lee and J. P. Rodrigue, 'Trade Reorientation and Its Effects on Regional Port Systems: The Korea-China Link along the Yellow Sea Rim', *Growth and Change*, 37:4 (December 2006), pp. 597–619, on p. 609.

115. G. Enkhtaivan, 'Energy Sector Development in Mongolia', *Northeast Asia Energy Focus*, 6:1 (Spring 2009), pp. 54–8, on p. 54.

116. For example, Cenozoic basalts from Mongolia. For more details: T. L. Barry, A. D. Saunders, P. D. Kempton, B. F. Windley, M. S. Pringle, D. Dorjnamjaa and S. Saandar, 'Petrogenesis of Cenozoic Basalts from Mongolia: Evidence for the Role of Aesthenspheric versus Metasomatized Lithospheric Mantle Sources', *Journal of Petrology*, 44:1 (January 2003), pp. 55–91.

117. X. Xu, 'China's Oil Strategy toward the Middle East', Post September 11 Update Report: Political, Economic, Social, Cultural, and Religious Trends in the Middle East and the Gulf and their Impact on Energy Supply, Security, and Pricing, The James A. Baker III Institute for Public Policy of Rice University, September 2002, at http://www.bakerinstitute.org/publications/PEC911Update_ChinasOilStrategyTowardsMiddleEast2.pdf [accessed 14 July 2011], p. 14.

118. Ibid.

119. H. Hakimian, 'From East to West Asia: Lessons of Globalization, Crisis and Economic Reform', *School of Oriental and African Studies (SOAS) Working Paper*, 82 (6 May 1998), at http://www.soas.ac.uk/economics/research/workingpapers/file28881.pdf [accessed 14 July 2011], p. 16.

120. J. Madsen, 'China's Policy in the Gulf Region: From Neglect to Necessity', Power and Interest News Report, 27 October 2006, at http://www.gees.org/documentos/Documen-01736.pdf [accessed 14 July 2011].

121. Ibid.

122. Yomiuri International Economic Society, 'Emerging China and the Asian Economy in the Coming Decade', *Symposium on International Economic Affairs November 2002 Occasional Paper*, 12 (Tokyo: Institute for International Monetary Affairs, March 2003), at www.iima.or.jp/pdf/paper12e.pdf [accessed 14 July 2011], p. 8.

123. Xu, 'China's Oil Strategy toward the Middle East', p. 11.

124. G. Zhang, 'China's Policies on Energy, Oil and Natural Gas in the New Century – Keynote Speech on the Sixth Sino-US Oil and Gas Forum', 28 June 2005, at http://www.usea.org/Archive/Speeches%20for%20Website/Guobao%20Remarks%20English.pdf [accessed 15 July 2011], p. 11.

125. Central Bank of Kuwait (CBK), 'International Trade from a Kuwaiti and Arab Perspective', Paper delivered on the occasion of the Annual Tacitus Lecture for the Guild of World Traders in London, UK, 22 January 1991, at http://www.cbk.gov.kw/PDF/Book2Eng/part11.pdf [accessed 15 July 2011], p. 2.

126. Calder, 'Sino-Japanese Energy Relations', p. 25.
127. Kelton, 'US Economic Statecraft in East Asia', p. 156.
128. Ibid., p. 160.
129. Plummer, 'The Global Economic Crisis and Its Implications for Asian Economic Cooperation', p. 13.
130. R. Huisken, 'The Outlook for US-China Relations', in R. Huisken (ed.), *Rising China: Power and Reassurance* (Canberra: The Australian National University E Press, 2009), pp. 9–20, on p. 18.
131. Q. Jia, 'Closer and More Balanced: China-US Relations in Transition', in R. Huisken (ed.), *Rising China: Power and Reassurance* (Canberra: The Australian National University E Press, 2009), p. 21–32, on p. 21.
132. J. Wang, 'China's Search for Stability with America', *Foreign Affairs*, 84:5 (September/October 2005), pp. 39–48.
133. G. Ji, 'Maritime Confidence-Building Measures (CBMs) in Northeast Asia', *Institute on Global Conflict and Cooperation (IGCC) Policy Paper – Northeast Asia Cooperation Dialogue II Conference Papers, Tokyo, Japan, 16–17 May 1994*, 9 (August 1994), p. 20.
134. Information Office of the State Council of the People's Republic of China, 'China's Energy Conditions and Policies' (December 2007), at http://en.ndrc.gov.cn/policyrelease/P020071227502260511798.pdf [accessed 15 July 2011], p. 16.
135. C. Parsons and J. Brown, 'The "Asian Premium" and Dependency on Gulf Oil', *Center for International Trade Studies (CITS) Working Papers*, CITS WP 2003–2002 (Japan: Yokohama National University, Faculty of Economics, November 2003), at http://www.econ.ynu.ac.jp/cits/sub3-2.htm [accessed 15 July 2011], p. 24.
136. B. D. Cole, '"Oil for the Lamps of China" – Beijing's 21st-Century Search for Energy', *McNair Paper*, 67 (Washington, DC: National Defense University Press, Institute for National Strategic Studies, 2003), at http://www.ndu.edu/inss/docUploaded/198_428.McNair.pdf [accessed 15 July 2011], p. 53.
137. Calabrese, 'The Consolidation of Gulf-Asia Relations', p. 4.
138. D. Kapur and R. Ramamurti, 'India's Emerging Competitive Advantage in Services', *Academy of Management Executive*, 15:2 (2001), pp. 20–33, on p. 20.
139. S. Ranganathan, 'Emerging India as a World Class Leader in the Knowledge Industry: Prospect for Human Resource Development', paper presented in LEC-Seminar Workshop on 'The Limits of Cultural Globalization', Jawaharlal Nehru University and Albert-Ludwigs-University Freiburg, June/July 2000, at http://www.zmk.uni-freiburg.de/CulturalGlobalization/Workshop/paper-ranganathan.pdf [accessed 8 July 2011], p. 6.
140. Ibid.
141. J. Rautava, 'Is India Emerging as a Global Economic Powerhouse Equal to China?', *Bank of Finland Institute for Economies in Transition (BOFIT) Online*, 2 (Helsinki: BOFIT, 2005), at http://www.suomenpankki.fi/fi/suomen_pankki/organisaatio/asiantuntijoita/Documents/bon0205.pdf [accessed 8 July 2011], p. 14.
142. Ibid., p. 16.
143. Kapur and Ramamurti, 'India's Emerging Competitive Advantage in Services', p. 20.
144. D. Ernst and B. Naughton, 'China's Emerging Industrial Economy: Insights from the IT Industry', in C. A. McNally (ed.), *China's Emergent Political Economy: Capitalism in the Dragon's Lair* (London: Routledge, 2008), pp. 39–59, on p. 48.
145. Ghosh, 'Poverty Reduction in China and India', p. 1.

146. Y. Chen and D. Jin, 'Who Benefits from the Emerging China? An International Inputs-Ouput Approach', *Far Eastern Studies*, 8 (March 2009), pp. 45–59.

147. P. Katel,'Emerging China', *CQ Researcher*, 15:40 (11 November 2005), pp. 957–80, on pp. 957, 959.

148. W. Overholt, 'China in the Global Financial Crisis: Rising Influence, Rising Challenges', *Washington Quarterly*, 33:1 (January 2010), pp. 21–34, on p. 23.

149. Ghosh, 'Poverty Reduction in China and India', p. 7.

150. Simon and Cao, *China's Emerging Technological Edge*, p. xviii.

151. Ibid., p. xix.

152. 'The Rise of the Gulf ', *Economist*, 387:8577 (26 April 2008), p. 15.

153. M. Sturm, J. Strasky, P. Adolf and D. Peschel, 'The Gulf Cooperation Council Countries Economic Structures, Recent Developments and Role in the Global Economy', *European Central Bank Occasional Paper Series*, 92 (July 2008), at http://www.ecb.int/pub/pdf/scpops/ecbocp92.pdf [accessed 10 July 2011], p. 8.

154. De Boer and Turner, 'Beyond Oil', p. 8.

155. Ibid., p. 12.

156. Ibid., p. 13.

157. Sturm, Strasky, Adolf and Peschel, 'The Gulf Cooperation Council Countries Economic Structures', p. 57.

158. De Boer and Turner, 'Beyond Oil', p. 8.

159. Sturm, Strasky, Adolf and Peschel, 'The Gulf Cooperation Council Countries Economic Structures', p. 8.

6 India and the Middle East

1. As former Chief of Indian Navy, Admiral Suresh Mehta is a noted commentator from India on the flow of trade through in the maritime sector including the supply of energy.

2. Kaplan, *Monsoon*, p. 128.

3. S. Itoh, 'Japan's Energy Strategy and Development of Energy Cooperation in the Asia-Pacific', *Economic Research Institute for Northeast Asia (ERINA) Report*, 77 (September 2007), pp. 35–48, on p. 44.

4. A. Kandel, 'The Significant Warming of Indo-Israeli Relations in the Post-Cold War Period', *Middle East Review of International Affairs*, 13:4 (December 2009), pp. 69–77, on pp. 69, 71.

5. Kaplan, *Monsoon*, pp. 7, 127.

6. Jensen, *The Development of a Global LNG Market*, p. 89.

7. Jaffe, 'Energy Security', p. 1.

8. A. Bubalo and M. P. Thirlwell, 'Energy Insecurity: China, India and Middle East Oil', *Lowy Institute for International Policy Issues Brief* (December 2004), at http://www.lowyinstitute.org/Publication.asp?pid=194 [accessed 15 July 2011], p. 5.

9. Kemp, *The East Moves West*, p. 7.

10. Bubalo and Thirlwell, 'Energy Insecurity', p. 5.

11. Kaplan, *Monsoon*, pp. 7–8.

12. Kemp, *The East Moves West*, p. 8.

13. Bubalo and Thirlwell, 'Energy Insecurity', p. 6.

14. Kaplan, *Monsoon*, p. 12.

15. Kemp, *The East Moves West*, p. 12.

16. Kandel, 'The Significant Warming of Indo-Israeli Relations in the Post-Cold War Period', p. 75.
17. Bubalo and Thirlwell, 'Energy Insecurity', p. 8.
18. Xu, 'China's Oil Strategy toward the Middle East', p. 10.
19. Rusko and Sasukumar, 'India and China', p. 113.
20. Itoh, 'Japan's Energy Strategy and Development of Energy Cooperation in the Asia-Pacific', p. 44.
21. M. Öğütçü and X. Ma, 'Growing Links in Energy and Geopolitics: China, Russia, and Central Asia', Centre for Energy, Petroleum and Mineral Law and Policy (CEPMLP) Research Network, at http://www.dundee.ac.uk/cepmlp/gateway/files.php?file=CEPMLP_IJ_Mar08-Growing_links_916741751.pdf [accessed 15 July 2011], p. 26.
22. Calabrese, 'The Consolidation of Gulf-Asia Relations', p. 3.
23. Ibid., p. 4.
24. Jaffe, 'Energy Security', p. 11.
25. Itoh, 'Japan's Energy Strategy and Development of Energy Cooperation in the Asia-Pacific', p. 35.
26. Kemp, *The East Moves West*, p. 4.
27. Davidson, 'Persian Gulf – Pacific Asia Linkages in the 21st Century', pp. 3–4.
28. Jaffe, 'Energy Security', p. 1.
29. Toichi, 'Energy Security in Asia and Japanese Policy', p. 1.
30. Kemp, *The East Moves West*, p. 7.
31. Ibid., p. 8.
32. Jensen, *The Development of a Global LNG Market*, pp. 6, 77, 88.
33. Insel and Tekce, 'Econometric Analysis of the Bilateral Trade Flows in the Gulf Cooperation Council Countries', p. 4.
34. Kemp, *The East Moves West*, p. 15.
35. Ibid., pp. 15–16.
36. Insel and Tekce, 'Econometric Analysis of the Bilateral Trade Flows in the Gulf Cooperation Council Countries', p. 9.
37. Ibid., p. 19, table B2 indicates that from 1997 to 2002, India is the second top trading partner for Bahrain; ninth for Kuwait; fourteenth for Oman; fourth for Qatar; tenth for Saudi Arabia; eleventh for UAE; and from 2003 to 2007, India is the third for Bahrain; first for Kuwait; fourth for Oman; third for Qatar; fourth for Saudi Arabia; second for UAE.
38. Kemp, *The East Moves West*, p. 12.
39. Ibid., p. 12.
40. Ibid., p. 16.
41. Jaffe, 'Energy Security', p. 11.
42. S. Fazl-e-Haider, 'Gwadar: An Emerging Centre of the New Great Game', *Istituto per gli Studi di Politica Internazionale (ISPI) [Institute for International Political Studies] Policy Brief*, 162 (October 2009), at http://www.ispionline.it/it/documents/PB_162_2009.pdf [accessed 16 July 2011], p. 2.
43. Öğütçü and Ma, 'Growing Links in Energy and Geopolitics', p. 26.
44. Itoh, 'Japan's Energy Strategy and Development of Energy Cooperation in the Asia Pacific', p. 37.
45. Toichi, 'Energy Security in Asia and Japanese Policy', p. 93.

46. Itoh, 'Japan's Energy Strategy and Development of Energy Cooperation in the Asia Pacific', p. 44.

7 The Energy Giants

1. This chapter was reviewed by Prof Stephen Nagy (Chinese University of Hong Kong) and it acknowledges his contributions.
2. V. Smil, *Energy in World History* (Boulder, CO: Westview Press, 1994), p. 211.
3. Ibid.
4. L. E. Hein, *Fueling Growth: The Energy Revolution and Economic Policy in Postwar Japan* (Cambridge, MA and London: Council on East Asian Studies, Harvard University, 1990), p. 2.
5. K. Ohkawa and H. Rosovsky, *Japanese Economic Growth: Trend Acceleration in the Twentieth Century* (Palo Alto, CA and London: Stanford University Press and Oxford University Press, 1973), p. 194.
6. K. Calder and M. Ye, *The Making of Northeast Asia* (Palo Alto, CA: Stanford University Press, 2010), p. 14.
7. Ibid., p. 14.
8. X. Li, 'China Protests Japan's Diaoyu Islands Stance', *China Daily*, 28 February 2009, at http://www.chinadaily.com.cn/cndy/2009-02/28/content_7521979.htm [accessed 27 April 2010]; or Xinhua, 'China Holds Indisputable Sovereignty over Diaoyu Islands – FM', *China Daily* (19 July 2009), at http://www.chinadaily.com.cn/china/2009-07/19/content_8446416.htm [accessed 27 April 2010] (citation by Stephen Nagy in his review of this chapter).
9. Calder and Ye, *The Making of Northeast Asia*, p. 14.
10. Smil, *Energy in World History*, p. 237.
11. Hein, *Fueling Growth*, p. 30.
12. Ibid., p. 20.
13. K. Wu, B. Usukh and B. Tsevegjav, 'Energy Cooperation in Northeast Asia: The Role of Mongolia', *Ritsumeikan Journal of Asia Pacific Studies*, 26 (December 2009), pp. 83–98, p. 85.
14. E. Wishnick, 'China as a Risk Society', *East-West Center Working Papers: Politics, Governance, and Security Series*, 12 (September 2005), at http://www.eastwestcenter.org/fileadmin/stored/pdfs/PSwp012.pdf [accessed 19 July 2011], p. 23.
15. R. K. Morse and G. He, 'The World's Greatest Coal Arbitrage: China's Coal Import Behavior and Implications for the Global Coal Market', *Program on Energy and Sustainable Development Working Paper*, 94 (Palo Alto, CA: Stanford University, Freeman Spogli Institute for International Studies, 5 August 2010), at http://iis-db.stanford.edu/pubs/22966/WP_94_Morse_He_Greatest_Coal_Arbitrage_5Aug2010.pdf [accessed 19 July 2011], p. 4.
16. Ibid.
17. P. Knights and M. Hood (eds), *Coal and the Commonwealth: The Greatness of an Australian Resource* (Brisbane: The University of Queensland, October 2009), p. 6.
18. Morse and He, 'The World's Greatest Coal Arbitrage', p. 3.
19. Ibid., p. 1.
20. Ibid., p. 19.
21. Kaplan, *Monsoon*, p. 271.
22. Knights and Hood (eds), *Coal and the Commonwealth*, p. 91.

23. Kaplan, *Monsoon*, p. 8.
24. Massachusetts Institute of Technology (MIT) Coal Energy Study Advisory Committee Members and Study Participants, *The Future of Coal – Options for a Carbon Constrained World* (Cambridge, MA: MIT, 2007), p. 5.
25. R. Ekawan, M. Duchêne and D. Goetz, 'The Evolution of Hard Coal Trade in the Pacific Market', *Energy Policy*, 34:14 (September 2006), pp. 1853–66, on p. 1855.
26. E. Wyciszkiewicz, 'Prospects for Energy Cooperation in North-East Asia', *Polish Institute of International Affairs (PISM) Research Papers*, 2 (August 2006), at http://kms1. isn.ethz.ch/serviceengine/Files/ISN/93294/ipublicationdocument_singledocument/ aada7013-c295-4850-b20c-822b9bff2d11/en/2006_2.pdf [accessed 20 July 2011], p. 2.
27. T. Yamazaki, K. Aso and J. Chinju, 'Japanese Potential of CO2 Sequestration in Coal Seams', *Applied Energy*, 83:9 (September 2006), pp. 911–20, on p. 911.
28. Ibid., pp. 912–13.
29. Knights and Hood (eds), *Coal and the Commonwealth*, p. 92.
30. D. Von Hippel, T. Savage, P. Hayes, 'Overview of the Northeast Asia Energy Situation', *Energy Policy* (July 2009), doi:10.1016/j.enpol.2009.07.004, p. 5.
31. J. Sasaki, *Modes of Traditional Mining Techniques* (Tokyo: United Nations University, 1980), p. 2.
32. N. Murakushi, *Technology and Labour in Japanese Coal Mining* (Tokyo: United Nations University, 1980), p. 1.
33. M. Allen, 'Undermining the Occupation: Women Coalminers in 1940s Japan', *POR-TAL Journal of Multidisciplinary International Studies*, 7:2 (July 2010), at http://epress. lib.uts.edu.au/ojs/index.php/portal/article/view/1518/1882 [accessed 20 July 2011], p. 8.
34. D. Yergin, *The Prize: The Epic Quest for Oil, Money, and Power* (Great Britain: Simon and Schuster, 1991), p. 545.
35. N. Swanström, M. Weissmann and E. Björnehed, 'Introduction', in N. Swanström (ed.), *Conflict Prevention and Conflict Management in Northeast Asia* (Washington, DC and Sweden: Central Asia-Caucasus Institute & Silk Road Studies Program, Johns Hopkins and Uppsala, 2005), pp. 7–36, on p. 33.
36. R. Dannreuther, 'Asian Security and China's Energy Needs', *International Relations of the Asia Pacific*, 3:2 (August 2003), pp. 197–219, on p. 199.
37. S.-Y. Chung, 'Reviving NEASPEC to Address Regional Environmental Problems in Asia', *SAIS Review*, 28:2 (Summer-Fall 2008), pp. 157–72, on pp. 159–60. Stephen Nagy's consultation for this paper points out another example of Kitakyushu worked assiduously in this area with cities in China such as Dalian in training resources and expertise to cooperate and improve coal management. He argues that local level initiatives such as the one in Kitakyushu are also at the vanguard of environmental cooperation. Details of this city-level cooperation will become available in his upcoming volume on regionalism currently at manuscript stage. He can be contacted at nagystephen@cuhk.edu.hk for more details.
38. S. Harris, 'Institutionalising Northeast Asia: The Energy Market', *Australian National University, Department of International Relations, Research School of Pacific and Asian Studies: Working Paper*, 2008/6 (Canberra, December 2008), at http://ips.cap.anu.edu. au/ir/pubs/work_papers/08-6.pdf [accessed 20 July 2011], p. 15.
39. Chung, 'Reviving NEASPEC to Address Regional Environmental Problems in Asia', p. 159.
40. Wishnick, 'China as a Risk Society', p. 29.

41. Knights and Hood (eds), *Coal and the Commonwealth*, p. 92.
42. H. Katayama, 'Ecological Modernization in Northeast Asia', in S. Tabata (ed.), *Energy and Environment in Slavic Eurasia: Toward the Establishment of the Network of Environmental Studies in the Pan-Okhotsk Region* (Sapporo: Hokkaido University, Slavic Research Center, 2008), p. 195.
43. Ibid., pp. 195–6.
44. Calder, 'East Asia and the Middle East', p. 5.
45. K. Zou, 'Transnational Cooperation for Managing the Control of Environmental Disputes in East Asia', *Journal of Environmental Law*, 16:3 (2004), pp. 341–60, on p. 343.
46. Von Hippel, Savage and Hayes, 'Overview of the Northeast Asia Energy Situation', p. 6.
47. Harris, 'Institutionalising Northeast Asia', p. 8.
48. Knights and Hood (eds), *Coal and the Commonwealth*, p. 7.
49. M. Ujihira and K. Hashimoto, 'Outbursts of Coal and Gas and Preventive Measures', *Memoirs of the Faculty of Engineering, Hokkaido University*, 14:3 (December 1976), pp. 25–32, on p. 28.
50. Yergin, *The Prize*, p. 545.
51. Ibid., p. 547.
52. Ekawan, Duchêne and Goetz, 'The Evolution of Hard Coal Trade in the Pacific Market', p. 1853
53. Dannreuther, 'Asian Security and China's Energy Needs', p. 197.
54. P. Bustelo, 'China and the Geopolitics of Oil in the Asian Pacific Region', *Elcano Royal Institue Working Paper*, 38/2005 (9 September 2005), at http://www.ucm.es/info/eid/pb/BusteloWPoil05eng.pdf [accessed 20 July 2011], p. 11.
55. Yergin, *The Prize*, p. 546.
56. Wishnick, 'China as a Risk Society', p. 22.
57. Katayama, 'Ecological Modernization in Northeast Asia', p. 198.
58. Harris, 'Institutionalising Northeast Asia', p. 6.
59. Von Hippel, Savage and Hayes, 'Overview of the Northeast Asia Energy Situation', p. 4.
60. Morse and He, 'The World's Greatest Coal Arbitrage', p. 19.
61. Kaplan, *Monsoon*, p. 282.
62. Ekawan, Duchêne and Goetz, 'The Evolution of Hard Coal Trade in the Pacific Market', p. 1854.
63. Ibid., p. 1860.
64. Knights and Hood (eds), *Coal and the Commonwealth*, p. 5.
65. Ibid., p. 90.
66. Yergin, *The Prize*, p. 545.
67. Wishnick, 'China as a Risk Society', p. 22.
68. MIT Coal Energy Study Advisory Committee Members and Study Participants, *The Future of Coal*, p. ix.
69. Wyciszkiewicz, 'Prospects for Energy Cooperation in North-East Asia', p. 33.
70. Von Hippel, Savage and Hayes, 'Overview of the Northeast Asia Energy Situation', p. 2.
71. P. Bardhan, *Awakening Giants Feet of Clay: Assessing the Economic Rise of China and India* (Princeton, NJ: Princeton University Press, 2010), p. 119.
72. Xinhua, 'Solar Power Plants to Spring up in China', *Sina English*, 10 January 2009, at http://english.sina.com/technology/p/2009/0110/210591.html [accessed 18 June 2010].
73. Smil, *Energy in World History*, p. 214.
74. Bardhan, *Awakening Giants Feet of Clay*, p. 117.

75. T. Mito, *State Power and Multinational Oil Corporations: The Political Economy of Market Intervention in Canada and Japan* (Fukuoka: Kyushu University Press, 2001), p. 129.
76. P. Duus, *Modern Japan* (Boston, MA: Houghton Mifflin Company, 1998), p. 323.
77. Bardhan, *Awakening Giants Feet of Clay*, p. 48.
78. Ibid., p. 126.
79. L. J. Lau, 'The Role of Government in Economic Development: Some Observations from the Experience of China, Hong Kong, and Taiwan', in M. Aoki, H.-K. Kim and M. Okuno-Fujiwara (eds) *The Role of Government in East Asian Economic Development: Comparative Institutional Analysis* (Oxford: Clarendon Press, 1997), pp. 41–73, on p. 48.
80. H.-K. Kim and J. Ma, 'The Role of Government in Acquiring Technological Capability: The Case of the Petrochemical Industry in East Asia', in M. Aoki, H.-K. Kim and M. Okuno-Fujiwara (eds) *The Role of Government in East Asian Economic Development: Comparative Institutional Analysis* (Oxford: Clarendon Press, 1997), pp. 101–33, p. 103.
81. Özçelik, 'The Japanese Foreign Policy of the Middle East between 1904-1998', p. 137.
82. N. Swanström, 'An Asian Oil and Gas Union: Prospects and Problems', *China and Eurasia Forum Quarterly*, 3:3 (November 2005), pp. 81–97, on p. 89.
83. Toichi, 'Energy Security in Asia and Japanese Policy', p. 1.
84. S. H. Ahn and M. T. Jones, 'Northeast Asia's Kovykta Conundrum: A Decade of Promise and Peril', *Asia Policy*, 5 (January 2008), pp. 105–40, on pp. 110–11.
85. A. Austin, D. Bochkarev and W. van der Geest, 'Energy Interests and Alliances: China, America and Africa', *EastWest Institute Policy Paper*, 7/2008 (August 2008), at http://www.ewi.info/energy-interests-and-alliances-china-america-and-africa [accessed 21 July 2011], p. 21.
86. D. Zha, 'China's Energy Security: Domestic and International Issues', *Survival*, 48:1 (Spring 2006), pp. 179–90, on p. 183.
87. Ibid., pp. 180, 183.
88. Ibid.
89. IEA, *China's Worldwide Quest for Energy Security*, pp. 50–1.
90. D. H. Rosen and T. Houser, 'China Energy: A Guide for the Perplexed', China Balance Sheet: A Joint Project by the Center for Strategic and International Studies and the Peterson Institute for International Economics, May 2007, at http://www.iie.com/publications/papers/rosen0507.pdf [accessed 21 July 2011], p. 30.
91. Ibid.
92. IEA, *China's Worldwide Quest for Energy Security*, pp. 50–1.
93. Zha, 'China's Energy Security: Domestic and International Issues', p. 183.
94. Swanström, 'An Asian Oil and Gas Union', p. 88.
95. Parsons and Brown, 'The "Asian Premium" and Dependency on Gulf Oil', p. 2.
96. Ibid., p. 4.
97. Ibid., p. 5.
98. Ibid., p. 6.
99. Ibid., p. 13.
100. R. Soligo and A. Jaffe, 'China's Growing Energy Dependence: The Costs and Policy Implications of Supply Alternatives', paper prepared in conjunction with an energy study 'China and Long-range Asia Energy Security: An Analysis of the Political, Economic and Technological Factors Shaping Asian Energy Markets' sponsored by the Center for International Political Economy and the James A. Baker III Institute for Public Policy, 2 November 2004, at http://www.bakerinstitute.org/publications/chinas-growing-

energy-dependence-the-costs-and-policy-implications-of-supply-alternatives [accessed 21 July 2011], pp. 6–7.

101. Cole, '"Oil for the Lamps of China"', p. 28.

102. Ahn and Jones, 'Northeast Asia's Kovykta Conundrum', pp. 110–11.

103. A. Blinick, 'The Kazah-China Oil Pipeline: "A Sign of the Times"', *Center on China's Transnational Relations Working Paper*, 21 (Hong Kong: The Hong Kong University of Science and Technology, 2006), at http://www.cctr.ust.hk/materials/working_papers/WorkigPaper22-Blinick.pdf [accessed 21 July 2011].

104. W. Jiang, *Fueling the Dragon: China's Quest for Energy Security and Canada's Opportunities* (Vancouver: Asia Pacific Foundation of Canada, 2005), p. 5.

105. Ibid., p. 5.

106. Thorpe and Mitra, 'Growing Economic Interdependence of China and the Gulf Cooperation Council', p. 115.

107. K. Wu, F. Fesharaki, S. B. Westley and W. Prawiraatmadja, 'Six Steps toward Increased Energy Security in the Asia Pacific Region', East-West Center, 25 August 2008, at http://www.eastwestcenter.org/index.php?id=3820&print=1 [accessed 1 January 2009].

108. Thorpe and Mitra, 'Growing Economic Interdependence of China and the Gulf Cooperation Council', p. 112.

109. Calabrese, 'The Consolidation of Gulf-Asia Relations', p. 5.

110. Swanström, 'An Asian Oil and Gas Union', p. 89.

111. Wu, Fesharaki, Westley and Prawiraatmadja, 'Six Steps toward Increased Energy Security in the Asia Pacific Region'.

112. Ibid.

113. IEA, *China's Worldwide Quest for Energy Security*, p. 52.

114. Calabrese, 'The Consolidation of Gulf-Asia Relations', p. 3.

115. Thorpe and Mitra, 'Growing Economic Interdependence of China and the Gulf Cooperation Council', p. 116.

116. Ibid.

117. Ibid.

118. M. Ögütçü, 'Foreign Direct Investment and Importance of the "Go West" Strategy in China's Energy Sector', Directorate for Financial, Fiscal and Enterprise Affairs, OECD, March 2002, at http://www.oecd.org/dataoecd/1/35/2085596.pdf [accessed 21 July 2011] (This paper builds on IEA, *China's Worldwide Quest for Energy Security* of which Ögütçü is the main author), p. 6.

119. IEA, *China's Worldwide Quest for Energy Security*, p. 58.

120. Calabrese, 'The Consolidation of Gulf-Asia Relations', p. 2.

121. Toichi, 'Energy Security in Asia and Japanese Policy', p. 2.

122. Cole, '"Oil for the Lamps of China"', p. 25.

123. Ibid.

124. Bardhan, *Awakening Giants Feet of Clay*, p. 130.

125. Hein, *Fueling Growth*, p. 216.

126. Mito, *State Power and Multinational Oil Corporations*, p. 149.

127. Diamond, *Collapse*, p. 377.

128. G. Bahgat, 'The Development of Middle-East Natural Gas Markets', *Energy Studies Review*, 10:1 (2002), pp. 42–8, on p. 44.

129. F. Fesharaki, K. Wu and S. Banaszak, 'Natural Gas: The Fuel of the Future in Asia', *Asia Pacific Issues – Analysis from the East-West Center*, 44 (June 2000), at http://www.eastwestcenter.org/fileadmin/stored/pdfs/api044.pdf [accessed 21 July 2011], p. 3.

130. H.-J. Doh, 'Energy Cooperation in Northeast Asia: Prospects and Challenges', *East Asian Review*, 15:3 (Autumn 2003), pp. 85–110, on p. 94.

131. China has the largest coal output in the world (2.23 billion tonnes in 2005); projected to make up more than 50 per cent of the world's coal increase in terms of supply and demand over the period of 2007–32 (Source: R. K. Lester and E. S. Steinfeld, 'The Coal Industry in China (and Secondarily India)', *Industrial Performance Center, MIT Working Paper Series*, MIT-IPC-07-001 (January 2007), at http://web.mit.edu/ipc/publications/pdf/07-001.pdf [accessed 21 July 2011], p. 1 (also see MIT Coal Energy Study Advisory Committee Members and Study Participants, *The Future of Coal*, Chapter 5)).

132. F. Leverett and J. Bader, 'Managing China-US Energy Competition in the Middle East', *Washington Quarterly*, 29:1 (Winter 2005–6), pp. 187–201, on p. 197.

133. Bahgat, 'The Development of Middle-East Natural Gas Markets', p. 47.

134. Doh, 'Energy Cooperation in Northeast Asia', p. 94.

135. Ibid.

136. Ibid.

137. Fesharaki, Wu and Banaszak, 'Natural Gas', p. 2.

138. Doh, 'Energy Cooperation in Northeast Asia', p. 90.

139. Cole, '"Oil for the Lamps of China"', p. 30.

140. Kobayashi, 'Corporate Strategies of Saudi Aramco', p. 18.

141. Cole, '"Oil for the Lamps of China"', p. 30.

142. Ibid.

143. Kobayashi, 'Corporate Strategies of Saudi Aramco', p. 18.

144. N. Al Kudsi, 'Time to Reflect on Silk Road', *China Daily*, 8 April 2011, at http://www.chinadaily.com.cn/opinion/2011-04/08/content_12290373_2.htm [accessed 21 July 2011]; Leverett and Bader, 'Managing China-US Energy Competition in the Middle East', p. 192.

145. Doh, 'Energy Cooperation in Northeast Asia', p. 88.

146. K. Yamaguchi and K. Cho, 'Natural Gas in China', The Institute of Energy Economics Japan, August 2003, at http://eneken.ieej.or.jp/en/data/pdf/221.pdf [accessed 21 July 2011], p. 6.

147. Ibid., p. 5.

148. Soligo and Jaffe, 'China's Growing Energy Dependence', pp. 9–11.

149. Ibid.

150. Ibid.

151. Leverett and Bader, 'Managing China-US Energy Competition in the Middle East', p. 189.

152. Soligo and Jaffe, 'China's Growing Energy Dependence', pp. 9–11.

153. Calder, 'East Asia and the Middle East', p. 6.

154. Doh, 'Energy Cooperation in Northeast Asia', p. 90.

155. Suttmeier, 'The Japanese Nuclear Power Option', pp. 132–3.

156. Newby, *Sino-Japanese Relations*, p. 26.

157. Calder, 'East Asia and the Middle East', p. 8.

158. Leverett and Bader, 'Managing China-US Energy Competition in the Middle East', p. 197.

159. Calder, 'East Asia and the Middle East', p. 6.

160. IEA, *China's Worldwide Quest for Energy Security*, p. 66.

161. Fesharaki, Wu and Banaszak, 'Natural Gas', p. 4.

162. M. Naitoh, 'The Recent Political Situation in the Middle East and the Oil Supply: A Summary of Questions at the Japan-US Joint Seminar', Japan Petroleum Energy Center, 30 November 2006, at http://www.pecj.or.jp/english/division/MiddleEast/061130_Nnaitoh2.pdf [accessed 21 July 2011], p. 2.

163. Candland, 'The U.S. Greater Middle East Initiative'.

164. Ibid.

165. Fesharaki, Wu and Banaszak, 'Natural Gas', p. 3

166. Ibid., p. 6.

167. S. W. Lewis, 'Energy Security in Northeast Asia: The Potential for Cooperation among the Major Energy Consuming Economies of China, Japan and the United States', The James A. Baker III Institute for Public Policy of Rice University, 18 July 2005, at http://www.rice.edu/energy/publications/docs/SIIS_SWLEWIS_chinajapanUScoopera-tion_071805.pdf [accessed 21 July 2011], p. 12.

168. Kobayashi, 'Corporate Strategies of Saudi Aramco', p. 26.

169. Fesharaki, Wu and Banaszak, 'Natural Gas', p. 7.

170. Lewis, 'Energy Security in Northeast Asia', p. 9.

171. Doh, 'Energy Cooperation in Northeast Asia', p. 97.

172. D. Hall, 'Regional Shrimp, Global Trees, Chinese Vegetables: The Environment in Japan-East Asia Relations', in P. J. Katzenstein and T. Shiraishi (eds), *Beyond Japan: The Dynamics of East Asian Regionalism* (Ithaca and London: Cornell University Press, 2006), pp. 188–210, on p. 191.

173. Bardhan, *Awakening Giants Feet of Clay*, pp. 121–2.

174. Hein, *Fueling Growth*, p. 42.

175. Ibid., p. 46.

176. Calder and Ye, *The Making of Northeast Asia*, pp. 114–5.

177. Friedman, *The Next Decade*, p. 232.

178. Ibid.

179. Mito, *State Power and Multinational Oil Corporations*, pp. 193–4.

8 China and Its Energy Needs

1. M. J. Economides and X. Wang, 'Energy for China', paper presented at the 'Behind the Gas Pump' Conference in Institute for Energy, Law & Enterprise, University of Houston, Houston, Texas, on 17 January 2003, at http://www.beg.utexas.edu/energyecon/documents/behind_the_gas_pump/Economides_Wang_China_Energy_Behind_the_Pump.pdf [accessed 25 July 2011], p. 1.

2. B. H. Mohamed, 'China in the Middle East: Perspectives from the Arab World', *Arab Insight: Bringing Middle Eastern Perspectives to Washington*, 2:2 (Summer 2008), pp. 67–75, on p. 67.

3. Ibid., p. 68.

4. Zha, 'China's Energy Security', p. 180.

5. J. K. Douglas, M. B. Nelson and K. L. Schwartz, 'Rising in the Gulf: How China's Energy Demands Are Transforming the Middle East', *Al Nakhlah – The Fletcher School Journal for Issues Related to Southwest Asia and Islamic Civilization* (Spring 2007), at http://kms1.isn.ethz.ch/serviceengine/Files/ISN/30176/ichaptersec-tion_singledocument/46e9eeb4-9c6b-471c-82a1-22e0997476a8/en/3_nelson-2.pdf [accessed 25 July 2011], p. 6.

6. IEA, *China's Worldwide Quest for Energy Security*, pp. 50–1.

7. Ibid., p. 52.
8. Cole, '"Oil for the Lamps of China"', p. 51.
9. Douglas, Nelson and Schwartz, 'Rising in the Gulf', p. 1.
10. R. W. Hu, 'Promoting China-U.S. Energy Cooperation: Issues and Prospects', paper prepared for the 2008 Northeast Asia Energy Outlook Seminar, Korea Economic Institute Policy Forum, Washington, DC, 6 May 2008, at www.keia.org/Publications/Other/HuFINAL.pdf [accessed 25 July 2011], p. 7.
11. Cociancich and Parenti, 'Will Iran Meet China's Energy Demand?'.
12. IEA, *China's Worldwide Quest for Energy*, p. 64.
13. Cociancich and Parenti, 'Will Iran Meet China's Energy Demand?'.
14. Ibid.
15. N. Norling, 'Russia's Energy Leverage over China and the Sinopec-Rosneft Deal', *China and Eurasia Forum Quarterly*, 4:4 (November 2006), pp. 31–8, on p. 32.
16. D. Child, 'Opportunities for Alberta's Oil and Gas Industry in China's Emerging Economy', Alberta School of Business, the University of Alberta, ID# 1073107 BUEC 463, 15 December 2004, at http://www.business.ualberta.ca/Centres/CABREE/Energy/Oil.aspx [accessed 25 July 2011], p. 8.
17. N. Swanström, 'China and Central Asia: A New Great Game or Traditional Vassal Relations?', *Journal of Contemporary China*, 14:45 (November 2005), pp. 569–84, on p. 578.
18. M. E. Herberg, 'The Emergence of China throughout Asia: Security and Economic Consequences for the U.S.', United States Senate Committee on Foreign Relations, 2005 Congressional Hearing, Testimony, 7 June 2005, at http://www.globalsecurity.org/military/library/congress/2005_hr/050607-herberg.pdf [accessed 25 July 2011], p. 5.
19. Asia Pacific Energy Research Centre, *Energy in China, Transportation, Electric Power and Fuel Markets* (Tokyo: Asia Pacific Energy Research Center, 2004), p. 49.
20. R. Bahl, *Superpower? The Amazing Race between China's Hare and India's Tortoise* (New York: Portfolio/Penguin, 2010), p. 45.
21. Ibid., p. 97.
22. B. Chellaney, *Asian Juggernaut: The Rise of China, India, and Japan* (New York: HarperCollins, 2010), p. 107.
23. Simpfendorfer, *The New Silk Road*, pp. 40, 45.
24. J. E. Stiglitz, *Freefall: Free Markets and the Sinking of the Global Economy* (London: Allen Lane, 2010), p. 191.
25. Chellaney, *Asian Juggernaut*, p. 91.
26. Bahl, *Superpower?*, p. 96.
27. Davidson, *The Persian Gulf and Pacific Asia*, p. 39.
28. Bahl, *Superpower?*, pp. 45, 96.
29. Soligo and Jaffe, 'China's Growing Energy Dependence', p. 4.
30. IEA, *China's Worldwide Quest for Energy*, p. 51.
31. Zha, 'China's Energy Security', p. 183.
32. Ibid.
33. Ibid.
34. Soligo and Jaffe, 'China's Growing Energy Dependence', p. 4.
35. IEA, *China's Worldwide Quest for Energy*, p. 52.
36. Mohamed, 'China in the Middle East', p. 74.
37. Öğütçü, 'Foreign Direct Investment and Importance of the "Go West" Strategy in China's Energy Sector'.
38. Soligo and Jaffe, 'China's Growing Energy Dependence', p. 4.

39. IEA, *China's Worldwide Quest for Energy*, p. 52.

40. Ibid., p. 58.

41. Norling, 'Russia's Energy Leverage over China and the Sinopec-Rosneft Deal', p. 32.

42. C. F. Bergsten, C. Freeman, N. R. Lardy and D. J. Mitchell, 'Energy Implications of China's Growth', in *China's Rise: Challenges and Opportunities* (Washington, DC: Peterson Institute for International Economics, 2008), chapter 7, pp. 137–68, on pp. 144–5.

43. For more on this aspect, please refer to: A. Austin, *Energy and Power in China: Domestic Regulation and Foreign Policy* (London: The Foreign Policy Centre, April 2005), at http://fpc.org.uk/fsblob/448.pdf [accessed 25 July 2011], p. x.

44. Bergsten, Freeman, Lardy and Mitchell, 'Energy Implications of China's Growth', p. 157.

45. IEA, *China's Worldwide Quest for Energy*, p. 75.

46. J. Calabrese, 'China and Iran: Mismatched Partners', *The Jamestown Foundation Occasional Papers* (August 2006), at http://www.jamestown.org/uploads/media/Jamestown-ChinaIranMismatch.pdf [accessed 25 July 2011], p. 4.

47. Austin, Bochkarev and van der Geest, 'Energy Interests and Alliances', p. 21.

48. Douglas, Nelson and Schwartz, 'Rising in the Gulf', p. 7.

49. Ibid., p. 6.

50. Ibid.

51. Zha, 'China's Energy Security', p. 181.

52. Swanström, 'China and Central Asia', p. 571.

53. Child, 'Opportunities for Alberta's Oil and Gas Industry in China's Emerging Economy', p. 10.

54. Ibid., p. 7.

55. Herberg, 'The Emergence of China throughout Asia', p. 11.

56. Ibid., p. 6.

57. Cociancich and Parenti, 'Will Iran Meet China's Energy Demand?'.

58. Jiang, *Fueling the Dragon*, p. 5.

59. Ibid.

60. Cociancich and Parenti, 'Will Iran Meet China's Energy Demand?'.

61. Information Office of the State Council of the People's Republic of China, 'China's Energy Conditions and Policies', p. 43.

62. Zha, 'China's Energy Security', p. 183.

63. Ibid., p. 181.

64. Douglas, Nelson and Schwartz, 'Rising in the Gulf', p. 2.

65. Ibid., p. 7.

66. Mohamed, 'China in the Middle East', p. 73.

67. Ibid., pp. 73, 74.

68. Ibid., p. 75.

69. Hu, 'Promoting China-U.S. Energy Cooperation', p. 6.

70. Ibid., p. 7. Hu characterizes dependence on US-maintained peace in the region as 'free-riding' on US-provided open access.

71. Ibid., pp. 6–7.

9 Addressing the UAE Natural Gas Crisis: Strategies for a Rational Energy Policy

1.   This chapter is an abstract of a larger work appearing in J. Stern and B. Fattouh (eds), *Natural Gas Markets in the Middle East and North Africa* (Oxford: Oxford Institute for Energy Studies/Oxford University Press, 2011). It was first published in *Dubai Initiative Policy Brief* (Belfer Center for Science and International Affairs, Harvard Kennedy School, August 2010).

2.   For a detailed study on the Dolphin natural gas pipeline project, see generally, Dargin, *The Dolphin Project*.

3.   Beyond Petroleum (BP), 'Natural Gas: Proved Reserves', *BP Statistical Review of World Energy* (June 2009), p. 22; N. Kawach, 'UAE Gas Output Rises by 10 bcm in Five Years', *Emirates Business 24/7*, 15 December 2008, at http://www.emirates247.com/2.277/energy-utilities/uae-gas-output-rises-by-10bcm-in-five-years-2008-12-15-1.229384 [accessed 9 December 2010].

4.   Sharjah's most important gas deposits are at the offshore Mubarek field and the onshore Sajaa, Moveyeid and Kahaif fields. 'Country Profile: Emirates Sharjah', Oxford Business Group, at http://www.oxfordbusinessgroup.com/country.asp?country=59 [accessed 9 December 2010].

5.   There are other smaller amounts spread out in the other Emirates.

6.   This figure excludes gas which was flared or reinjected. Reinjected gas accounts for an additional 18 bcm per year. BP, 'Natural Gas', p. 24.

7.   Ibid., p. 27.

8.   S. Nambiar, 'Demand for Electricity to Increase 6%', *Emirates Business 24/7*, 2 March 2009, at http://www.emirates247.com/2.277/energy-utilities/demand-for-electricity-to-increase-6-2009-03-02-1.93927 [accessed 9 December 2010].

9.   Saudi Arabia's gas consumption in 2008 was 78.1 bcm versus 58.1 bcm by the UAE. BP, 'Natural Gas', p. 27; see generally, Kawach, 'UAE Gas Output Rises by 10 bcm in Five Years'.

10. 'Population Leaps to 8.19 Million', UAE Interact, 30 May 2010, at http://www.uaeinteract.com/docs/Population_leaps_to_8.19_million/41204.htm [accessed 9 December 2010].

11. Ibid.

12. The UAE contracted for amount of Dolphin gas is 18.61 bcm per year. However, because of a series of maintenance and inspection programs at a Qatar Gas facility in Ras Laffan during 2009, the exported quantity dropped below its contractual amount. 'Qatar's Gas Supply to UAE will be Down 25 Pct', *Zawya Dow Jones*, 10 February 2010.

13. Most of the LNG is shipped to Japan, with a lesser quantity exported to South Korea and India.

14. For a discussion on the impact of OPEC production cuts on Gulf associated gas production, see P. Salisbury, 'OPEC Faces up to Cost of Output Cuts', *Middle East Business Intelligence (MEED)*, 12 March 2009.

15. Dargin, 'Trouble in Paradise'.

16. K. Remo-Listana, 'Alternative Energy is an Answer to Dwindling Natural Gas Supplies', *Emirates Business 24/7*, 6 April 2009, at http://www.emirates247.com/2.277/energy-utilities/alternative-energy-is-an-answer-to-dwindling-natural-gas-supplies-2009-04-06-1.96739 [accessed 9 December 2010]. Power demand in Ajman is driven by rapid GDP growth, estimated at approximately 27 per cent per annum, with

demographic increases reaching 18 per cent per annum. A senior official at the Federal Electricity and Water Authority (FEWA) deflected responsibility, and instead, blamed the lack of adequate development planning on Ajman officials. See S. Writer, 'Utilities Supply Crunch in Northern Emirates', *Emirates Business 24/7*, 10 July 2008, at http://www.emirates247.com/2.277/energy-utilities/utilities-supply-crunch-in-northern-emirates-2008-07-10-1.222417 [accessed 9 December 2010]. Hassan Abdullah al-Ghasyah, FEWA's executive director of supply, supported this assessment with the statement that, 'local government authorities have not coordinated on precise water and power requirements with FEWA'. As a result of the alleged lack of coordination, al-Ghasyah stated that poor planning was the primary cause for the shortages and for the need for independent generating capacity. See 'UAE – Economic Update: Private Supply', Oxford Business Group, 8 August 2008, at http://www.oxfordbusinessgroup.com/economic_updates/private-supply [accessed 9 December 2010].

17. K. Maree, 'Coal Is Dubai's Best Option to Meet Rising Demand', *MEED*, 22 February 2008; 'UAE Cement Firms Turn to Coal', *Arabian Business*, 24 June 2007, at http://www.arabianbusiness.com/uae-cement-firms-turn-to-coal-58758.html [accessed 9 December 2010].

18. Fuel liquids can refer to diesel, medium fuel oil, crude oil, kerosene, or LPG. Dargin, 'Trouble in Paradise'; R. T. Ghazal, 'Ajman Hopes to be Next Mini Dubai', *The National*, 17 May 2008.

19. In the Northern Emirates, the local banks understand that any new projects will not be attached to the grid. Because of the uncertainty of future grid access, they refuse to fund many otherwise viable development projects.

20. 'Greater Supply Deficits Force Middle East to Focus on Domestic Needs', *Alexander's Gas and Oil Connections*, 12:9, 10 May 2007.

21. US Energy Information Administration, 'Country Analysis Briefs: United Arab Emirates, Electricity', at http://www.eia.doe.gov/emeu/cabs/UAE/Electricity.html [accessed 9 December 2010].

22. The consortium comprises KEPCO, Samsung, Hyundai and Doosan Heavy Industries, along with US firm Westinghouse, Toshiba of Japan and KEPCO subsidiaries. M. Coker, 'Corporate News: Korean Team to Build U.A.E. Nuclear Plant', *Wall Street Journal*, 28 December 2009, p. B3.

23. Reportedly, the cost of producing electricity at the Shams1 solar thermal plant at Madinat Zayed in Abu Dhabi would be about three to five times higher than the average cost of producing electricity from natural gas. The government would provide a direct subsidy by paying the different between the average costs of power generation and the actual costs of generation at Shams 1. C. Stanton, 'Green Subsidy for Solar Power', *The National*, 9 June 2010.

24. A. T. Crane and C. Swann, 'U.S. Dollar a Haven, but for How Long? Nuclear Power at Bay', *New York Times*, 20 May 2010, p. B2; S. Muthiah, 'Generation Asset Valuation: Are We at the Nadir for Gas-Fired Power Plants?', *Electric Light & Power*, 82:7 (November/December.2004), pp. 54–5.

25. K. Patel, 'Challenges and Prospects for the UAE Power Sub-Sector', *Zawya*, 18 March 2010.

26. 'Power Demand to Dictate More N-Deals in the UAE', *The Peninsula*, 9 January 2009.

27. S. Bierman and A. Daya, 'U.A.E. Bid for Caspian Gas May Test Russian Dominance', *Bloomberg Businessweek*, 5 May 2010.

28. 'ADNOC to Lift Curb on Oil Output', UAE Interact, 9 March 2010, at http://www.uaeinteract.com/docs/ADNOC_to_lift_curb_on_oil_output/40027.htm [accessed 9 December 2010].

29. Additionally, under the 'Plan Abu Dhabi 2030: Urban Structure Framework Plan', Abu Dhabi pledged to spend upwards of $15 billion until 2012 on massive urban construction.

30. S. McGinley, 'Abu Dhabi Construction Costs Down by 30%-TDIC', *Arabian Business*, 17 April 2010, at http://www.arabianbusiness.com/abu-dhabi-construction-costs-down-by-30-tdic-156855.html [accessed 9 December 2010]; N. Kawach, 'Abu-Dhabi Says Oil Project Cost Slashed 20 per cent', *Emirates Business 24/7*, 27 January 2009, at http://www.emirates247.com/2.277/energy-utilities/abu-dhabi-says-oil-project-cost-slashed-20-per-cent-2009-01-27-1.99678 [accessed 9 December 2010]; 'Building Materials Decline in Cost in UAE', *CityScape Intelligence* (24 November 2009).

31. BP, *BP Statistical Review of World Energy* (June 2010), p. 27.

32. T. Singh, 'Abu Dhabi Invests $1 Tn into Infrastructure', *Mena Infrastructure*, 3 November 2009, at http://www.menainfra.com/news/abu-dhabi-trillion-infrastructure-investment/ [accessed 9 December 2010].

33. H. M. Kumar, 'UAE Gas Demand Rises 7% Yearly, *Gulf News*, 18 May 2010, at http://gulfnews.com/business/oil-gas/uae-gas-demand-rises-7-yearly-1.628276 [accessed 9 December 2010].

34. The Institute of International Finance predicted that the UAE would have probably 3.3 per cent economic growth by 2011. However, the report indicated that under optimistic scenarios, UAE's 'growth could reach 2.7 per cent in 2010 and 4.2 per cent in 2011' if debt-laden Dubai successfully resolves its debt issues and accelerates reforms. 'IIF Expects 4.4 pct Gulf Economic Growth', *AFP*, 18 May 2010.

35. 'ADNOC to Press Ahead with 5-Year Plan', *Maktoob Business* (2 June 2009), at http://en.news.maktoob.com/20090000004516/ADNOC_to_press_ahead_with_5-year_plan/Article.htm [accessed 9 December 2010].

36. The most pessimistic forecast was announced by Khalid al-Awadi, Gas Operations Manager at Emirates General Petroleum Corporation (Emarat), who calculated that in 2020, Emirati gas demand would reach 155 bcm per year in 2020. However, al-Awadi was optimistic that increased imports, domestic capacity expansion, nuclear plans and renewable energy would be able to meet the demand increase. Kumar, 'UAE Gas Demand Rises 7% Yearly'.

37. A. Yee, 'Chemical City Is a Step Nearer', *The National*, 23 December 2010. See generally, J. Dargin, 'The Development of a Gulf Carbon Platform: Mapping out the Gulf Cooperation Council Carbon Exchange', *Dubai Initiative Working Paper*, 1 (Dubai and Cambridge: Dubai School of Government; Belfer Center for Science and International Affairs, Harvard Kennedy School, May 2010), at http://belfercenter.ksg.harvard.edu/files/Dargin%20-%20DI%20Working%20Paper%201.PDF [accessed 9 December 2010].

38. 'Second Phase of Al-Khaleej Launched as Domestic Demand Grows', *Business Monitor*, 11 May 2010.

39. One such alternative feedstock being explored is ethane in liquid petroleum gas condensate. R. Shamseddine, 'Gulf Petrochemical Firms Seek Alternatives to Gas', *Arabian Business*, 9 June 2010, at http://www.arabianbusiness.com/gulf-petrochemical-firms-seek-alternatives-gas-281950.html [accessed 9 December 2010].

40. The UAE attempted to reform electricity tariffs and gasoline prices several times previously. In April 2010, the UAE attempted to liberalize gasoline prices. These incremental movements, combined with the increase in price for Qatari gas and the refusal of IOCs to produce Emirati gas fields for a less than adequate return on investment, e.g., Conoco-Phillips, will likely increase budgetary burdens, therefore, spurring greater pricing reform. 'UAE Planning to Increase Petrol Prices', *Gulf Daily News*, 19 April 2010, at http://www.gulf-daily-news.com/NewsDetails.aspx?storyid=276080 [accessed 9 December 2010].

10 Conclusion

1. For further reading with regards to the contents of p. 176, please refer to S. R. Nagy, 'Opportunity in Crisis: Sino-Japanese Relations after the Earthquake', *East Asia Forum*, 2 June 2011, at http://www.eastasiaforum.org/?p=18565 and S. R. Nagy 'Regional Regime and Norm Building: Redefining Japan's Regional Role in East Asia through Environmental and Human Security', *Tamkang Journal of International Affairs*, 15:1 (2011), pp. 1–38.

WORKS CITED

Abdullah, B., 'The Growing Economic Presence of Gulf Countries in the Mediterranean Region', *Mediterranean Yearbook: Med.2009* (2009), pp. 203–9, at http://www.iemed.org/anuari/2009/aarticles/a203.pdf [accessed 22 December 2010].

Abo-Kazleh, M., 'Transformations in Japanese Foreign Policy toward the Middle East: From Low to More Active Political Engagement', *Uluslararasi Hukuk ve Politika (Review of International Law & Politics)*, 5:17 (2009), pp. 165–93.

'ADNOC to Lift Curb on Oil Output', UAE Interact, 9 March 2010, at http://www.uaeinteract.com/docs/ADNOC_to_lift_curb_on_oil_output/40027.htm [accessed 9 December 2010].

'ADNOC to Press Ahead with 5-Year Plan', *Maktoob Business* (2 June 2009), at http://en.news.maktoob.com/20090000004516/ADNOC_to_press_ahead_with_5-year_plan/Article.htm [accessed 9 December 2010].

Aharonovitz, G. D., 'Development and the Increasing Prices of Natural Resources: Have You Missed the Last Boat to Sustained Growth?', Washington State University, School of Economic Sciences, April 2008, at http://www.ses.wsu.edu/people/Aharonovitz/nr_prices_dev_2.pdf [accessed 24 January 2011].

Ahn, S. H. and M. T. Jones, 'Northeast Asia's Kovykta Conundrum: A Decade of Promise and Peril', *Asia Policy*, 5 (January 2008), pp. 105–40.

Al Kudsi, N., 'Time to Reflect on Silk Road', *China Daily*, 8 April 2011, at http://www.chinadaily.com.cn/opinion/2011-04/08/content_12290373_2.htm [accessed 21 July 2011].

Al-Rodhan, K. R., *The Saudi and Gulf Stock Markets: Irrational Exuberance or Markets Efficiency?* (Washington, DC: Center for Strategic and International Studies, 2005), at http://csis.org/files/media/csis/pubs/051025_saudi_gulf_mrkts.pdf [accessed 24 June 2011].

Alesina, A., E. Glaeser and B. Sacerdote, 'Why Doesn't the US Have a European-Style Welfare State?', *Brookings Papers on Economic Activity*, 2001:2 (2001), pp. 187–254.

Allen, M., 'Undermining the Occupation: Women Coalminers in 1940s Japan', *PORTAL Journal of Multidisciplinary International Studies*, 7:2 (July 2010), at http://epress.lib.uts.edu.au/ojs/index.php/portal/article/view/1518/1882 [accessed 20 July 2011].

Alles, D. L. (ed.), 'Asian Air Pollution', Western Washington University, 18 December 2009, at http://fire.biol.wwu.edu/trent/alles/AirPollution.pdf [accessed 22 December 2010].

Anderson, R. S., 'Asia: Important to All of Us', *Phi Delta Kappan – Problems and Promises of Education in Asia*, 39:3 (December 1957), pp. 81–3.

Armitage, N., 'From Crisis to Kyoto and Beyond: The Evolution of Environmental Concerns in Japanese Official Development Assistance', *Graduate School of International Development Nagoya University Discussion Papers*, 176, November 2009, at http://www.gsid.nagoya-u.ac.jp/bpub/research/public/paper/article/176.pdf [accessed 7 July 2011].

Armstrong, K., G. Rozman, S. S. Kim and S. Kotkin (eds), *Korea at the Center: Dynamics of Regionalism in Northeast Asia* (Armonk, NY: ME Sharpe, 2006).

Asia Business Council, 'Containing Pandemic and Epidemic Diseases in Asia' (2010), at http://www.asiabusinesscouncil.org/docs/DiseaseBriefing.pdf [accessed 22 December 2010].

Asia Pacific Energy Research Centre, *Energy in China, Transportation, Electric Power and Fuel Markets* (Tokyo: Asia Pacific Energy Research Center, 2004).

Austin, A., *Energy and Power in China: Domestic Regulation and Foreign Policy* (London: The Foreign Policy Centre, April 2005), at http://fpc.org.uk/fsblob/448.pdf [accessed 25 July 2011].

Austin, A., D. Bochkarev and W. van der Geest, 'Energy Interests and Alliances: China, America and Africa', *EastWest Institute Policy Paper*, 7/2008 (August 2008), at http://www.ewi.info/energy-interests-and-alliances-china-america-and-africa [accessed 21 July 2011].

Aydin, A., 'Choosing Sides: Economic Interdependence and Interstate Disputes', *Journal of Politics*, 70:4 (October 2008), pp. 1098–108.

Bahgat, G., 'The Development of Middle-East Natural Gas Markets', *Energy Studies Review*, 10:1 (2002), pp. 42–8.

Bahl, R., *Superpower? The Amazing Race between China's Hare and India's Tortoise* (New York: Portfolio/Penguin, 2010).

Bardhan, P., *Awakening Giants Feet of Clay: Assessing the Economic Rise of China and India* (Princeton, NJ: Princeton University Press, 2010).

Barry, T. L., A. D. Saunders, P. D. Kempton, B. F. Windley, M. S. Pringle, D. Dorjnamjaa and S. Saandar, 'Petrogenesis of Cenozoic Basalts from Mongolia: Evidence for the Role of Aesthensospheric versus Metasomatized Lithospheric Mantle Sources', *Journal of Petrology*, 44:1 (January 2003), pp. 55–91.

Bergsten, C. F., C. Freeman, N. R. Lardy and D. J. Mitchell, 'Energy Implications of China's Growth', in *China's Rise: Challenges and Opportunities* (Washington, DC: Peterson Institute for International Economics, 2008), chapter 7, pp. 137–68.

Bernard, A. B., J. B. Jensen, S. J. Redding and P. K. Schott, 'Firms in International Trade', *Journal of Economic Perspectives*, 21:3 (Summer 2007), pp. 105–30.

Beyond Petroleum (BP), 'Natural Gas: Proved Reserves', *BP Statistical Review of World Energy* (June 2009).

—, *BP Statistical Review of World Energy* (June 2010).

Bierman, S., and A. Daya, 'U.A.E. Bid for Caspian Gas May Test Russian Dominance', *Bloomberg Businessweek*, 5 May 2010.

Blinick, A., 'The Kazah-China Oil Pipeline: "A Sign of the Times"', *Center on China's Transnational Relations Working Paper*, 21 (Hong Kong: The Hong Kong University of Science and Technology, 2006), at http://www.cctr.ust.hk/materials/working_papers/WorkigPaper22-Blinick.pdf [accessed 21 July 2011].

Brahmbhatt, M., and L. Christiaensen, 'Rising Food Prices in East Asia: Challenges and Policy Options', Faculty of Economics, Thammasat University, May 2008, at http://econ.tu.ac.th/archan/rangsun/ec%20460/ec%20460%20readings/global%20issues/Food%20Crisis/Policy%20Issues/Rising%20Food%20Price%20in%20East%20Asia-%20Challenges%20and%20Policy.pdf [accessed 22 December 2010].

Bubalo, A., and M. P. Thirlwell, 'Energy Insecurity: China, India and Middle East Oil', *Lowy Institute for International Policy Issues Brief* (December 2004), at http://www.lowyinstitute.org/Publication.asp?pid=194 [accessed 15 July 2011].

'Building Materials Decline in Cost in UAE', *CityScape Intelligence* (24 November 2009).

Bull, A., and S. Desai, 'U.S. Britain Press G8 to Help Poor Nations', *Reuters*, 26 June 2010, at http://in.reuters.com/article/2010/06/25/idINIndia-49637420100625 [accessed 15 August 2010].

Bustelo, P., 'China and the Geopolitics of Oil in the Asian Pacific Region', *Elcano Royal Institue Working Paper*, 38/2005 (9 September 2005), at http://www.ucm.es/info/eid/pb/BusteloWPoil05eng.pdf [accessed 20 July 2011].

Calabrese, J., 'China and Iran: Mismatched Partners', *The Jamestown Foundation Occasional Papers* (August 2006), at http://www.jamestown.org/uploads/media/Jamestown-ChinaIranMismatch.pdf [accessed 25 July 2011].

—, 'The Consolidation of Gulf-Asia Relations: Washington Tuned in or out of Touch?', *Middle East Institute Policy Brief*, 25 (June 2009), at http://www.mei.edu/Portals/0/Publications/Consolidation-of-Gulf-Asia.pdf [accessed 5 July 2011].

Calder, K., 'East Asia and the Middle East: A Fateful Energy Embrace', *The China and Eurasia Forum Quarterly*, 3:3 (November 2005), pp. 5–9.

—, 'Sino-Japanese Energy Relations: Prospects for Deepening Strategic Competition', Paper presented at the conference on Japan's Contemporary Challenges in Honor of the Memory of Asakawa Kanichi, Yale University, New Haven, Connecticut, 9–10 March 2007, at http://eastasianstudies.research.yale.edu/japanworld/calder.pdf [accessed 24 January 2011].

Calder, K., and M. Ye, *The Making of Northeast Asia* (Palo Alto, CA: Stanford University Press, 2010).

Caldicott, H., *If You Love This Planet: A Plan to Heal the Earth*, rev. and updated edn (New York and London: WW Norton, 2009).

Candland, C., 'The U.S. Greater Middle East Initiative: Implications for Persian Gulf Economies and Polities', *Iranian Journal of International Affairs* (Spring 2007), at http://www.wellesley.edu/Polisci/Candland/USGMEI.pdf [accessed 5 July 2011].

Central Bank of Kuwait (CBK), 'International Trade from a Kuwaiti and Arab Perspective', Paper delivered on the occasion of the Annual Tacitus Lecture for the Guild of World Traders in London, UK, 22 January 1991, at http://www.cbk.gov.kw/PDF/Book2Eng/part11.pdf [accessed 15 July 2011].

Chellaney, B., *Asian Juggernaut: The Rise of China, India, and Japan* (New York: HarperCollins, 2010).

Chen, Y., and D. Jin, 'Who Benefits from the Emerging China? An International Inputs-Ouput Approach', *Far Eastern Studies*, 8 (March 2009), pp. 45–59.

Child, D., 'Opportunities for Alberta's Oil and Gas Industry in China's Emerging Economy', Alberta School of Business, the University of Alberta, ID# 1073107 BUEC 463, 15 December 2004, at http://www.business.ualberta.ca/Centres/CABREE/Energy/Oil.aspx [accessed 25 July 2011].

'China Enthusiastic about "Blood-sweating" Horse', *People's Daily*, 5 August 2002, at http://english.peopledaily.com.cn/200208/05/eng20020805_100885.shtml [accessed 12 July 2011].

Chung, S.-Y., 'Reviving NEASPEC to Address Regional Environmental Problems in Asia', *SAIS Review*, 28:2 (Summer-Fall 2008), pp. 157–72.

Cociancich, M., and F. M. Parenti, 'Will Iran Meet China's Energy Demand? The Effects of Globalisation on the Energy Demand Allocation and on the Strengthening of Iran's Market Power', Paper for the Sixth Pan-European Conference on International Relations, Session 6–10: Greater Asia, The Middle East, and Energy Security, IPE, Developing Countries and Development, 14 September 2007, University of Turin, Italy, 12–15 September 2007, at http://www.turin.sgir.eu/uploads/Cociancich-Cociancich%20Iran%20China.pdf [accessed 24 January 2011].

Coker, M., 'Corporate News: Korean Team to Build U.A.E. Nuclear Plant', *Wall Street Journal*, 28 December 2009, p. B3.

Cole, B. D., '"Oil for the Lamps of China" – Beijing's 21st-Century Search for Energy', *McNair Paper*, 67 (Washington, DC: National Defense University Press, Institute for National Strategic Studies, 2003), at http://www.ndu.edu/inss/docUploaded/198_428.McNair.pdf [accessed 15 July 2011].

Cooper, W. H., 'US-Japan Economic Relations: Significance, Prospects, and Policy Options', *Congressional Research Service Report for Congress* (2007), at http://www.fas.org/sgp/crs/row/RL32649.pdf [accessed 22 December 2010].

'Country Profile: Emirates Sharjah', Oxford Business Group, at http://www.oxfordbusinessgroup.com/country.asp?country=59 [accessed 9 December 2010].

Crane, A. T., and C. Swann, 'U.S. Dollar a Haven, but for How Long? Nuclear Power at Bay', *New York Times*, 21 May 2010, p. B2.

Cumings, B., *Korea's Place in the Sun: A Modern History* (New York: WW Norton, 1997).

Dannreuther, R., 'Asian Security and China's Energy Needs', *International Relations of the Asia Pacific*, 3:2 (August 2003), pp. 197–219.

Dargin, J., *The Dolphin Project: The Development of a Gulf Gas Initiative* (Oxford: Oxford Institute for Energy Studies Press, January 2008).

—, 'Trouble in Paradise – The Widening Gulf Gas Deficit', *Middle East Economic Survey*, 29 September 2008.

—, 'Lights Out in the Gulf', *Alexander's Gas and Oil Connections*, 13:21 (2008), at http://www.gasandoil.com/goc/news/ntm84847.htm [accessed 1 January 2010].

—, 'The Islamization of Project Finance in the Gulf', *Oil and Gas Financial Journal*, 6:2 (2009), at http://belfercenter.ksg.harvard.edu/files/xstandard/Islamic%20Finance%20 Dargin.pdf [accessed 24 June 2011].

—, 'The Development of a Gulf Carbon Platform: Mapping Out the Gulf Cooperation Council Carbon Exchange', *Dubai Initiative Working Paper*, 1 (Dubai and Cambridge: Dubai School of Government; Belfer Center for Science and International Affairs, Harvard Kennedy School, May 2010), at http://belfercenter.ksg.harvard.edu/files/Dargin%20 -%20DI%20Working%20Paper%201.PDF [accessed 9 December 2010].

Davidson, C. M., *The Persian Gulf and Pacific Asia: From Indifference to Interdependence* (New York: Columbia University Press, 2010).

—, 'Persian Gulf – Pacific Asia Linkages in the 21st Century: A Marriage of Convenience?', *Kuwait Programme on Development, Governance and Globalisation in the Gulf States*, 7 (London: London School of Economics and Political Science, The Centre for the Study of Global Governance, January 2010), at http://www.lse.ac.uk/collections/LSEKP/ documents/Davidson%20paper.pdf [accessed 7 July 2011].

De Boer, K., and J. M. Turner, 'Beyond Oil: Reappraising the Gulf States', *McKinsey Quarterly* (January 2007), at http://mkqpreview1.qdweb.net/Middle_East/Beyond_oil_Reappraising_the_Gulf_States_1902 [accessed 22 December 2010], pp. 7–17.

Dent, C. M., 'The International Political Economy of Northeast Asian Economic Integration', in C. M. Dent and D. W. F. Huang (eds), *Northeast Asian Regionalism: Learning from the European Experience* (London: RoutledgeCurzon, 2002), pp. 65–95.

Diamond, J., *Collapse: How Societies Choose to Fail or Succeed* (London: Penguin, 2006).

Doane, D. L., *Cooperation, Technology, and Japanese Development: Indigenous Knowledge, the Power of Networks, and the State* (Boulder, CO: Westview Press, 1998).

Doh, H.-J., 'Energy Cooperation in Northeast Asia: Prospects and Challenges', *East Asian Review*, 15:3 (Autumn 2003), pp. 85–110.

Douglas, J. K., M. B. Nelson and K. L. Schwartz, 'Rising in the Gulf: How China's Energy Demands Are Transforming the Middle East', *Al Nakhlah – The Fletcher School Journal for Issues Related to Southwest Asia and Islamic Civilization* (Spring 2007), at http://kms1.isn. ethz.ch/serviceengine/Files/ISN/30176/ichaptersection_singledocument/46e9eeb4-9c6b-471c-82a1-22e0997476a8/en/3_nelson-2.pdf [accessed 25 July 2011].

Duus, P., *Modern Japan* (Boston, MA: Houghton Mifflin Company, 1998).

Economides, M. J., and X. Wang, 'Energy for China', paper presented at the 'Behind the Gas Pump' Conference in Institute for Energy, Law & Enterprise, University of Houston, Houston, Texas, on 17 January 2003, at http://www.beg.utexas.edu/energyecon/ documents/behind_the_gas_pump/Economides_Wang_China_Energy_Behind_the_ Pump.pdf [accessed 25 July 2011].

Eghbalnia, Y., 'Natural Resource Curse: Special Experience of the Persian Gulf States', Munich Personal RePEc Archive Paper No. 22325, 30 July 2006, at http://mpra.ub.uni-muenchen.de/22325/1/MPRA_paper_22325.pdf [accessed 24 January 2011].

Ekawan, R., M. Duchêne and D. Goetz, 'The Evolution of Hard Coal Trade in the Pacific Market', *Energy Policy*, 34:14 (September 2006), pp. 1853–66.

Enkhtaivan, G., 'Energy Sector Development in Mongolia', *Northeast Asia Energy Focus*, 6:1 (Spring 2009), pp. 54–8.

Ernst, D., and B. Naughton, 'China's Emerging Industrial Economy: Insights from the IT Industry', in C. A. McNally (ed.), *China's Emergent Political Economy: Capitalism in the Dragon's Lair* (London: Routledge, 2008), pp. 39–59.

European Commission, *The World in 2025: Rising Asia and Socio-Ecological Transition* (Luxembourg: Office for Official Publications of the European Communities, 2009).

Fazl-e-Haider, S., 'Gwadar: An Emerging Centre of the New Great Game', *Istituto per gli Studi di Politica Internazionale (ISPI) [Institute for International Political Studies] Policy Brief*, 162 (October 2009), at http://www.ispionline.it/it/documents/PB_162_2009.pdf [accessed 16 July 2011].

Fesharaki, F., K. Wu and S. Banaszak, 'Natural Gas: The Fuel of the Future in Asia', *Asia Pacific Issues – Analysis from the East-West Center*, 44 (June 2000), at http://www.eastwest-center.org/fileadmin/stored/pdfs/api044.pdf [accessed 21 July 2011].

Finfacts Team, 'Asia's Rising "Clean Technology Tigers" – China, Japan, and South Korea – to Overtake United States', *Finfacts Ireland Business & Personal Finance Portal*, 20 November 2009, at http://www.finfacts.ie/irishfinancenews/article_1018490.shtml [accessed 22 December 2010].

Freeman, C. W., and M. Goodman, 'Crafting US Economic Strategy toward Asia: Lessons Learned from 30 Years of Experience', *A Report of the CSIS Asia Economic Task Force* (Washington, DC: Center for Strategic and International Studies (CSIS), October 2008), at http://csis.org/files/media/csis/events/081016_freeman_craftusecon_web.pdf [accessed 22 December 2010].

Friedman, G., *The Next Decade: Where We've Been – and Where We're Going* (New York: Doubleday, 2011).

Ghazal, R. T., 'Ajman Hopes to be Next Mini Dubai', *The National* (17 May 2008).

Ghosh, J., 'Poverty Reduction in China and India: Policy Implications of Recent Trends', *Department of Economic and Social Affairs Working Paper*, 92:ST/ESA/2010/DWP/92 (January 2010), at http://www.un.org/esa/desa/papers/2010/wp92_2010.pdf [accessed 8 July 2011].

Goodstein, D. L., *Out of Gas: The End of the Age of Oil* (New York and London: WW Norton and Company, 2004).

Gould, A., 'Resisting Postmodernity: Swedish Social Policy in the 1990s', *Social Work & Society: Series on European Services in Transition (I)*, 3:1 (2005), pp. 72–84, at http://www.socwork.net/2005/1/articles/473/Gould2005.pdf [accessed 13 January 2011].

Gray, S., and M. I. Blejer, 'The Gulf Cooperation Council Region: Financial Market Development, Competitiveness, and Economic Growth', in M. D. Hanouz, S. El Diwany and

T. Yousef (eds), *The Arab World Competitiveness Report 2007 – Sustaining the Growth Momentum* (Geneva: World Economic Forum, 2007), pp. 41–51.

'Greater Supply Deficits Force Middle East to Focus on Domestic Needs', *Alexander's Gas and Oil Connections*, 12:9 (10 May 2007).

Gulf Research Center, *India's Growing Role in the Gulf: Implications for the Region and the United States* (Dubai: Gulf Research Center and the Nixon Center, 2009), at http:// www.cftni.org/Monograph-Indias-Growing-Role-in-the-Gulf.pdf [accessed 12 July 2011].

Hakimian, H., 'From East to West Asia: Lessons of Globalization, Crisis and Economic Reform', *School of Oriental and African Studies (SOAS) Working Paper*, 82 (6 May 1998), at http://www.soas.ac.uk/economics/research/workingpapers/file28881.pdf [accessed 14 July 2011].

Hall, D., 'Regional Shrimp, Global Trees, Chinese Vegetables: The Environment in Japan-East Asia Relations', in P. J. Katzenstein and T. Shiraishi (eds), *Beyond Japan: The Dynamics of East Asian Regionalism* (Ithaca, NY: Cornell University Press, 2006), pp. 188–210.

Halperin, C. J., *Russia and the Golden Horde: The Mongol Impact on Medieval Russian History* (Bloomington, IN and Indianapolis, IN: Indiana University Press, 1987).

Hänggi, H., 'Interregionalism: Empirical and Theoretical Perspectives', paper prepared for the workshop 'Dollars, Democracy and Trade: External Influence on Economic Integration in the Americas', The Pacific Council on International Policy, Los Angeles, CA; The Center for Applied Policy Research, Munich, 18 May 2000, at http://www.ipw. unisg.ch/org/ipw/web.nsf/SysWebRessources/h%C3%A4nggi/$FILE/Haenggi.pdf [accessed 1 September 2010].

Harris, S., 'Institutionalising Northeast Asia: The Energy Market', *Australian National University, Department of International Relations, Research School of Pacific and Asian Studies: Working Paper*, 2008/6 (Canberra, December 2008), at http://ips.cap.anu.edu. au/ir/pubs/work_papers/08-6.pdf [accessed 20 July 2011].

Hayashi, N., *The Japanese Economy Today – 50 Years after World War II*, Series of the Research Institute for Economics, No. 2 (Japan: Osaka University of Economics and Law, 1996).

Heal, G., 'Are Oil Producers Rich?', in M. Humphreys, J. D. Sachs and J. E. Stiglitz (eds), *Escaping the Resource Curse* (New York: Columbia University Press, 2007), pp. 155–72.

Hein, L. E., *Fueling Growth: The Energy Revolution and Economic Policy in Postwar Japan* (Cambridge, MA and London: Council on East Asian Studies, Harvard University, 1990).

Heintz, J., R. Pollin and H. Garrett-Peltier, *How Infrastructure Investments Support the U.S. Economy: Employment, Productivity and Growth* (US: Political Economy Research Institute and Alliance for American Manufacturing, January 2009), at http://www. americanmanufacturing.org/wordpress/wp-content/uploads/2009/01/peri_aam_ finaljan16_new.pdf [accessed 30 June 2011].

Herberg, M. E., 'The Emergence of China throughout Asia: Security and Economic Consequences for the U.S.', United States Senate Committee on Foreign Relations, 2005 Congressional Hearing, Testimony, 7 June 2005, at http://www.globalsecurity.org/military/library/congress/2005_hr/050607-herberg.pdf [accessed 25 July 2011].

Hirano, K., 'Sengo Nihon no Kokusai Bunka Kōryū' ('International Cultural Relations of Postwar Japan'), in K. Hirano (ed.), *Sengo Nihon no Kokusai Bunka Kōryū* (*International Cultural Relations of Postwar Japan*) (Tokyo: Keisō Shobō, 2005), pp. 81–129.

Hofmeister, J., *Why We Hate the Oil Companies: Straight Talk from an Energy Insider* (New York: Palgrave Macmillan, 2010).

Hopkins, T. K., I. Wallerstein, R. L. Bach, C. Chase-Dunn and R. Mukherjee, *World-Systems Analysis: Theory and Methodology* (Beverly Hills, California: Sage, 1982).

Hsiao, F. S. T., M. W. Hsiao and A. Yamashita, 'The Impact of the US Economy on the Asia-Pacific Region: Does It Matter?', *Journal of Asian Economics*, 14:2 (April 2003), pp. 219–41.

Hu, R. W., 'Promoting China-U.S. Energy Cooperation: Issues and Prospects', paper prepared for the 2008 Northeast Asia Energy Outlook Seminar, Korea Economic Institute Policy Forum, Washington, DC, 6 May 2008, at www.keia.org/Publications/Other/HuFINAL.pdf [accessed 25 July 2011].

Huisken, R., 'The Outlook for US-China Relations', in R. Huisken (ed.), *Rising China: Power and Reassurance* (Canberra: The Australian National University E Press, 2009), pp. 9–20.

Huntington, S. P., *Political Order in Changing Societies* (New Haven, CT: Yale University Press, 1968).

'IIF Expects 4.4 pct Gulf Economic Growth', *AFP*, 18 May 2010.

Information Office of the State Council of the People's Republic of China, 'China's Energy Conditions and Policies' (December 2007), at http://en.ndrc.gov.cn/policyrelease/P020071227502260511798.pdf [accessed 15 July 2011].

Insel, A., and M. Tekce, 'Econometric Analysis of the Bilateral Trade Flows in the Gulf Cooperation Council Countries', Munich Personal RePEc Archive Paper No. 22130, 15 April 2010, at http://mpra.ub.uni-muenchen.de/22130/1/MPRA_paper_22130.pdf [accessed 5 July 2011].

International Energy Agency (IEA), *China's Worldwide Quest for Energy Security* (Paris: OECD/IEA, 2000).

International Fund for Agricultural Development (IFAD), *Environment and Natural Resource Management IFAD's Growing Commitment* (Rome: IFAD, February 2002), at http://www.ifad.org/pub/enviorn/EnvironENG.pdf [accessed 24 January 2011].

International Institute for Sustainable Development (IISD), 'Business Strategies for Sustainable Development', at http://www.iisd.org/business/pdf/business_strategy.pdf [accessed 24 January 2011]. (Based on the book *Business Strategy for Sustainable Development: Leadership and Accountability for the '90s* (Winnipeg: IISD, jointly with Deloitte and Touche and the World Business Council for Sustainable Development, 1992).

International Monetary Fund (IMF), 'Asia in the World Economy Asia's Importance Growing in Global Economy', *IMF Survey Online*, 12 May 2010, at http://www.imf.org/external/pubs/ft/survey/so/2010/car051210a.htm [accessed 22 December 2010].

Itoh, S., 'Can Russia Become a "Regional Power" in Northeast Asia? Implications from Contemporary Energy Relations with China and Japan' (Center for East Asian Studies

Monterey Institute of International Studies, May 2006), at http://gsti.miis.edu/CEAS-PUB/2007_Itoh.pdf [accessed 7 July 2011].

—, 'Japan's Energy Strategy and Development of Energy Cooperation in the Asia-Pacific', *Economic Research Institute for Northeast Asia (ERINA) Report*, 77 (September 2007), pp. 35–48.

Ivanov, V. I., 'Russian Crisis: Will Northeast Asia Links Help?', in T. Akaha (ed.), *Politics and Economics in Northeast Asia: Nationalism and Regionalism in Contention* (New York: St Martin's Press, 1999), pp. 227–46.

Jaffe, A. M., 'Energy Security: Oil-Geopolitical and Strategic Implications for China and the United States' (Houston, TX: The James A. Baker III Institute for Public Policy of Rice University, 2004), at http://www.rice.edu/energy/publications/docs/SIIS_AJAFFE_worldenergy071805.pdf [accessed 5 July 2011].

Jensen, J. T., *The Development of a Global LNG Market: Is It Likely? If So When?* (Oxford: Oxford Institute for Energy Studies, 2004), at http://www.jai-energy.com/pubs/Oxfordbook.pdf [accessed 7 July 2011].

Ji, G., 'Maritime Confidence-Building Measures (CBMs) in Northeast Asia', *Institute on Global Conflict and Cooperation (IGCC) Policy Paper – Northeast Asia Cooperation Dialogue II Conference Papers, Tokyo, Japan, 16-17 May 1994*, 9 (August 1994).

Jia, Q., 'Closer and More Balanced: China-US Relations in Transition', in R. Huisken (ed.), *Rising China: Power and Reassurance* (Canberra: The Australian National University E Press, 2009), p. 21–32.

Jiang, W., *Fueling the Dragon: China's Quest for Energy Security and Canada's Opportunities* (Vancouver: Asia Pacific Foundation of Canada, 2005).

Johannessen, P., 'Beyond Modernization Theory: Democracy and Development in Latin America' (Outstanding Senior Honors Thesis, Pi Sigma Alpha, the National Political Science Honor Society in the US, the University of Vermont, 2009), at http://www.uvm.edu/~polisci/Johannessen_Thesis-2009.pdf [accessed 13 January 2011].

Johns, T., and P. B. Eyzaguirre, 'Nutrition and The Environment', in *Nutrition: A Foundation for Development: Why Practitioners in Development Should Integrate Nutrition*, Environment Brief 5 of 12 (Geneva: Administrative Committee on Coordination/Sub-Committee on Nutrition, January 2002), at http://www.unscn.org/files/Publications/Briefs_on_Nutrition/Brief5_EN.pdf [accessed 24 January 2011].

Johnson, C. A., *MITI and the Japanese Miracle: The Growth of Industrial Policy, 1925-1975* (Palo Alto, CA: Stanford University Press, 1982).

Kandel, A., 'The Significant Warming of Indo-Israeli Relations in the Post-Cold War Period', *Middle East Review of International Affairs*, 13:4 (December 2009), pp. 69–77.

Kaplan, R. D., *Monsoon: The Indian Ocean and the Future of American Power* (New York: Random House, 2010).

Kapur, D., and R. Ramamurti, 'India's Emerging Competitive Advantage in Services', *Academy of Management Executive*, 15:2 (2001), pp. 20–33.

Katayama, H., 'Ecological Modernization in Northeast Asia', in S. Tabata (ed.), *Energy and Environment in Slavic Eurasia: Toward the Establishment of the Network of Environmen-*

tal Studies in the Pan-Okhotsk Region (Sapporo: Hokkaido University, Slavic Research Center, 2008).

Katel, P., 'Emerging China', *CQ Researcher*, 15:40 (11 November 2005), pp. 957–80.

Kates, R. W., T. M. Parris and A. A. Leiserowitz, 'What is Sustainable Development', *Environment: Science and Policy for Sustainable Development*, 47:3 (April 2005), pp. 8–21.

Kaufman, S., 'Obama's Trip Underscores Asia's Importance', US Department of State's Bureau of International Information Programs, 29 October 2010, at http://www.america.gov/st/peacesec-english/2010/October/20101029142757nehpets5.151629e-04.html?CP.rss=true [accessed 22 December 2010].

Kawach, N., 'UAE Gas Output Rises by 10 bcm in Five Years', *Emirates Business 24/7*, 15 December 2008, at http://www.emirates247.com/2.277/energy-utilities/uae-gas-output-rises-by-10bcm-in-five-years-2008-12-15-1.229384 [accessed 9 December 2010].

—, 'Abu-Dhabi Says Oil Project Cost Slashed 20 per cent', *Emirates Business 24/7*, 27 January 2009, at http://www.emirates247.com/2.277/energy-utilities/abu-dhabi-says-oil-project-cost-slashed-20-per-cent-2009-01-27-1.99678 [accessed 9 December 2010].

Keller, W., and S. R. Yeaple, 'Multinational Enterprises, International Trade, and Productivity Growth: Firm-Level Evidence from the United States', *Review of Economics and Statistics*, 91:4 (November 2009), pp. 821–31.

Kelton, M., 'US Economic Statecraft in East Asia', *International Relations of the Asia-Pacific*, 8:2 (April 2008), pp. 149–74.

Kemp, G., *The East Moves West: India, China and Asia's Growing Presence in the Middle East* (Washington, DC: Brookings Institution, 2010).

Kennedy, J. R., and R. J. Orr, 'The "New Market" for Emerging Markets Infrastructure: China, Other New Players and Revised Game Rules', *Collaboratory for Research on Global Projects Working Paper*, 32 (Palo Alto, CA: Stanford University, April 2007), at http://crgp.stanford.edu/publications/working_papers/GCR3_April07_Proceedings_3_v2.pdf [accessed 24 June 2011].

Kim, H.-K., and J. Ma, 'The Role of Government in Acquiring Technological Capability: The Case of the Petrochemical Industry in East Asia', in M. Aoki, H.-K. Kim and M. Okuno-Fujiwara (eds), *The Role of Government in East Asian Economic Development: Comparative Institutional Analysis* (Oxford: Clarendon Press, 1997), pp. 101–33.

King, S. D., *Losing Control: The Emerging Threats to Western Prosperity* (New Haven, CT: Yale University Press, 2010).

Knights, P., and M. Hood (eds), *Coal and the Commonwealth: The Greatness of an Australian Resource* (Brisbane: The University of Queensland, October 2009).

Kobayashi, Y., 'Corporate Strategies of Saudi Aramco' (The James A. Baker III Institute for Public Policy of Rice University, March 2007), at http://www.rice.edu/energy/publications/docs/NOCs/Papers/NOC_Kobayashi%20SAramco.pdf [accessed 12 July 2011].

Kornblut, A. E., and B. Harden, 'In Japan, Obama Stresses Asia's Role in U.S. economy', *Washington Post*, 14 November 2009, at http://www.washingtonpost.com/wp-dyn/content/article/2009/11/13/AR2009111304272.html [accessed 22 December 2010].

Ku, H., and A. Zussman, 'Lingua Franca: The Role of English in International Trade', *Journal of Economic Behavior and Organization*, 75:2 (August 2010), pp. 250–60.

Kumar, H. M., 'UAE Gas Demand Rises 7% Yearly, *Gulf News*, 18 May 2010, at http://gulfnews.com/business/oil-gas/uae-gas-demand-rises-7-yearly-1.628276 [accessed 9 December 2010].

Lall, S. V., H. Selod and Z. Shalizi, 'Rural-Urban Migration in Developing Countries: A Survey of Theoretical Predictions and Empirical Findings', *World Bank Policy Research Working Paper*, 3915 (May 2006), at http://www-wds.worldbank.org/servlet/WDS-ContentServer/WDSP/IB/2006/05/05/000016406_20060505110833/Rendered/PDF/wps3915.pdf [accessed 24 January 2011].

Lau, L. J., 'The Role of Government in Economic Development: Some Observations from the Experience of China, Hong Kong, and Taiwan', in M. Aoki, H.-K. Kim and M. Okuno-Fujiwara (eds) *The Role of Government in East Asian Economic Development: Comparative Institutional Analysis* (Oxford: Clarendon Press, 1997), pp. 41–73.

Lau, L. J., and J. Park, 'The Sources of East Asian Economic Growth Revisited' (Stanford University and the State University of New York at Buffalo, September 2003), at http://www.stanford.edu/~ljlau/RecentWork/RecentWork/030921.pdf [accessed 22 December 2010].

Lee, J.-Y., and J. P. Rodrigue, 'Trade Reorientation and Its Effects on Regional Port Systems: The Korea-China Link along the Yellow Sea Rim', *Growth and Change*, 37:4 (December 2006), pp. 597–619.

Lester, R. K., and E. S. Steinfeld, 'The Coal Industry in China (and Secondarily India)', *Industrial Performance Center, MIT Working Paper Series*, MIT-IPC-07-001 (January 2007), at http://web.mit.edu/ipc/publications/pdf/07-001.pdf [accessed 21 July 2011].

Leverett, F., and J. Bader, 'Managing China-US Energy Competition in the Middle East', *Washington Quarterly*, 29:1 (Winter 2005–6), pp. 187–201.

Levin, R. C., 'Speeches & Statements: The Rise of Asia's Universities', Yale Office of Public Affairs & Communications, 1 February 2010, at http://opa.yale.edu/president/message.aspx?id=91 [accessed 22 December 2010].

Lewis, S. W., 'Energy Security in Northeast Asia: The Potential for Cooperation among the Major Energy Consuming Economies of China, Japan and the United States', The James A. Baker III Institute for Public Policy of Rice University, 18 July 2005, at http://www.rice.edu/energy/publications/docs/SIIS_SWLEWIS_chinajapanUScooperation_071805.pdf [accessed 21 July 2011].

Li, X., 'China Protests Japan's Diaoyu Islands Stance', *China Daily*, 28 February 2009, at http://www.chinadaily.com.cn/cndy/2009-02/28/content_7521979.htm [accessed 27 April 2010].

Lincoln, E., 'Japan: Using Power Narrowly', *Washington Quarterly*, 27:1 (Winter 2003–4), pp. 111–27.

Liu, X., *The Silk Road: Overland Trade and Cultural Interactions in Eurasia* (Washington, DC: American Historical Association, 1998).

Madsen, J., 'China's Policy in the Gulf Region: From Neglect to Necessity', Power and Interest News Report, 27 October 2006, at http://www.gees.org/documentos/Documen-01736.pdf [accessed 14 July 2011].

Majid, M., 'The Big Idea: US Diplomacy in Rising Asia: Through the Glass Darkly', *IDEAS Today – Deals, Denials and Declassification: Israeli-South African Nuclear Collaboration*, 5 (The London School of Economics and Political Science (LSE), September 2010), at http://www2.lse.ac.uk/IDEAS/publications/ideasToday/05/majid.pdf [accessed 22 December 2010], pp. 4–6.

Maree, K., 'Coal is Dubai's Best Option to Meet Rising Demand', *MEED*, 22 February 2008.

Margonelli, L., *Oil on the Brain: Petroleum's Long, Strange Trip to Your Tank* (New York: Broadway Books, 2008).

Martin, C., 'Crafting a US Response to the Emerging East Asia Free Trade Area', *Whitehead Journal of Diplomacy and International Relations*, 8:2 (Summer/Fall 2007), pp. 73–84.

Mason, S. A., and A. Muller, 'Transforming Environmental and Natural Resource Use Conflicts', in M. Cogoy and K. W. Steininger (eds), *The Economics of Global Environmental Change: International Cooperation for Sustainability* (Cheltenham, UK and Northampton, MA: Edward Elgar, 2007), pp. 225–72.

Massachusetts Institute of Technology (MIT) Coal Energy Study Advisory Committee Members and Study Participants, *The Future of Coal – Options for a Carbon Constrained World* (Cambridge, MA: MIT, 2007).

McCulley, P., and R. Toloui, 'Asia Rising', *Time*, 13 September 2007, at http://www.time.com/time/magazine/article/0,9171,1661477,00.html [accessed 22 December 2010].

McGinley, S., 'Abu Dhabi Construction Costs Down by 30%-TDIC', *Arabian Business*, 17 April 2010, at http://www.arabianbusiness.com/abu-dhabi-construction-costs-down-by-30-tdic-156855.html [accessed 9 December 2010].

Meng, B., and S. Inomata, 'Production Networks and Spatial Economic Interdependence: An International Input-Output Analysis of the Asia Pacific Region', *Institute of Developing Economies Discussion Paper*, 185 (March 2009), at https://ir.ide.go.jp/dspace/bitstream/2344/818/1/ARRIDE_Discussion_no.185_BoMENG.pdf [accessed 3 January 2011].

Middle East Studies Association (MESA), 'Description', at http://www.mesa.arizona.edu/about/description.htm [accessed 20 June 2011].

Mito, T., *State Power and Multinational Oil Corporations: The Political Economy of Market Intervention in Canada and Japan* (Fukuoka: Kyushu University Press, 2001).

Mohamed, B. H., 'China in the Middle East: Perspectives from the Arab World', *Arab Insight: Bringing Middle Eastern Perspectives to Washington*, 2:2 (Summer 2008), pp. 67–75.

Mohan, R. C., 'India and the Asian Security Architecture', in M. J. Green and B. Gills (eds), *Asia's New Multilateralism: Cooperation, Competition and the Search for Community* (New York: Columbia University Press, 2009), pp. 128–53.

Morita, A., *Made in Japan: Akio Morita and Sony* (London: HarperCollins Business, 1994).

Morse, R. K., and G. He, 'The World's Greatest Coal Arbitrage: China's Coal Import Behavior and Implications for the Global Coal Market', *Program on Energy and Sustainable Devel-*

opment Working Paper, 94 (Palo Alto, CA: Stanford University, Freeman Spogli Institute for International Studies, August 2010), at http://iis-db.stanford.edu/pubs/22966/ WP_94_Morse_He_Greatest_Coal_Arbitrage_5Aug2010.pdf [accessed 19 July 2011].

Muller-Kraenner, S., 'China's and India's Emerging Energy Foreign Policy', *German Development Institute Discussion Paper*, 15/2008 (Bonn: German Development Institute, 2008), at http://www.die-gdi.de/CMS-Homepage/openwebcms3.nsf/(ynDK_contentByKey)/ANES-7HJAZ8/$FILE/DP%2015.2008.pdf [accessed 8 July 2011].

Murakushi, N., *Technology and Labour in Japanese Coal Mining* (Tokyo: United Nations University, 1980).

Muthiah, S., 'Generation Asset Valuation: Are We at the Nadir for Gas-Fired Power Plants?', *Electric Light & Power,* 82:7 (November/December.2004), pp. 54–5.

Nagasu, K., and Y. Sakamoto, *Jichitai no Kokusai Kōryū: Hirakareta Chihō o Mezashite* (*International Cooperation of Local Governments: Toward Open Local Regions*) (Tokyo: Gakuyō Shobō, 1983).

Nagy, S., and T. W. Lim, 'The Future Trend of Inter-Regionalism in East Asia', Paper presented at the conference 'Major Trends in the Contemporary World', College of International Studies of Tamkang University, March 2011 (unpublished at the time of this writing).

Naitoh, M., 'The Recent Political Situation in the Middle East and the Oil Supply: A Summary of Questions at the Japan-US Joint Seminar', Japan Petroleum Energy Center, 30 November 2006, at http://www.pecj.or.jp/english/division/MiddleEast/061130_ Nnaitoh2.pdf [accessed 21 July 2011].

Nakanishi, H., 'Overcoming the Crises: Japanese Diplomacy in the 1970s', in M. Iokibe (ed.), *The Diplomatic History of Postwar Japan, Winner of the 1999 Yoshida Shigeru Prize*, trans. R. D. Eldrige (Abingdon: Routledge, 2009), pp. 108–43.

Nambiar, S., 'Demand for Electricity to Increase 6%', *Emirates Business 24/7*, 2 March 2009, at http://www.emirates247.com/2.277/energy-utilities/demand-for-electricity-to-increase-6-2009-03-02-1.93927 [accessed 9 December 2010].

Nasr, S. V. R., *Meccanomics: The March of the New Muslim Middle Class* (Oxford: Oneworld, 2010).

National Science Foundation (NSF), Division of Science Resources Statistics, *Asia's Rising Science and Technology Strength: Comparative Indicators for Asia, the European Union, and the United States*, NSF 07-319 (Arlington, VA: NSF, 2007).

Newby, L., *Sino-Japanese Relations: China's Perspective* (London: Routledge, 1988).

Nicol, B., 'Introduction: Postmodernism and Postmodernity' in *The Cambridge Introduction to Postmodern Fiction* (Cambridge: Cambridge University Press, 2009).

Nissanke, M., and E. Thorbecke, 'Linking Globalization to Poverty in Asia, Latin America and Africa', *United Nations University WIDER Policy Brief*, 3 (2010), at http://www.wider.unu.edu/publications/policy-briefs/en_GB/unupb3-2010/_ files/83351175411204184/default/Policy%20Brief%20no%203%202010-Web-.pdf [accessed 22 December 2010].

Noland, M., 'United States Economic Policy toward Asia', *East-West Center Working Papers*, 103 (June 2009), at http://www.eastwestcenter.org/fileadmin/stored/pdfs/econwp103. pdf [accessed 22 December 2010].

Norling, N., *First Kabul Conference on Partnership, Trade, and Development in Greater Central Asia* (Washington, DC and Sweden: Central Asia-Caucasus Institute & Silk Road Studies Program and the First Kazakhstan President Foundation, 2006), at http://www. silkroadstudies.org/new/docs/0604Kabul.pdf [accessed 12 July 2011].

—, 'Russia's Energy Leverage over China and the Sinopec-Rosneft Deal', *China and Eurasia Forum Quarterly*, 4:4 (November 2006), pp. 31–8.

Öğütçü, M., 'Foreign Direct Investment and Importance of the "Go West" Strategy in China's Energy Sector', Directorate for Financial, Fiscal and Enterprise Affairs, OECD, March 2002, at http://www.oecd.org/dataoecd/1/35/2085596.pdf [accessed 21 July 2011].

Öğütçü, M., and X. Ma, 'Growing Links in Energy and Geopolitics: China, Russia, and Central Asia', Centre for Energy, Petroleum and Mineral Law and Policy (CEPMLP) Research Network, at http://www.dundee.ac.uk/cepmlp/gateway/files.php?file=CEPMLP_IJ_ Mar08-Growing_links_916741751.pdf [accessed 15 July 2011].

Ohkawa, K., and H. Rosovsky, *Japanese Economic Growth: Trend Acceleration in the Twentieth Century* (Palo Alto, CA and London: Stanford University Press and Oxford University Press, 1973).

Oren, M. B., *Power, Faith, and Fantasy: America in the Middle East, 1776 to the Present* (New York and London: WW Norton, 2007).

Ostrom, E., *Governing the Commons: the Evolution of Institutions for Collective Action* (Cambridge: Cambridge University Press, 1990).

Overholt, W., 'China in the Global Financial Crisis: Rising Influence, Rising Challenges', *Washington Quarterly*, 33:1 (January 2010), pp. 21–34.

Özçelik, S., 'The Japanese Foreign Policy of the Middle East between 1904-1998: Resource, Trade and Aid Diplomacy', *Humanity & Social Sciences Journal*, 3:2 (2008), pp. 129–42.

Panagariya, A., 'India and China: Trade and Foreign Investment', *Stanford Center for International Development Working Paper*, 302 (Stanford, CA: Stanford University, November 2006), at http://www.stanford.edu/group/siepr/cgi-bin/siepr/?q=system/files/shared/ pubs/papers/pdf/SCID302.pdf [accessed 6 July 2011].

Parker, E. G. M., and T. C. Shaffer, 'India and China: The Road Ahead', *South Asia Monitor*, 120 (1 July 2008), at http://csis.org/files/media/csis/pubs/sam120.pdf [accessed 5 July 2011].

Parsons, C., and J. Brown, 'The "Asian Premium" and Dependency on Gulf Oil', *Center for International Trade Studies (CITS) Working Papers*, CITS WP 2003-2002 (Japan: Yokohama National University, Faculty of Economics, November 2003), at http://www. econ.ynu.ac.jp/cits/sub3-2.htm [accessed 15 July 2011].

Patel, K., 'Challenges and Prospects for the UAE Power Sub-Sector', *Zawya*, 18 March 2010.

Plummer, M. G., 'The Global Economic Crisis and Its Implications for Asian Economic Cooperation', *East-West Center Policy Studies*, 55 (2009), at http://www.eastwestcenter. org/fileadmin/stored/pdfs/ps055.pdf [accessed 14 July 2011].

'Population Leaps to 8.19 Million', UAE Interact, 30 May 2010, at http://www.uaeinter-act.com/docs/Population_leaps_to_8.19_million/41204.htm [accessed 9 December 2010].

'Power Demand to Dictate More N-Deals in the UAE', *The Peninsula*, 9 January 2009.

Pradhan, S., 'India's Economic and Political Presence in the Gulf: A Gulf Perspective', in Gulf Research Center, *India's Growing Role in the Gulf: Implications for the Region and the United States* (Dubai: Gulf Research Center and the Nixon Center, 2009), at http://www.cftni.org/Monograph-Indias-Growing-Role-in-the-Gulf.pdf [accessed 12 July 2011], pp. 15–39.

'Qatar's Gas Supply to UAE will be Down 25 Pct', *Zawya Dow Jones*, 10 February 2010.

Qureshi, M. S., and G. Wan, 'Trade Expansion of China and India Threat or Opportunity', *United Nations University World Institute for Development Economics Research (UNU-WIDER) Research Paper*, 2008/08 (February 2008), at http://www.environmentportal.in/files/rp2008-08.pdf [accessed 6 July 2011].

Ranganathan, S., 'Emerging India as a World Class Leader in the Knowledge Industry: Prospect for Human Resource Development', paper presented in LEC-Seminar Workshop on 'The Limits of Cultural Globalization', Jawaharlal Nehru University and Albert-Ludwigs-University Freiburg, June/July 2000, at http://www.zmk.uni-freiburg.de/CulturalGlobalization/Workshop/paper-ranganathan.pdf [accessed 8 July 2011].

Rautava, J., 'Is India Emerging as a Global Economic Powerhouse Equal to China?', *Bank of Finland Institute for Economies in Transition (BOFIT) Online*, 2 (Helsinki: BOFIT, 2005), at http://www.suomenpankki.fi/fi/suomen_pankki/organisaatio/asiantunti-joita/Documents/bon0205.pdf [accessed 8 July 2011].

Remo-Listana, K., 'Alternative Energy is an Answer to Dwindling Natural Gas Supplies', *Emirates Business 24/7*, 6 April 2009, at http://www.emirates247.com/2.277/energy-utilities/alternative-energy-is-an-answer-to-dwindling-natural-gas-supplies-2009-04-06-1.96739 [accessed 9 December 2010].

Roberts, P., *The End of Oil: On the Edge of a Perilous New World* (Boston, MA and New York: Houghton Mifflin, 2005).

Romulo, B. D., 'Asia's Rising Middle Class', *Manila Bulletin*, 29 September 2010, at http://www.mb.com.ph/node/279682/a [accessed 22 December 2010].

Rosen, D. H. and T. Houser, 'China Energy: A Guide for the Perplexed', China Balance Sheet: A Joint Project by the Center for Strategic and International Studies and the Peterson Institute for International Economics, May 2007, at http://www.iie.com/publications/papers/rosen0507.pdf [accessed 21 July 2011].

Rostow, W. W., *The Stages of Economic Growth: A Non-Communist Manifesto* (Cambridge: Cambridge University Press, 1960).

Rothkopf, D., *Superclass: The Global Power Elite and the World They are Making* (New York: Farrar, Straus and Giroux, 2008).

Roubini, N., 'Japan's Economic Crisis: Comments for the Panel Discussion on "Business Practices and Entrepreneurial Spirit in Japan and the United States"', 12 November 1996, at http://library.thinkquest.org/28837/japan.pdf [accessed 27 June 2011].

Rozman, G., *Northeast Asia's Stunted Regionalism: Bilateral Distrust in the Shadow of Globalization* (New York and Cambridge: Cambridge University Press, 2004).

Rusko, C. J., and K. Sasikumar, 'India and China: From Trade to Peace?', *Asian Perspective*, 31:4 (October 2007), pp. 99–123.

Ryan, L., 'The "Asian Economic Miracle" Unmasked', *International Journal of Social Economics*, 27:7–10 (2000), pp. 802–15.

Saeed, K., 'Sustainable Trade Relations in a Global Economy' (Worcester Polytechnic Institute, January 1998), at http://www.wpi.edu/Images/CMS/SSPS/08.pdf [accessed 24 January 2011].

Sager, A., and G. Kemp, 'Introduction', in Gulf Research Center, *India's Growing Role in the Gulf: Implications for the Region and the United States* (Dubai: Gulf Research Center and the Nixon Center, 2009), at http://www.cftni.org/Monograph-Indias-Growing-Role-in-the-Gulf.pdf [accessed 11 July 2011], pp. 11–13.

Sahlgren, G. H., 'The United States-South Korea Free Trade Agreement: An Economic and Political Analysis', *Competitive Enterprise Institute Issue Analysis*, 10 (October 2007), at http://cei.org/pdf/6189.pdf [accessed 24 January 2011].

Salisbury, P., 'OPEC Faces up to Cost of Output Cuts', *Middle East Business Intelligence* (*MEED*), 12 March 2009.

Sasaki, J., *Modes of Traditional Mining Techniques* (Tokyo: United Nations University, 1980).

Schuman, M., 'What Asia Can Really Teach America', *Time*, 4 February 2010, at http://www.time.com/time/business/article/0,8599,1959065,00.html [accessed 22 December 2010].

Schumpeter, J. A., *Business Cycles: A Theoretical, Historical, and Statistical Analysis of the Capitalist Process* (New York, London: McGraw-Hill, 1964).

Schwenninger, S. R., 'US/Europe: Shaping a New Model of Economic Development', in C. Degryse (ed.), *Social Developments in the European Union 2009: Eleventh Annual Report* (Brussels: European Trade Union Institute, 2010), pp. 23–36.

'Second Phase of Al-Khaleej Launched as Domestic Demand Grows', *Business Monitor*, 11 May 2010.

Shamseddine, R., 'Gulf Petrochemical Firms Seek Alternatives to Gas', *Arabian Business*, 9 June 2010, at http://www.arabianbusiness.com/gulf-petrochemical-firms-seek-alternatives-gas-281950.html [accessed 9 December 2010].

Shorenstein APARC, 'No One Can Now Ignore or Overlook the Importance of Asia, Says APARC Director Dr. Gi-Wook Shin', Korean Studies Program (KSP) News, Freeman Spogli Institute for International Studies at Stanford University, 19 July 2010, at http://fsi.stanford.edu/news/no_one_can_now_ignore_or_overlook_the_importance_of_asia_says_aparc_director_dr_giwook_shin_20100719/ [accessed 22 December 2010].

Silverthorne, S., 'The Rise of Innovation in Asia', Harvard Business School Working Knowledge, 7 March 2005, at http://hbswk.hbs.edu/item/4676.html [accessed 22 December 2010].

Simon, D. F., and C. Cao, *China's Emerging Technological Edge: Assessing the Role of High-End Talent* (Cambridge: Cambridge University Press, 2009).

Simpfendorfer, B., *The New Silk Road: How a Rising Arab World Is Turning Away from the West and Rediscovering China* (Basingstoke: Palgrave MacMillan, 2009).

Singh, T., 'Abu Dhabi Invests $1 Tn into Infrastructure', *Mena Infrastructure*, 3 November 2009, at http://www.menainfra.com/news/abu-dhabi-trillion-infrastructure-investment/ [accessed 9 December 2010].

Smil, V., *Energy in World History* (Boulder, CO: Westview Press, 1994).

—, *Energy in Nature and Society: General Energetics of Complex Systems* (London and Cambridge, MA: The MIT Press, 2008).

Smith, J., N. Clark and K. Yusoff, 'Interdependence', *Geography Compass*, 1:3 (May 2007), pp. 340–59.

Soligo, R., and A. Jaffe, 'China's Growing Energy Dependence: The Costs and Policy Implications of Supply Alternatives', paper prepared in conjunction with an energy study 'China and Long-range Asia Energy Security: An Analysis of the Political, Economic and Technological Factors Shaping Asian Energy Markets' sponsored by the Center for International Political Economy and the James A. Baker III Institute for Public Policy, 2 November 2004, at http://www.bakerinstitute.org/publications/chinas-growing-energy-dependence-the-costs-and-policy-implications-of-supply-alternatives [accessed 21 July 2011].

Somjee, A. H., 'India: A Challenge to Western Theories of Development', in H. J. Wiarda (ed.), *Non-Western Theories of Development: Regional Norms Versus Global Trends* (Fort Worth, TX: Harcourt Brace College Publishers, 1999), pp. 44–63.

Soubbotina, T. P., 'What is Development?', *Beyond Economic Growth: An Introduction to Sustainable Development, Second Edition* (Washington, DC: the World Bank, 2004), at http://www.worldbank.org/depweb/english/beyond/beyondco/beg_all.pdf [accessed 3 June 2011], pp. 7–11.

Srinivasan, T. N., 'China and India: Economic Performance, Competition and Cooperation: An Update', Economic Growth Center, Yale University, February 2004, at http://www.econ.yale.edu/~srinivas/C&I%20Economic%20Performance%20Update.pdf [accessed 6 July 2011].

—, 'Economic Reforms and Global Integration', in F. R. Frankel and H. Harding (eds), *The India-China Relationship: What the United States Needs to Know* (Washington, DC: Woodrow Wilson Center Press, 2004), pp. 219–66.

Stanton, C., 'Green Subsidy for Solar Power', *The National*, 9 June 2010.

Stewart, D., 'Japan: The Power of Efficiency', in G. Luft and A. Korin (ed.), *Energy Security Challenges for the 21st Century: A Reference Handbook* (Santa Barbara, CA: Praeger Security International, 2009), pp. 176–90.

Stiglitz, J. E., *Freefall: Free Markets and the Sinking of the Global Economy* (London: Allen Lane, 2010).

Sturm, M., J. Strasky, P. Adolf and D. Peschel, 'The Gulf Cooperation Council Countries Economic Structures, Recent Developments and Role in the Global Economy', *European Central Bank Occasional Paper Series*, 92 (July 2008), at http://www.ecb.int/pub/pdf/scpops/ecbocp92.pdf [accessed 10 July 2011].

Summers, L. H., 'The U.S.-India Economic Relationship in the 21st Century: Remarks to the U.S.-India Business Council', US Government National Economic Council, 2 June 2010, at http://www.whitehouse.gov/administration/eop/nec/speeches/us-india-economic-relationship [accessed 22 December 2010].

Suttmeier, R. P., 'The Japanese Nuclear Power Option: Technological Promise and Social Limitations', in R. A. Morse (ed.), *The Politics of Japan's Energy Strategy: Resources-Diplomacy-Security* (Berkeley: Institute of East Asian Studies Research Papers and Policy Studies, 1981), pp. 106–33.

Suzuki, M., 'Realization of a Sustainable Society – Zero-Emission Approaches', Introductory Articles, Zero Emissions Forum, United Nations University, at http://archive.unu.edu/zef/publications_e/suzuki_intro_ZE.pdf [accessed 10 June 2011].

Swanström, N., 'An Asian Oil and Gas Union: Prospects and Problems', *China and Eurasia Forum Quarterly*, 3:3 (November 2005), pp. 81–97.

—, 'China and Central Asia: A New Great Game or Traditional Vassal Relations?', *Journal of Contemporary China*, 14:45 (November 2005), pp. 569–84.

Swanström, N., M. Weissmann and E. Björnehed, 'Introduction', in N. Swanström (ed.), *Conflict Prevention and Conflict Management in Northeast Asia* (Washington, DC and Sweden: Central Asia-Caucasus Institute & Silk Road Studies Program, Johns Hopkins and Uppsala, 2005), pp. 7–36.

The Middle East Partnership Initiative (MEPI), 'About MEPI', U.S. Department of State, MEPI, at http://mepi.state.gov/about-us.html [accessed 5 July 2011].

The National Bureau of Asian Research, 'Emerging Leaders in East Asia', *National Bureau of Asian Research Project Notes* (May 2008), at http://www.nbr.org/downloads/pdfs/PSA/EL_PN_May08.pdf [accessed 22 December 2010].

'The Rise of the Gulf ', *Economist*, 387:8577 (26 April 2008), p. 15.

The Task Force on the Future of American Innovation, 'The Knowledge Economy: Is the United States Losing its Competitive Edge?', *Benchmarks of Our Innovation Future*, 16 February 2005, at http://www.futureofinnovation.org/PDF/Benchmarks.pdf [accessed 22 December 2010].

Thorpe, M., and S. Mitra, 'Growing Economic Interdependence of China and the Gulf Cooperation Council', *China & World Economy*, 16:2 (March–April 2008), pp. 109–24.

Toichi, T., 'Energy Security in Asia and Japanese Policy', *Asia-Pacific Review*, 10:1 (May 2003), pp. 44–51.

Townsend, J., and A. King, 'Sino-Japanese Competition for Central Asian Energy: China's Game to Win', *China and Eurasia Forum Quarterly*, 5:4 (November 2007), pp. 23–45.

'UAE – Economic Update: Private Supply', Oxford Business Group, 8 August 2008, at http://www.oxfordbusinessgroup.com/economic_updates/private-supply [accessed 9 December 2010].

'UAE Cement Firms Turn to Coal', *Arabian Business*, 24 June 2007, at http://www.arabianbusiness.com/uae-cement-firms-turn-coal-58758.html [accessed 9 December 2010].

'UAE Planning to Increase Petrol Prices', *Gulf Daily News*, 19 April 2010, at http://www.gulf-daily-news.com/NewsDetails.aspx?storyid=276080 [accessed 9 December 2010].

Ujihira, M., and K. Hashimoto, 'Outbursts of Coal and Gas and Preventive Measures', *Memoirs of the Faculty of Engineering, Hokkaido University*, 14:3 (December 1976), pp. 25–32.

United Nations Environment Programme (UNEP), *From Conflict to Sustainable Development: Assessment and Clean-up in Serbia and Montenegro* (Switzerland: UNEP, 2004).

—, 'Alternative Policy Study: Reducing Air Pollution in Asia and the Pacific', *Global Environment Outlook (GEO)-2000*, at http://www.unep.org/geo2000/aps-asiapacific/index.htm [accessed 22 December 2010].

United Nations Millennium Project, *Innovation: Applying Knowledge in Development* (UN: Task Force on Science, Technology, and Innovation, 2005).

United States General Accounting Office (GAO), 'Emerging Infectious Diseases: Asian SARS Outbreak Challenged International and National Responses', Report to the Chairman, Subcommittee on Asia and the Pacific, Committee on International Relations, House of Representatives, April 2004, at http://www.gao.gov/new.items/d04564.pdf [accessed 22 December 2010].

US Congress Office of Technology Assessment, *Technology Transfer to the Middle East OTA-l SC-173* (Washington, DC: US Congress Office of Technology Assessment, September 1984), at http://govinfo.library.unt.edu/ota/Ota_4/DATA/1984/8428.PDF [accessed 7 July 2011].

US Energy Information Administration, 'Country Analysis Briefs: United Arab Emirates, Electricity', at http://www.eia.doe.gov/emeu/cabs/UAE/Electricity.html [accessed 9 December 2010].

Verdoux, P., 'Transhumanism, Progress and the Future', *Journal of Evolution and Technology*, 20:2 (December 2009), pp. 49–69.

Vespignani, A., 'The Fragility of Interdependency', *Nature: News & Views*, 464 (15 April 2010), at http://polymer.bu.edu/hes/articles/nv-vespignani10.pdf [accessed 3 January 2011], pp. 984–85.

Von Hippel, D. F., and P. Hayes, 'Growth in Energy Needs in Northeast Asia: Projections, Consequences, and Opportunities', paper prepared for the 2008 Northeast Asia Energy Outlook Seminar, Korea Economic Institute Policy Forum, Washington, DC, 6 May 2008, at http://www.keia.org/Publications/Other/vonHippelFINAL.pdf [accessed 22 December 2010].

Von Hippel, D., T. Savage, P. Hayes, 'Overview of the Northeast Asia Energy Situation', *Energy Policy* (July 2009), doi:10.1016/j.enpol.2009.07.004.

Wallerstein, I., *The Modern World-system: Capitalist Agriculture and the Origins of the European World-economy in the Sixteenth Century* (New York: Academic Press, 1974).

Wang, J., 'China's Search for Stability with America', *Foreign Affairs*, 84:5 (September/October 2005), pp. 39–48.

Weerahewa, J., and K. Meilke, 'Indo-China Trade Relationships: Implications for the South Asian Economies', The Ohio State University, Department of Agricultural, Environmental, and Development Economics, 22 June 2007, at http://aede.osu.edu/programs/anderson/trade/34Weerahewa.pdf [accessed 11 June 2011].

Werner, C., 'The New Silk Road: Mediators and Tourism Development in Central Asia', *Ethnology*, 42:2 (Spring 2003), pp. 141–59.

Wiarda, H. J., *Non-Western Theories of Development: Regional Norms versus Global Trends* (Fort Worth, TX: Harcourt Brace College Publishers, 1999).

Wickramasekera, P., 'Asian Labour Migration: Issues and Challenges in an Era of Globalization', *International Migration Papers*, 57 (International Labour Organization, August 2002), at http://www.ilo.org/public/english/protection/migrant/download/imp/imp57e.pdf [accessed 24 January 2011].

Willson, S., 'Wealth Funds Group Publishes 24-Point Voluntary Principles', *IMF Survey Online*, 15 October 2008, at http://www.imf.org/external/pubs/ft/survey/so/2008/new101508b.htm [accessed 24 June 2011].

Wishnick, E., 'China as a Risk Society', *East-West Center Working Papers: Politics, Governance, and Security Series*, 12 (September 2005), at http://www.eastwestcenter.org/fileadmin/stored/pdfs/PSwp012.pdf [accessed 19 July 2011].

World Economic Forum (WEF), 'EU Commissioner Mandelson Urges Europe to Look at a Rising Asia as an Opportunity, Not a Threat', 29 April 2005, at http://www2.weforum.org/en/media/Latest%20Press%20Releases/PRESSRELEASES139.html [accessed 22 December 2010].

World Health Organization (WHO), 'TB a Threat to Economic Progress in Asia: TB Control Must be Effectively Supported to Reverse Losses', 29 November 2006, at http://www.searo.who.int/LinkFiles/Events_JakPressRelease.pdf [accessed 22 December 2010].

Writer, S., 'Utilities Supply Crunch in Northern Emirates', *Emirates Business 24/7*, 10 July 2008, at http://www.emirates247.com/2.277/energy-utilities/utilities-supply-crunch-in-northern-emirates-2008-07-10-1.222417 [accessed 9 December 2010].

Wu, K., F. Fesharaki, S. B. Westley and W. Prawiraatmadja, 'Six Steps toward Increased Energy Security in the Asia Pacific Region', East-West Center, 25 August 2008, at http://www.eastwestcenter.org/index.php?id=3820&print=1 [accessed 1 January 2009].

Wu, K., B. Usukh and B. Tsevegjav, 'Energy Cooperation in Northeast Asia: The Role of Mongolia', *Ritsumeikan Journal of Asia Pacific Studies*, 26 (December 2009), pp. 83–98.

Wyatt, I. D., and K. J. Byun, 'Employment Outlook: 2008-18 – The US Economy to 2018: From Recession to Recovery', *Monthly Labor Review*, 132:11(November 2009), pp. 11–29.

Wyciszkiewicz, E., 'Prospects for Energy Cooperation in North-East Asia', *Polish Institute of International Affairs (PISM) Research Papers*, 2 (August 2006), at http://kms1.isn.ethz.ch/serviceengine/Files/ISN/93294/ipublicationdocument_singledocument/aada7013-c295-4850-b20c-822b9bff2d11/en/2006_2.pdf [accessed 20 July 2011].

Xinhua, 'Solar Power Plants to Spring up in China', *Sina English*, 10 January 2009, at http://english.sina.com/technology/p/2009/0110/210591.html [accessed 18 June 2010].

—, 'China Holds Indisputable Sovereignty over Diaoyu Islands – FM', *China Daily*, 19 July 2009, at http://www.chinadaily.com.cn/china/2009-07/19/content_8446416.htm [accessed 27 April 2010].

Xu, X., 'China's Oil Strategy toward the Middle East', Post September 11 Update Report: Political, Economic, Social, Cultural, and Religious Trends in the Middle East and the Gulf and their Impact on Energy Supply, Security, and Pricing', The James A. Baker III Institute for Public Policy of Rice University, September 2002, at http://www.bakerinstitute.org/publications/PEC911Update_ChinasOilStrategyTowardsMiddleEast2.pdf [accessed 14 July 2011].

Yamaguchi, K., and K. Cho, 'Natural Gas in China', The Institute of Energy Economics Japan, August 2003, at http://eneken.ieej.or.jp/en/data/pdf/221.pdf [accessed 21 July 2011].

Yamamoto, T., and S. Itoh (eds), *Fighting a Rising Tide: The Response to AIDS in East Asia* (Tokyo: Japan Center for International Exchange, 2006).

Yamazaki, T., K. Aso and J. Chinju, 'Japanese Potential of CO2 Sequestration in Coal Seams', *Applied Energy*, 83:9 (September 2006), pp. 911–20.

Yergin, D., *The Prize: The Epic Quest for Oil, Money, and Power* (New York: Simon and Schuster, 1991).

Yomiuri International Economic Society, 'Emerging China and the Asian Economy in the Coming Decade', *Symposium on International Economic Affairs November 2002 Occasional Paper*, 12 (Tokyo: Institute for International Monetary Affairs, March 2003), at www.iima.or.jp/pdf/paper12e.pdf [accessed 14 July 2011].

Yoshimatsu, H., 'Japan's Quest for Free Trade Agreements Constraints from Bureaucratic and Interest Group Politics', in M. Pangestu and L. Song (eds), *Japan's Future in East Asia and the Pacific: In Honour of Professor Peter Drysdale* (Canberra: Asia Pacific Press, Australian National University, 2007), pp. 80–102.

Zapf, W., 'Modernization Theory – and the Non-Western World', Paper presented to the conference 'Comparing Processes of Modernization', University of Potsdam, 15–21 December 2003, Wissenschaftszentrum Berlin für Sozialforschung (WZB), Beim Präsidenten, Emeriti Projekte, Best.-Nr. P 2004–003, June 2004, at http://bibliothek.wz-berlin.de/pdf/2004/p04-003.pdf [accessed 13 January 2011].

Zha, D., 'China's Energy Security: Domestic and International Issues', *Survival*, 48:1 (Spring 2006), pp. 179–90.

Zhang, G., 'China's Policies on Energy, Oil and Natural Gas in the New Century – Keynote Speech on the Sixth Sino-US Oil and Gas Forum', 28 June 2005, at http://www.usea.org/Archive/Speeches%20for%20Website/Guobao%20Remarks%20English.pdf [accessed 15 July 2011].

Zhang, S., 'The Environmental Impact of the Financial Crisis: Challenges and Opportunities', The Carnegie Endowment for International Peace, 11 April 2009, at www.carnegieendowment.org/events/?fa=eventDetail&id=1328http://www.carnegieendowment.org/events/?fa=eventDetail&id=1328 [accessed 1 April 2010].

Zhang, Z. X., 'Asian Energy and Environmental Policy: Promoting Growth While Preserving the Environment', Munich Personal RePEc Archive Paper No. 12224, January 2008, at http://mpra.ub.uni-muenchen.de/12224/ [accessed 24 June 2011].

Zou, K., 'Transnational Cooperation for Managing the Control of Environmental Disputes in East Asia', *Journal of Environmental Law*, 16:3 (2004), pp. 341–60.

INDEX

For Product Safety Concerns and Information please contact our EU
representative GPSR@taylorandfrancis.com
Taylor & Francis Verlag GmbH, Kaufingerstraße 24, 80331 München, Germany